PANZER ACES
OF THE WEHRMACHT
AND THE WAFFEN-SS

THE DEFINITIVE LIST

SUMMARY

INTRODUCTION

Several "Panzer Aces" lists can be found today on the internet. Most of them seem to have originated from an old Wikipedia article that included a list of German panzer aces. This article no longer exists: at the time of this writing it has been completely changed and turned into a sort of mini sociological treatise on the meaning of the term "ace", in which the accomplishments of the German soldiers are belittled in every possible way; the previous list of successful commanders has been suppressed and only the names of Knispel and Carius (not Wittmann...) have been merged in a general list of "Tank aces" of all nations in a new Wikipedia article called "List of aces of aces". Either way, all the available lists are incomplete and incorrect in many respects. Some commanders are given too high scores or, better to say, scores resulting from misunderstandings. Even worse, several figures are entirely fabricated. In the present book these "special cases" have been examined separately in an additional list. The opposite case of relevant commanders not included in the lists is also to be noted. It is also evident that the "aces" do not come homogeneously from all units; just to limit ourselves to the Tiger units; the actions of the *LSSAH*'s Tigers have been extensively investigated because of Wittmann, and so all commanders are well known and are listed; the same applies for the schwere Panzer-Abteilung 102/502, again thanks to a charismatic leader like Carius. On the contrary Tiger commanders belonging to other abteilungen are neglected not for lack of successes, but because their story has not been sufficiently researched. Wrong assessments have not spared even the most famous commander. Wittmann is credited with destroying 138 enemy tanks, a claim that, for lack of better, is usually repeated in every book or website. This number comes from the addition of 117 Soviet tanks with 21 British tanks. Both figures are wrong. For the eastern front it's too low: he destroyed 117 AFVs as Tiger commander, but, before that, at least 7 as StuG III commander in "Barbarossa"; the assault guns were part of the artillery arm, so in the first years these "kills" were counted separately. For the Invasion front it's too high: in Villers-Bocage he destroyed 11 tanks; he correctly spoke of a total of 21 "armoured vehicles", but the German war correspondents turned the dozen of carriers and half-tracks also into "tanks".

The present work is the result of an accurate research on both primary and secondary sources. Mistakes and omissions are everywhere, however all the relevant information that could be identified on books and on the internet has been carefully scrutinized, all data have been compared and evaluated. The aim is to provide the reader with a finally reliable list of the most successful German panzer commanders in World War II, with a focus on the number of enemy vehicles and guns destroyed by each of them.

Essentially this is accomplished through a new, and somehow definitive in its structure, collection of biographies of "aces" who managed to reach a personal total of no less than 20 enemy tank "kills" (30 for the Tiger commanders); the most successful gunners have been also included. Of course much remains to be done: many of the biographies are incomplete; in several cases even a portrait of the soldier is lacking. Furthermore there is still a large group of commanders, maybe around 50 of them, which should be included in the list; for the moment it has not been possible to establish with sufficient accuracy their personal number of "kills". Both the list and biographies are obviously open to further addition and improvement based on primary sources yet to be discovered. The author is not happy with the term "ace": it has become prominent in contemporary popular culture, but the German military did not recognize the concept of a panzer ace during the war. However, keeping this limitation in mind, this is the term that better summarize what we are talking about.

In a work based on the number of tanks (and, collaterally, AT guns) destroyed, a main question arises: are these figures reliable? The issue leads itself to much confusion; it is difficult even to establish the meaning of terms such as "destroyed", "knocked out", "put out of action", "eliminated", "disabled", and the difference between them. A "kill" credited to a commander didn't always mean that the enemy tank was permanently destroyed. A total loss occurred when the AT shell achieved a penetration of the hull, resulting in the explosion or in the complete burning out of the vehicle. But the outcome of the firefight was not always so clear. The enemy vehicle can be hit and apparently destroyed but in fact still left in repairable condition. Sometimes tanks that were accounted as "hits" can be salvaged by an advancing enemy resulting in no total loss for him. On the contrary enemy tanks that got little damage became a total loss if captured and destroyed by advancing friendly forces. Most important: many tanks that were actually destroyed can be rendered operable again. From early 1943 onwards, on the eastern front German troops started to identify a large number of entirely rebuild machines. The Red Army was infact intensifying the salvaging of a great number of tanks that for the western standard would have been considered beyond repair. This was possible because the Soviet tank, tipically the T-34, was a crude machine (and perhaps so effective for this very reason). In the west too the Allies managed not to write off a good number of their heavily damaged tanks, even if in smaller proportion. The Germans, for their part, during the course of the war entrained an innumerable quantity of crippled panzers for depot-level maintenance; in their own way they even managed to create completely new vehicles, for example 31 StuG IVs were built by re-utilising the hulls of destroyed Panzer IVs; destroyed Panthers and Tigers were brought to a new life as Bergepanther and Bergetiger; etcetera. Finally it must be remembered the not unusual case of damaged tanks that were potentially recoverable but were instead cannibalized for spare parts. Those tanks became infact total losses, but in some way they "survived" within other tanks. In the German army claims made by combat units were carefully scrutinized by regimental and/or divisional commands in order to avoid double counting. Moreover similar to the fighter units of the Luftwaffe each claim required, to be validated, a subsequent evidence of the destruction. And in this regard it should be noted that the consequence of a hit were witnessed not only by the commander, but by the whole crew, by other panzer crews and by the grenadiers on the ground. There are several examples where claims were found to be entirely accurate when enemy losses were counted, as when German troops held an area after a battle and were able to prevent enemy forces from recovering their vehicles. The German High Command was well aware of the problem of the enemy's recovered/repairable vehicles and, consequently, figures of Soviet losses were reduced by 20 percent from 1 December 1942 to 30 June 1943, and by a dramatic 50 percent from 1 July 1943 onwards. The Allied losses too were reduced by routinely dividing the claims by two. This does not mean that German units claims were untruthful, but simply that, for a variety of circumstances, a proportion of destroyed AFVs can be brought back to action by the enemy. As regards to Soviet tanks it should be noted that Krivosheev's data relate exclusively to total losses; 1997 tracked AFVs in the Battle of Berlin alone (fifteen days). As for the Anglo-American losses, these are the figures established by historians: ~4000 tracked AFVs in Normandy (eighty-five days), 733 in the Ardennes (forty days).

The following is a list of the most successful panzer commanders and gunners of WWII. Names are not sorted merely by the number of enemy AFVs destroyed. Another assessment criterion has been adopted, depending on two considerations.

-the first consideration is that the commander alone was responsible for the outcome of the combat, he deserved full credit for a success and beared full responsability in case of failure; the gunner had also a decisive task, but still led by the commander.

-the second is that give battle in the West was much more hazardous for the German panzer crews, essentially because of the complete air superiority of the Allies. It was also much more discouraging: the US Army logistics was too powerful; a gigantic wave of resources that steadily submerged and nullified any military success.

On this basis a virtual score has been created, and names have been positioned according to this. Of course only the real score will appear on the list. For each Soviet AFV the commander gets a virtual score of "1", while the gunner "0,5", (ideally with another "0,5" shared by the rest of the crew). For the destruction of an Allied AFV the score doubles: "2" for the commander and "1" for the gunner. This makes the list more reflective of reality: for the Germans, both psychologically and materially, 20-25 destroyed Allied tanks were of a greater importance than 50 Soviets. By the way, the Luftwaffe adopted this same unwritten rule: just compare Marseille with Hartmann. In case of equivalent score then priority is given to the fallen soldiers. As a result Knispel is not at the top of our list. The destruction of 126 Soviet AFVs as gunner and 42 as commander brings to him a virtual score of: 63 (126/2) plus 42, that is "105". Surpassed by Wittmann with his 124+ Soviet and 11 Allied AFVs and a virtual score of "146+". Is the top belonging to Carius? Carius, not unlike Wittmann, was always where the danger was; many actions were planned following his advice and when the time came he was in the leading panzer. In this situation it is likely that victories obtained together with others may have been attributed to him alone, and that his final "official" score of more than 150 enemy AFVs destroyed is exaggerated. The fair and frank lieutenant in his later life hinted that the real total was something above the hundred; so for him the lowest estimate (110) has been taken into account; if we include the lone Allied tank, that gives a virtual score of "112". He is infact joined by Bölter, one of his comrades in the s.PzAbt 502. Bölter didn't stand under the spotlight, but was in the Panzerwaffe since the start of the war and his victories also should reach the number of 110.

THE LIST

Michael Wittmann 1

7+ soviet tanks, **2**+ soviet AT guns, (as StuG III commander).
117 soviet tanks, **130** soviet AT guns, (as Tiger I commander).
11+ british tanks, **2** british AT guns, (as Tiger I commander).

Johannes Bölter 2

7+ french tanks, (as Panzer IV commander).
10 soviet tanks, (as Panzer IV commander).
85+ soviet tanks, (as Tiger I commander).
100+ soviet AT guns, (as Pz IV/Tiger I commander).
5~(?) american tanks, (as Tiger I commander).

Otto Carius 3

110~ soviet tanks, **100**+ soviet AT guns, (as Tiger I commander).
1 american tank, (as Jagdtiger commander).

Albert Kerscher 4

107 soviet tanks, **50**+ soviet AT guns, (as Tiger I commander).

Kurt Knispel 5

12 soviet tanks, (as Panzer IV gunner).
114+ soviet tanks, (as Tiger I gunner).
42 soviet tanks, (as Tiger II commander).
100+ soviet AT guns, (as gunner and commander).

Karl Körner 6

102+ soviet tanks, **26** soviet AT guns, (as Tiger II commander).

Helmut Wendorff 7

68+ soviet tanks, (as Tiger I commander).
15+ allied tanks, (as Tiger I commander).

Paul Egger 8

60~ soviet tanks, (as StuG III/Tiger I commander).
7+ british tanks, (as Tiger I commander).
20+ soviet tanks, (as Tiger II commander).

Ernst Barkmann 9

10+ soviet tanks, (as Panzer III gunner/commander).
34+ soviet tanks, (as Panther commander).
20+ american tanks, (as Panther commander).

Heinz Deutsch   10
44 allied tanks, (as StuG III commander).

Helmut Höhno   11
83 soviet tanks, (as Panzer IV/Tiger I commander).

Hans Strippel   12
36 soviet tanks, (as Panzer III/Panzer IV commander).
40+ soviet tanks, (as Panther commander).

Erich Litzke   13
76+ soviet tanks, (mostly as Tiger I/Tiger II commander).

Hermann Bix   14
2 soviet tanks, (as Panzer III commander).
45~ soviet tanks, (as Panzer IV/Panther commander).
28 soviet tanks, (as Jagdpanther commander).

Franz Bäke   15
10 french/british tanks, (as Panzer 35(t) commander).
33+ soviet tanks, (as Panzer IV commander).
16+ soviet tanks, (as Panther commander).
3 soviet tanks, (using hand-held weapons).
3+(?) allied tanks, (as Panther commander).

Bodo Spranz   16
72 soviet tanks, (as StuG commander).
4 soviet tanks, (using hand-held weapons).

August Kaminski   17
20~ allied and soviet tanks, (as Panzerjäger I commander).
50+ soviet tanks, (as Nashorn commander).

Franz Fischer   18
73 soviet tanks, (as Panzer IV/Panther commander).

Georg Hurdelbrink   19
36 allied tanks, (as Jagdpanzer IV commander).

Wilhelm Knauth   20
68+ soviet tanks, (as Tiger I commander).

Hubert "Hugo" Primozic   21
68 soviet tanks, (as StuG III commander).

Emil Seibold   22
55 soviet tanks, (as T-34/Panzer IV commander).
5(?) allied tanks, (as Panzer IV commander).
9 soviet tanks, (as Panzer IV commander).

Rudolf Larsen   23
66+ soviet tanks, (as Panther commander).

Karl Brommann   24
66 soviet tanks, (as Tiger II commander).

Konrad Sauer   25
65 soviet tanks, (as StuG III commander).

Rudolf Roy   26
10 soviet tanks, (as Panzerjäger commander).
26 british tanks, (as Jagdpanzer IV commander).

Hermann Eckardt   27
5~ allied tanks, (as Panzer IV commander).
50~ soviet tanks, (as StuG/Panzer IV commander).

Theodor Hönniger   28
60+ soviet tanks, (as Panzer IV/Panther commander).

Josef Brandner   29
61 soviet tanks, (as StuG III/IV commander).

Albert Witte   30
56 soviet and allied tanks, (as StuG commander).

Heinz Timpe   31
59 soviet tanks, (as StuG commander).

Hans-Christian Stock   32
58+ soviet tanks, (as StuG commander).

Hans-Babo von Rohr 33
52 soviet tanks, (as Panther commander).
6 soviet tanks, (using hand-held weapons).

Hans Bunzel 34
48+ soviet tanks, (mostly as Panzer IV commander).
7+ allied tanks, (as Panther commander).

Jürgen Brandt 35
20~ soviet tanks, (as Tiger I commander).
20~ allied tanks, (as Tiger I commander).
1 american tank, (as Tiger II commander).

Horst Giese 36
58+ soviet tanks, (as Panzerjäger/Panther commander).

Wilhelm Bachor 37
57 soviet tanks, (mostly as StuG commander).

Herbert Elsner 38
56 soviet tanks, (mostly as Panther commander).

Josef Rohrbacher 39
56 soviet tanks, (as StuG commander).

Alois Kalss 40
35~ soviet tanks, (as Tiger I commander).
2 soviet tanks, (using hand-held weapons).
5~ allied tanks, (as Tiger I commander).
10+(?) soviet tanks, (as Tiger II commander).

Albert Ernst 41
55 soviet tanks, (as Nashorn commander).

Johannes Kochanowski 42
55 soviet tanks, (as StuG commander).

Richard Engelmann 43
54 soviet tanks, (as StuG commander, 1 using hand-held weapons).

Konrad Heubeck 44
52 soviet and allied tanks, (as Panther commander).

Wilhelm "Willi" Fey   45
30~ allied tanks, (as Tiger I commander).

Gerhard Brehme   46
45+ soviet tanks, (as Panzer III/Panzer IV commander).
5~ soviet tanks, (as Panther commander).

Friedrich Arnold   47
51 soviet tanks, (as StuG III commander).

Balthasar Woll   48
80 soviet tanks, (as Tiger I gunner).
11+(?) british tanks, (as Tiger I gunner).

Heinrich Rondorf   49
50~ soviet tanks, (as Tiger I/Jagdpanther commander).
2(?) allied tanks, (as Jagdtiger commander).

Heinrich Mausberg   50
53 soviet tanks, (as Tiger I/Tiger II commander).

Josef Jakwert   51
50 soviet tanks, (as towed PaK and as StuG commander).
1 soviet tank, (using hand-held weapons).

Walter Wolf   52
5~ allied tanks, (as Panzer IV gunner).
50~ soviet tanks, (as Panzer IV/Panther commander).

Norbert Kujacinski   53
51+ soviet tanks, (mostly as Panther commander).

Johann Müller   54
50+ soviet tanks, (as Tiger I commander).

Kurt Göring   55
50+ soviet tanks, (as Panzer IV/Tiger I commander).

Oskar Schäfer   56
50+ soviet tanks, (mostly as Tiger II commander).

Konrad Weinert   57
50~ soviet tanks, (as Tiger I commander).

Felix Adamowitsch   58
50~ soviet tanks, (as StuG commander).

Josef Dallmeier   59
50~ soviet tanks, (as Hetzer commander).

Gerhard Fischer   60
50~ soviet tanks, (mostly as Panther commander).

Karl Ketterer   61
50~ soviet tanks, (as Panzer IV/Panther commander).

Hans-Jochen Kühn   62
50~ soviet tanks, (as StuG III commander).

Hans-Joachim Weißflog   63
40~ soviet tanks, (as Panzer III(?)/Panzer IV commander).
5+ allied tanks, (as Panther commander).

Alfred Montag   64
40~ soviet tanks, (as StuG commander).
5+ american tanks, (as StuG commander).

Paul Senghas   65
49 soviet tanks, (as Panzer IV commander).

Kurt Kannenberg   66
20+ soviet tanks, (as Tiger I commander).
14+ allied tanks, (as Tiger II commander).

Johannes Spielmann   67
48 soviet tanks, (as StuG commander).

Erich Zillmann   68
48 soviet tanks, (as StuG commander).

Waldemar Lutz   69
47 soviet tanks, (as StuG III commander).

Ahrend Höper   70
47 soviet tanks, (as StuG commander).

Roland Paul 71
37 soviet tanks, (as StuG III commander).
8(?) allied tanks, (as Jagdpanzer IV commander).

Heinrich Kling 72
46+ soviet tanks, (as Tiger I commander).

Berndt Lubich von Milovan 73
46 soviet tanks, (as StuG commander).

Karl-Friedrich Nökel 74
2+ allied tanks, (as Panzer III commander).
40~ soviet tanks, (as Panzer IV/Panther commander).

Oskar Röhrig 75
35+ soviet tanks, (as Panzer III/IV commander).
5+ american tanks, (as Tiger I commander).

Fritz Scherf 76
36 soviet tanks, (as StuG III commander).
6 allied tanks, (as StuG III commander).

Josef Schwarzenbacher 77
43 soviet tanks, (as StuG gunner).
20+ soviet tanks, (as StuG commander).

Heinz Gärtner 78
70~ soviet tanks, (as Tiger I gunner).
10~(?) soviet tanks, (as Tiger II commander).

Eduard Müller 79
46 soviet tanks, (as StuIG 33B/StuG commander).

Felix Przedwojewski 80
45 soviet tanks, (as StuG commander).

Franz Riedel 81
20~ soviet tanks, (as Panzerjäger gunner/comm, Panzer IV comm).
10+ allied tanks, (as Panzer IV commander).
10~ soviet tanks, (as Panzer IV commander).

Friedrich Banach 82
43+ soviet tanks, (as Panzer IV commander).

Georg Bose   83
43 soviet tanks, (as StuG III/Jagdpanzer IV commander).
1 soviet tank, (using hand-held weapons).

Karl Pfreundtner   84
43 soviet tanks, (as StuG III commander).

Wilhelm Günther   85
42+ soviet tanks, (as Panzer IV commander).

Fritz Amling   86
42+ soviet tanks, (as StuG III commander).

Herbert Amann   87
42 soviet tanks, (as StuG III commander).

Georg Schäfer   88
41+ soviet tanks, (as Panzer IV/Panther commander).

Eberhard Schmalz   89
12+ soviet tanks, (as Marder III commander).
29 soviet tanks, (as StuG commander).

Walther Oberloskamp   90
40+ soviet tanks, (as StuG III commander).

Richard Schramm   91
40~ soviet tanks, (as StuG commander).

Kurt Schumacher   92
40~(?) soviet tanks, (as Panzer IV commander).

Thomas Amselgruber   93
20+ soviet tanks, (as Tiger I commander).
10~ allied tanks, (as Tiger I commander).

Wilhelm von Malachowski   94
40+ soviet tanks, (as StuG III commander).

Heinz Scharf   95
40+ soviet tanks, (as StuG III commander).

Paul Wegener 96
40+ soviet tanks, (as StuG III commander).

Helmut Schwalb 97
40 soviet tanks, (as StuG commander).

Gottfried Tornau 98
40 soviet tanks, (as StuG III commander).

Karl-Heinz Warmbrunn 99
44 soviet tanks, (as Tiger I gunner).
8 soviet tanks, (as Tiger I commander).
5 allied tanks, (as Tiger I commander, 1 as gunner).

Helmut Harth 100
60 soviet tanks, (as Panzer IV gunner/commander).

Friedrich "Fritz" Tadje 101
39 soviet tanks, (as StuG III commander).

Georg Diers 102
39~ soviet tanks, (as Tiger II commander).

Diddo Diddens 103
38+ soviet tanks, (as StuG III commander).

Otto Angel 104
38 soviet tanks, (as StuG/Hetzer commander).

Heinz Baurmann 105
38 soviet tanks, (as StuG commander).

Friedrich "Fritz" Henke 106
38 soviet tanks, (as StuG III commander).

Josef Karl 107
38 soviet tanks, (mostly as Marder III commander).

Ludwig Laubmeier 108
38 soviet tanks, (as StuG III commander).

Josef Rampel 109
20+ soviet tanks, (as Panzer IV commander).
17+ soviet tanks, (as Tiger I commander).

Werner Stehle 110
19 allied tanks, (as StuG commander).

Ulf-Ola Olin 111
30+ soviet tanks, (as Panther commander, 1 using hand-held weapons).
2+(?) allied tanks, (as Jagdpanther commander).

Robert Eichert 112
36+ soviet tanks, (as Panzer IV commander).

Alfredo Carpaneto 113
35+ soviet tanks, (as Tiger I commander).

Gerhard Brandt 114
35 soviet tanks, (as StuG III commander).

Richard Krämer 115
35 soviet tanks, (as StuG III commander).

Hans Dauser 116
34+ soviet tanks, (as Panther commander).

Rudolf Haen 117
30~ soviet tanks, (as StuG commander).
2+(?) allied tanks, (as StuG commander).

Fritz Biermeier 118
33+ soviet tanks, (as Panzer IV commander).

Franz Staudegger 119
2 soviet tanks, (using hand-held weapons).
22 soviet tanks, (as Tiger I commander).
10~ soviet tanks, (as Tiger II commander).

Karl Buckel 120
30+ soviet tanks, (as StuG commander).
2 soviet tanks, (using hand-held weapons).

Gerhard Niemeck 121
32 soviet tanks, (as Panzer III/IV commander).

Karl Kloskowski 122
20+ soviet and allied tanks, (as Panzer III/Panzer IV commander).

Kurt Kirchner 123
30+ soviet tanks, (as StuG III commander).

Herbert Meißner 124
30+ soviet tanks, (as StuG commander).

Alfred Egghardt 125
30+ soviet tanks, (as StuG commander, 6 using hand-held weapons).

Otto Heymann 126
30+ soviet tanks, (as Panzer IV commander).

Karl Rettlinger 127
30+ soviet tanks, (as StuG commander).

Fritz Scherer 128
30+(?) soviet tanks, (as StuG commander).

Gottwald Stier 129
30+ soviet tanks, (as StuG commander).

Johann Straub 130
30+(?) soviet tanks, (as StuG commander).

Josef Trägner 131
30+ soviet tanks, (as StuG commander).

Franz Bayer 132
10~ soviet tanks, (as Panzer IV commander).
10~ soviet tanks, (as Tiger I commander).
10~ soviet tanks, (as Panther commander).
1 soviet tank, (using hand-held weapons).

Andreas von Rakowitz 133
30 soviet tanks, (as StuG commander).

Werner Pietsch 134
30~ soviet tanks, (as Panzer IV commander).

Willy Hein   135
30~(?) soviet tanks, (as StuG commander).

Franz Holzinger   136
30~(?) soviet tanks, (as StuG commander).

Heinz Kramer   137
50+ soviet tanks, (as Tiger I gunner/commander).

Hans Malkomes   138
24+ soviet and allied tanks, (as Panther commander).

Johann Veith   139
? soviet tanks.
20~(?) american tanks, (as Panther commander).

Albert Bausch   140
29 soviet tanks, (as StuG commander).

Alfred Großrock   141
29 soviet tanks, (as StuG III/Panther commander).

Martin Buhr   142
29 soviet tanks, (as StuG III commander).

Walter Scherf   143
29 soviet tanks, (mostly as Tiger I commander).

Kurt Schließmann   144
29 soviet tanks, (as StuG commander).

Heinz Pieper   145
28 soviet tanks, (as Panzerjäger commander).

Wolfgang von Bostell   146
28 soviet tanks, (as Panzerjäger/StuG commander).

Karl-Heinrich Banze   147
27+ soviet tanks, (as StuG III commander).

Reinhold Ertel   148
27+ soviet tanks, (as StuG III commander).

Ernst Alex 149
27+ soviet tanks, (as StuG III commander).

Carl Bath 150
3+ soviet tanks, (as towed PaK commander).
15 soviet tanks, (as Ferdinand gunner).
8 allied tanks, (as Jagdpanther commander).

Albert Blaich 151
26+ soviet tanks, (mostly as Panzer IV commander).

Horst Naumann 152
26+ soviet tanks, (as StuG III commander).

Ludwig Neigl 153
26+ soviet tanks, (as Nashorn commander).

Josef Beginen 154
25+ soviet tanks, (mostly as Panther commander).

Willi Eßlinger 155
25+ soviet tanks, (as Marder III commander).

Friedrich Dath 156
25+ soviet tanks, (as StuG commander).

Wolfgang Hartelt 157
25+ soviet tanks, (as Panther commander).

Rolf Truxa 158
25+ soviet tanks, (as StuG commander).

Hans Flügel 159
25~ soviet tanks, (as Panzer III/Panther commander).

Alfred Rubbel 160
25~(?) soviet tanks, (as Panzer IV/Tiger I/Tiger II commander).

Wolfgang Röhder 161
23+ soviet and allied tanks, (as StuG commander).

Heinrich Becker   162
23+ soviet tanks, (as Panzer III/IV commander).

Heinrich Teriete   163
? soviet tanks, (as StuG III commander).
22+ soviet tanks, (as Ferdinand (Elefant) commander).

Richard von Rosen   164
10~ soviet tanks, (as Tiger I commander).
2~ allied tanks, (as Tiger I commander).
10~ soviet tanks, (as Tiger II commander).

Heinz Buchner   165
51 soviet tanks, (as Panzer III/Tiger I gunner).

Heinz Angelmaier   166
23 soviet tanks, (as StuG commander).

Günter Chrzonsz   167
23 soviet tanks, (as StuG III commander).

Eugen Metzger   168
23 soviet tanks, (as StuG commander).

Johann Eggers   169
46+ soviet tanks, (as Panzer III/IV gunner).

Erwin Bohlken   170
22 soviet tanks, (as Panther commander).

Klaus Wagner   171
22 soviet tanks, (as StuG commander).

Kurt Zitzen   172
22 soviet tanks, (as StuG III commander).

Georg Gransee   173
21+ soviet tanks, (as Panzer III/IV commander).

Anton Grünert   174
21+ soviet tanks, (as StuG III commander).

Bernhard Sowada 175
21 soviet tanks, (as StuG III commander).

Franz Kretschmer 176
21 soviet tanks, (as Ferdinand (Elefant) commander).

Heinrich Köhler 177
21 soviet tanks, (as StuG commander).

Karl-Heinrich Gsell 178
20+ soviet tanks, (as Panzer IV commander).

Hanns Magold 179
20+ soviet tanks, (as StuG commander).

Wolfgang Eichler 180
20+ soviet tanks, (as Panzer IV commander).

Walter Rappholz 181
20+ soviet tanks, (mostly as Marder II commander).

Albert Dressel 182
20~ soviet tanks, (as Panzer IV commander).

Bernhard Himmelskamp 183
40 soviet tanks, (as Panzer IV gunner).

Heinrich Hendricks 184
38 soviet tanks, (as Panzer IV gunner).

Robert Rahlenbeck 185
15+ soviet tanks, (as commander/gunner in captured T-34).

INTRODUCTION

The four or five men -six for the Ferdinand/Elefant and the Jagdtiger- inside the machine are all volunteers.

-the tank commander is responsible for the vehicle and its crew. He indicates targets to the gunner, gives fire orders and observes the effects. He gives his orders by intercom to the driver and the radio operator, and by speaking tube and touch signals to the gunner and loader; by radio he receives orders and reports to his unit commander.

-the gunner fires the main gun and the co-axial machine gun; he assists the commander with observation.

-the loader loads and mantains the turret armament under the order of the gunner; he is also responsible for the care of ammunition; he replaces the radio operator if the latter becomes a casualty.

-the driver operates the vehicle under the orders of the commander; he assists with observation, reporting the presence of the enemy or obstacles; he is responsible to the commander for the care and maintenance of the vehicle.

-the radio operator when not actually transmitting always keeps his radio set to "receive". He operates the intercom system and records any important messages; he fires the bow machine gun; if the loader becomes a casualty he takes over his duties.

In the assault guns or jagdpanzers it worked somewhat differently. These vehicles were not equipped with a rotating turret, and even greater responsability was placed on the driver: in combat, with quick maneuvers, he has to get the right firing position for the gunner. In the StuG the loader also acted as radio operator, but in the Jagdpanzer IV that job moved to the commander. Contrary to what one might think, the crew of a panzer rarely remained the same for a long period. If the panzer was rendered inoperable for whatever reason, a leading commander had to temporary take over another vehicle; usually he didn't bring with him his crew, he simply went alone to replace a subordinate commander in the new vehicle. The composition of the crew changed also in the very common evenience that one or more men became casualties. Moreover, when the unit undertook a period of training and reorganization proven gunners would became commanders, so a new gunner had to be found, sometimes he was the former loader, other times a gunner coming from a disbanded crew, or directly from a gunnery course.

Until the summer of 1943 the Germans fought for total victory. For the common soldier this meant extinguishing the disgrace that had descended over the country with the Treaty of Versailles. For the Waffen-SS it was the creation of an empire ruled by the National Socialist idea and spanning from

Brittany to the Urals and from the North Cape to Crete; a community of nations freed from the Judeo-Bolshevism in the east, and from the Cultural Marxism of the cosmopolites and their accomplices in the west. For a moment at Prokhorovka and over the Psel this distant dream must have seemed still attainable.

The men have to endure the suffocating heat of June-August, or the unbearable cold when the flesh and the clothing stick on the steel surface. In the night the panzers are positioned behind the combat outposts of the grenadiers; one man stands on watch in the turret, the others sleep as long as the situation permits; the best time is when they can stretch under the hull in the freshness of the summer night. After a while they became one only thing with the panzer, and the machine itself through them acquired a soul, rised to a living creature; a tiger, a panther. When the moment comes, bodies and minds are completely devoted to one aim, to hit first, to overcome the human beings on the other side. Death was everywhere. Snipers were the nightmare of the commanders. In the Red Army very soon a large number of specialists are trained to target the man on the turret. And yet the field of view through slits in the cupola is too narrow. Carius develops a tecnique: at irregular intervals he emerges head and shoulders, keeping moving, for few precious seconds. On the contrary Wittmann always has a scissors periscope installed in his Tiger, a habit from his time with the assault guns battalion where each vehicle had one of these useful devices. In the west too, many are hit, particularly during the fighting in the forested terrain in autumn and winter 1944-45. For the panzer itself the most dangerous opponent more often is not the group of enemy vehicles, but the lone well concealed tank or AT gun. Wittmann repeats that the advancing T-34s give him little concern, but that he has fear of the isolated gun waiting in ambush. Almost a premonition we should say. In the east capture is to be avoided at all costs. Untold crew members shoot themselves after being surrounded by the Soviets. On the Invasion front and in Italy several panzer men are killed in cold blood, especially by the Canadians and New Zealanders it would seem.

The end comes in the most diverse ways but also with different destinies for the crew. When Wendorff's Tiger I is destroyed two survivors are trapped inside. In fear of being burned alive the eighteen years old loader shoots himself. The gunner cannot reach his pistol and so he lies, waiting for the inconceivable. But no! The English men climb on the machine, valiant arms in olive-brown uniform bring him away... to life.

BIOGRAPHIES

Adamowitsch Felix, born on 20 November 1919 in Salzburg, Austria, the son of a company manager. He joined the Wehrmacht in December 1938 being posted to Artillerie-Regiment 41 in Ulm. Promoted to *Leutnant* on April 1st 1940, he volunteered for the Sturmartillerie and in "Barbarossa" was with the Sturmgeschütz-Abteilung 185 in command of his own vehicle. He fought in the northern sector and received the EK II on 29 September 1941 for the destruction of a number of bunkers and tanks. On April 1st 1942 he was promoted to *Oberleutnant* and then transferred to the Sturmgeschütz-Abteilung 904 which was being formed at the time. He was awarded the EK I on 28 August 1943 and the Deutsches Kreuz in Gold on 29 February 1944. Promoted to *Hauptmann* and in command of the 3rd battery in the upgraded Sturmgeschütz-Brigade 904, he distinguished himself during the battles along the lower Narew. In the time period 10-13 September 1944 facing six Soviet armour-led attacks, each about 20-30 tanks strong, he personally eliminates 20 tanks (his subordinate vehicles a further 37). He then played a major role in the relief of the encircled 129.Infanterie-Division: with his battery he breaks the Soviet ring enabling the division to escape at the last moment. He is mentioned by name in the Wehrmachtbericht and on 20 October awarded the Ritterkreuz. Wounded five times during the war, he reached a total of around 50 tank "kills". In 1957 he joined the Bundeswehr retiring in 1979 as an *Oberst*. He passed away on 10 February 2013.

Alex Ernst, born on the 1st of March 1915 near the town of Schweidnitz (today Świdnica, Poland; possibly in the hamlet of Seifersdorf, today Pogorzała), fifty kilometers southwest of Breslau. He joined the Wehrmacht in 1935 being posted to Artillerie-Regiment 29 in Kassel. He fought in the Polish campaign receiving the EK II on 16 September 1939. Promoted to *Oberwachtmeister* on October 1st 1940, he took part in "Barbarossa" as platoon leader in the 1st battery, Sturmgeschütz-Abteilung 243. On 26 June in the tank battle at Yavoriv (in German reports under the Polish name of Jaworów) and during a night attack on the 27/28, he eliminates a total of 10 enemy tanks establishing the conditions for a swift advance on Lemberg. During the continued advance, at the railway station of Kopyčynci (fifty kilometers south of Ternopil) he opens fire from very close range on a Soviet armoured train destroying its heavy 15-cm gun. On 2 July he is awarded the EK I. His greatest achievement came on the 27 July when, launching himself in pursuit at the head of the 1.Gebirgs-Division, he secures the crossing over the Southern Bug at Bratslav. For this action, in which he is seriously wounded, and for reaching a personal total of 27 tank "kills" he is awarded the Ritterkreuz on August 1st 1941. Transferred to the Reserve as instructor, on June 1st 1943 he was promoted to *Leutnant*. In 1944 he may have fought in the area of Uman; then shortly before the end of the war he was critically injured having both his legs amputated. Promoted to *Oberleutnant* on April 1st 1945. He passed away on 25 October 1965.

Amann Herbert, born on 11 October 1919 in the small town of Dossenheim (five kilometers north of Heidelberg). He was posted to a number of artillery battalions taking part in the Battle of France and in the invasion of the Soviet Union. Promoted to *Leutnant* on November 1st 1941, he received the EK II on July 1st 1942. After a period of training in the Sturmgeschütz-Ersatz-Abteilung 200, in December 1942 he was sent again to the eastern front with the Sturmgeschütz-Abteilung 905, fighting in southern Russia. He received the EK I on 21 August 1943.

On the night of 8/9 January 1944 in the area northwest of Kirovograd an enemy armoured group of the 67th Tank Brigade succeeded in thrusting through the front of the 10.Panzergrenadier-Division and onto the command post of the XXXXVII.Panzerkorps in Mala Vyska. *Oberleutnant* Amann, in command of the 1st battery, leads his sturmgeschütze in a counterattack that inflicts heavy losses on the enemy stabilizing the situation. Few days later he is fatally wounded while in combat southeast of Novomirgorod and dies on 12 (or 13) January in the Hauptverbandsplatz of the Sanitätskompanie 2/61. On 10 February he was posthumously awarded the Ritterkreuz and promoted to *Hauptmann*. He destroyed a total of 42 enemy tanks.

Amling Fritz, born on 17 January 1916 in the small town of Preußisch Holland (today Pasłęk), eighty kilometers southeast of Danzig. He joined the Wehrmacht in late 1937, in the Artillerie-Regiment 24. With the 24.Infanterie-Division he took part in the Poland campaign and the Battle of France. In October 1941 he was sent to the eastern front with the newly formed Sturmgeschütz-Abteilung 202; he fought in the battle of Moscow and was awarded the EK II on 26 January. On 25 November 1942 the Soviets launched operation "Mars" with the aim of encircling and destroying the German forces in the Rzhev salient. Amling, despite being wounded, in a few days of combat in support of the 78.Infanterie-Division, with his StuG III eliminates no less than 40 enemy tanks (gunner Bruno Guskowski). On 7 December 1942 he had already received the EK I, but after further successes he was awarded the Ritterkreuz on 11 December, as *Wachtmeister* and platoon leader in the 3rd battery, for reaching a personal total of 56 "kills". Promoted to *Oberwachtmeister*, in March 1943 he was transferred to the Sturmgeschütz-Ersatz-und Ausbildungs-Abteilung 300 in Neisse as instructor, never to return to the front again. He passed away on 6 March 1994.

Notes. The recommendation for the Ritterkreuz seems to indicate a total of "56 Soviet tanks". This should be the sum of the 40 "kills" of 10-11 December with previous kills. If not, "56" could mean tanks, AT guns and other vehicles combined.

Amselgruber Thomas, born on 18 December 1905 in the village of Kirchweidach (eighty kilometers east of München). He joined the Allgemeine SS in München in July 1931; later he was placed in charge of the garage of the *Reichsführer-SS* in Berlin. In 1940 he joined the *LSSAH* assault gun battalion, at first as a driver, then in "Barbarossa" as a StuG III driver. In 1943 he was selected for the newly formed Tiger company. Promoted to *SS-Hauptscharführer* he was awarded the EK I on 2 July 1943. During "Zitadelle" he destroys 8 T-34s and 18 AT guns, but on 12 July he is wounded in the left hand losing four fingers. In December 1943 he was transferred to the schwere SS-Panzer-Abteilung 101; there he was promoted to *Standartenoberjunker* and then to *SS-Untersturmführer* on 20 April 1944. In Normandy, in mid-June he took command of the 3rd company. On 23 June in ambush position beside the Villers-Bocage Caen road he destroys 5 British tanks. Three days later in support of a counterattack of *Hitlerjugend* west of Caen against "Epsom", he eliminates 3 more tanks and, together with another Tiger, wipes out the British infantry. On 28 June he destroys two Shermans before his Tiger (turret number 331) is disabled by several hits. Injured to the left leg he escapes on foot taking with him the badly wounded gunner. During the fighting in Hungary, on 14 February 1945 he was awarded the Deutsches Kreuz in Gold. Fate unknown.

With Wittmann.

Tiger 331 in Normandy.

Angel Otto, born on 20 February 1913 in the village of Oberntief (fifty kilometers west of Nürnberg). He joined the Wehrmacht in April 1934 and took part in the early campaigns of the war with Artillerie-Regiment 103, 4.Panzer-Division. In 1942 he was sent to Schweinfurt for training in the Sturmartillerie, and in March 1943 joined the Sturmgeschütz-Abteilung 185. He received both classes of the EK.

In early 1945 while returning from leave he cannot make it back to his Sturmgeschütz-Brigade 185 and so he reported to Panzerjäger-Abteilung 6 in Frankfurt/Oder. This battalion had been destroyed in central Poland and now was being re-equipped with the Hetzer in order to be incorporated in the newly formed Panzer-Jagd-Brigade 104 (renamed "Kampfgruppe Munzel" on 15 February). On 7 March during the fighting for Körlin in eastern Pomerania, Angel is attacked by a force of 9 T-34s and 4 IS-2s. Reportedly, in just seven minutes he is able to destroy 6 of the T-34s. Three days later, despite battle damage to his Hetzer, he eliminates a further 8 tanks. For these actions, as well as raising his total of tank "kills" to 38, he is awarded the Ritterkreuz on 15 March as *Unteroffizier der Reserve* and platoon leader in Kampfgruppe Munzel; he is simultaneously promoted to *Feldwebel*. He may have been still in combat in the time period 20-23 April southwest of Stettin. He passed away on 14 October 2002.

Angelmaier Heinz, born on 22 July 1918 in Ulm. He joined the Wehrmacht in 1938, at first posted to Artillerie-Regiment 41, then in the Artillerie-Batterie 690 E (Kurze Bruno 28 cm railway guns). In February 1940 he was promoted to *Unteroffizier* and transferred to the 1st battery, Lehr-und Ersatzabteilung für Eisenbahnartillerie (motorisiert) 100. He took part in the Battle of France and was promoted to *Wachtmeister* in August 1940. On September 1st 1940 he was promoted to *Leutnant der Reserve*; he then volunteered for the Sturmartillerie and in November was posted to the Sturmgeschütz-Abteilung 192 as platoon leader in the 1st battery. He fought in the battle of Brest-Litovsk receiving the EK II on 20 July 1941. On 20 August he was severely wounded; four days later was awarded the EK I, however he had to leave his unit. In May 1942 he was transferred to the Sturmgeschütz-Abteilung 203 as platoon leader in the 3rd battery. In July during the advance towards the Caucasus he was given command of the whole battery and on September 1st he was promoted to *Oberleutnant*. On August 1st 1943, during the deployment in the Dnieper area he was promoted to *Hauptmann*; on 12 October he was awarded the Deutsches Kreuz in Gold. He then fought in the area of Krivoy Rog and in Cherkassy. In April 1944 he was posted to the Sturmgeschütz-Schule Burg, then he was given command of the 3rd battery, Sturmgeschütz-Ersatz-Abteilung 500 in Posen. On 27 October he took command of the whole Sturmgeschütz-Brigade 279 after the death in combat of *Major* Hoppe.

In East Prussia, on the 19 January 1945 he was ordered to support the defense of Breitenstein (today Ul'yanovo) with two of his batteries. This large village had to be held until 19:00, in order to enable the 56.Infanterie-Division to complete its withdrawal over the Inster (Instruč) river. Angelmaier found that the German infantry had pulled back along the road to Moulinen (possibly the present hamlet of Mikhaylovka) and that the flak guns charged with covering the retreat were in the process of dismantling. He immediately shuttled the infantry into favourable defensive positions, then used some of the remaining forces to create a kampfgruppe with both grenadiers and 6 sturmgeschütze. In a bold counterthrust he recaptures the northeastern part of the village ejecting the Soviets

from the Breitenstein estate; he then withdraws according to plan with the division's last elements over the Inster at Scherden (possibly the present hamlet of Ryabinovka). During the second half of January in the area Breitenstein-Insterburg the Brigade's 19 operational sturmgeschütze eliminated: 5 IS-2s (as well as another 3 immobilized), 5 KV-85s, 35 T-34s, 5 heavy assault guns, 61 heavy AT guns, 3 tractors, 29 trucks, 7 artillery pieces. For these successes and for his personal total of 23 tank "kills" he was awarded the Ritterkreuz on 18 February 1945. On 20 February he was given acting command of a battalion in the Fallschirm-Panzergrenadier-Division 2 "Hermann Göring". On 9 May he was taken prisoner by the Soviets in the Sudeten region; he managed to escape and surrender to US forces. He passed away on 12 January 2014, aged 95.

StuG IV and grenadiers in East Prussia, early 1945.

Arnold Friedrich, born on 10 May 1919 in Karlsruhe. He joined the Wehrmacht in November 1937; in early 1941 he attended an assault gun course in Jüterbog and became StuG commander. In "Barbarossa" he fought in the central sector receiving the EK II on 18 August 1941 and the EK I a week later. On 9 October 1942 he was awarded the Deutsches Kreuz in Gold as *Leutnant der Reserve* in the 2nd battery, Sturmgeschütz-Abteilung 201. In 1943 he was transferred to the newly formed Sturmgeschütz-Abteilung 237 as *Oberleutnant* and platoon leader in the 2nd battery. In the region of Smolensk in the time period 8 August-22 September 1943 he destroys 22 enemy tanks, bringing his total to 51. In one action, while assigned to the 35.Infanterie-Division, he launches a counterattack with only two vehicles and a handful of grenadiers, retaking the old defensive line and then holding this position for a whole night until reinforcements arrive. Repeatedly wounded, on 16 November 1943 he is awarded the Ritterkreuz. In 1944 he was assigned to the Sturmgeschütz-Ersatz und Ausbildungs-Abteilung 500, then after being promoted to *Hauptmann*, he was posted as instructor at the Sturmgeschütz-Schule in Burg. In the last days of the war he was allegedly wounded again in combat and taken prisoner by the French. He passed away on September 1st 2006.

Bachor Wilhelm, born on 4 May 1921 in the village of Kelbassen (today Kiełbasy), sixty kilometers southeast of Allenstein (Olsztyn). After a period of training in the Reiter-Ersatz-Regiment 1, he was assigned to the 1.Kavallerie-Division and took part in the Western Campaign. On 14 November 1940 he received the EK II. On the eastern front, in November 1941, the division was disbanded and reformed as the 24.Panzer-Division. With this unit Bachor fought in Stalingrad, however he was wounded and evacuated in time from the city. In early 1943 he returned to the division which was in the process of reconstitution in the west. He fought in southern Ukraine and in Romania and was awarded the EK I on 25 December 1943 and the Deutsches Kreuz in Gold on 28 June 1944 as *Unteroffizier* in the 12th company, Panzer-Regiment 24.

Promoted to *Oberwachtmeister* and platoon leader, he would distinguish himself in East Prussia. On 18 March 1945 he was deployed with his sturmgeschütz northeast of Grunenfeld, near Heiligenbeil. All on his own he was tasked with mantaining his position, despite strong enemy artillery and AT gun fire, in order to both support the hard-pressed grenadiers and counter any potential enemy armoured attacks. At around 13:00 the Soviets began a breakthrough attempt with 11 medium/heavy tanks and assault guns, abundant infantry and ground attack aircrafts. In a bitter firefight at close range the sturmgeschütz is hit twice, but manages to eliminate six AFVs. When the remaining enemy vehicles turn around and try to escape, Bachor, on his own initiative, decides to pursue them: he destroys two additional tanks and immobilizes a ISU-152 assault gun with his last 4 rounds of high-explosive ammunition. By this time he had reached a total of 57 tank "kills", along with over 90 AT guns, artillery pieces and mortars, and in May he was awarded the Ritterkreuz. During the course of the war he partecipated in over fifty separate armoured engagements and was wounded nine times. He passed away on 20 March 2008.

Notes. In April 1943 the Panzer-Abteilung 127 of the disbanded 27.Panzer-Division became the new III.Abteilung of the 24.Panzer-Division; soon after, in July, it was converted to Panzer-Sturmgeschütz-Abteilung. - His nomination for the Ritterkreuz was not forwarded or may have been lost by the corps due to the military situation. A second nomination, which was submitted after the German capitulation, was not processed. The order commission of the OdR processed the case in 1982 and decided: "Knight's Cross yes, 8 May 1945".

Two generations of T-34 knocked out in the area of Heiligenbeil, March 1945.

Bäke Dr. Franz, born on 28 February 1898 in the village of Schwarzenfels (eighty kilometers east of Frankfurt am Main). In May 1915 he volunteered for the German army and was posted to an infantry regiment on the western front; in 1916 he earned the EK II. He was discharged in January 1919 only to enlist soon after in the Freikorps Epp. In parallel he studied medicine and became Doctor of Medical Dentistry in 1923. On March 1st 1933 he joined the SA (his final rank would be *SA-Standartenführer* as of August 1944). In 1938 he was again mobilized for full-time service as an officer in the 6.Panzer-Division and took part in the Poland campaign. In the Battle of France he leads the 1st company to Dunkirk and then in the breakthrough to the southeast. With the 3,7 cm gun of his light panzer 35(t) he manages to destroy several enemy vehicles with multiple hits on the flanks. On June 1st he was awarded the EK I. He took little part in the first phase of "Barbarossa", however in December he was given command of the 1st company, Panzer-Regiment 11. In February 1942 he leads a small force in the battle for the Rzhev salient, and with his short barreled Panzer IV destroys 2 T-34s. In December 1942 the re-equipped division was committed to the west of Stalingrad in operation "Wintergewitter". Bäke, now *Major* and in command of the 2nd battalion, Panzer-Regiment 11, leads his unit within forty-eight kilometers from the pocket, personally destroying, with a long barreled Panzer IV, a dozen enemy tanks; then in the following retreat behind the Donets he eliminates another dozen tanks. On 11 January 1943 he is awarded the Ritterkreuz.

In "Zitadelle" he leads his battalion on the right flank of the southern pincer, personally destroying another ten enemy tanks, followed by several more during the withdrawal. On August 1st he is awarded the Eichenlaub. In late 1943 he was appointed regimental commander and ordered to form an ad-hoc reinforced tank unit. This is Schweres Panzer-Regiment Bäke consisting of 34 Tigers I and 46 Panthers, supported by self-propelled artillery, a mechanized engineer battalion and, at a later stage, also by a Gebirgsjäger battalion. In late January 1944, in the battle against the Soviet forces encircled in the Balabanivka area (midway between Uman and Vinnytsia), in five days the regiment eliminates 268 Soviet AFVs and 156

42

AT guns for the complete loss of four panzers. Of this total, Bäke accounted for more than 10 tanks with his Panther and, at the age of 46, 3 tanks in close combat. Next, his panzers together with a kampfgruppe of the *LSSAH* manage to open a route of escape for the units encircled in the Cherkassy pocket, destroying another 250 enemy tanks and assault guns. During this battle he personally eliminates another 5 tanks. On 21 February he is awarded the Schwertern. In March the regiment was trapped in the Kaments-Podolsky pocket along with the entire 1.Panzer-Armee; it formed one of the spearheads moving west and effected a link up with the II.SS-Panzerkorps. In May 1944 he was promoted to *Oberstleutnant* and put in command of Panzer-Brigade 106 "Feldherrnhalle". In the night of 7-8 September, in a ill-advised attack against a US infantry division, his unit took very heavy losses. In the following weeks, always leading aboard his Panther, he may have knocked out a few Allied tanks.

On 10 March he was given command of Panzer-Division Feldherrnhalle 2. With this unit he fights during the retreat through Hungary and Slovakia. Promoted to *Generalmajor* he surrenders the remnants of his division to the Americans on 8 May. When the men are handed over to Soviet forces, he manages to slip with a small group through the enemy lines to the west. In 1947, after two years of internment, Dr. Bäke resumed his dental practice in the town of Hagen. During World War II he partecipated in over 400 (four hundred) tank combat missions, survived 13 times to penetrating hits on his panzer and was wounded seven times in combat. He died in a car accident on 12 December 1978. The Bundeswehr provided an honour guard at his funeral.

Notes. He is credited with destroying 79 enemy tanks. F. Kurowski in his "Panzer Aces" provides a detailed description of Bäke's combats, each time precisely reporting the number of "kills". These figures seem to come from war time documentation or in any case from some other relevant source, and so may be considered reliable. From all this we get a total of at least 70 enemy tanks eliminated by Bäke in the course of WWII.

Banach Friedrich, born on 2 January 1916 in Rotthausen (a district of Gelsenkirchen, in the Ruhr region). After a period in the Reichsarbeitsdienst, in November 1937 he joined the Wehrmacht being posted to Panzer-Regiment 5; one year later he was transferred to Panzer-Regiment 36, 4.Panzer-Division. He took part in the early campaigns receiving the EK II on 4 November 1939 and the EK I on 30 September 1940. With his regiment -which in the meantime had been assigned to the newly formed 14.Panzer-Division- he fought in "Barbarossa" and then during the advance on Stalingrad in 1942; on 7 August he was wounded by a shrapnel in the face. On 24 November 1942 he was awarded the Deutsches Kreuz in Gold as *Feldwebel* in the 4th company; few days later in the course of an attack against a Soviet cavalry division he takes over a leaderless zug from his unit. Skilfully utilizing the terrain he works his way into the enemy flank and destroys 5 guns; without waiting for the other panzers, he thrusts further forwards knocking out an armoured car and penetrating into a densely packed Soviet supply unit which is totally surprised and scattered. Since the start of the war he had eliminated 43 Soviet tanks as well as numerous guns of all kind, and on 30 November 1942 he was awarded the Ritterkreuz. Promoted to *Oberfeldwebel*, he was killed in action on 13 March 1943 in Zaporozhye. He may have reached a total of 48 tank "kills".

Banze Karl-Heinrich, born on 24 February 1911 in the town of Hofgeismar (twenty kilometers north of Kassel). On October 1st 1933 he joined the Reichswehr being posted to Artillerie-Regiment 70 in Koblenz. With the Sturmgeschütz-Abteilung 244 he took part in "Barbarossa" receiving the EK II and the EK I respectively on 24 July and on 27 September 1941. During the second battle of Kharkov, on 14 May 1942, as *Oberwachtmeister* and platoon leader in the 1st battery, acting in support of the 113.Infanterie-Division he engages a Soviet tank formation all on his own and destroys 13 tanks (out of a total of 36 by the whole abteilung). By doing so he raised his personal total of tank "kills" to 24, a feat for which the day after he was mentioned by name in the Wehrmachtbericht. In the following days he managed to eliminate three more tanks, and on 27 May 1942 was awarded the Ritterkreuz. Promoted to *Leutnant*, he was captured in Stalingrad and reportedly died in February 1943 at a prisoner-of-war camp in Dubrovka (in European Russia).

Notes. He was listed as missing in action until 1951 when, at the request of his family, he was formally declared dead by the district court of his hometown. The date of death was retroactive to December 31, 1945.

Barkmann Ernst, born on 25 August 1919 in the village of Kisdorf (sixty kilometers south of Kiel), the son of a farmer. He joined the NSDAP on September 1st 1938 then in the following months served in the Reichsarbeitsdienst. On April 1st 1939 he enlisted in the Waffen-SS and was assigned to the SS-Standarte "Germania" headquartered in Hamburg. He fought in the Poland campaign as a machine gunner in the ninth company of the third battalion, receiving a promotion to *SS-Rottenführer*, the infantry assault badge and the wound badge. During "Barbarossa" he was seriously wounded near Dniepropetrovsk in July; he received the EK II, but spent the remainder of 1941 in convalescence. In early 1942 he was posted for a time as an instructor of SS volunteers in the Netherlands. In winter 1942/43 he was sent back to *Das Reich*, this time in the divisional panzer regiment as a gunner in a Panzer III Ausf.J in the second company of the first battalion. During the large scale operations to annihilate Mobile Group Popov he proves to be an excellent gunner, therefore he is promoted to *SS-Unterscharführer* and is given command of his own Panzer III. He takes part in the ensuing recapture of Kharkov scoring several "kills". Still with the Panzer III he fights in "Zitadelle" and then to the Mius. In August he is transferred in the fourth company, in command of one of the new Panther Ausf.D. In the course of the defensive battles in southern Ukraine he destroys several enemy tanks and is awarded the EK I.

47

In Normandy he was in command of a Panther Ausf.A in the fourth company, SS-Panzer-Regiment 2. On 8 July he destroys his first Sherman, two more on 12 July. The day after, in ambush position, he destroys two Shermans and an AT gun, then the Panther takes a hit in the front armor but can be brought to the repair company. On 14 July with a replacement vehicle he manages to recover 4 panzers left behind in no-man's land and to score three more kills; several wounded German prisoners are also freed. On 20 and 21 July he destroys four more Shermans. At dawn on 27 July he finds himself cut off from the rest of the company; some retreating grenadiers tell him of a long column of tanks and vehicles on the road to Coutances (thirty kilometers west of Saint-Lô); this is infact "Operation Cobra", the US First Army long-planned breakthrough to the south. Barkmann moves his Panther behind an earth mound with bushes, only 100 meters from a main crossroad. From this ideal position he destroys the two point tanks, followed by several carriers, jeeps and ammunition trucks; two more approaching Shermans are eliminated. The Allies call for an air strike and the Panther is hit several times. Other Shermans close in, but three more are eliminated as well. The Panther is repaired and, with two panzers in tow, reaches Coutances on July 28. The town is already occupied, so Barkmann drives westwards, crossing over the American march route several times, to Granville (on the Atlantic coast!). Here he has the panzers blown up, then he leads the crews through the gulf of Avranches at low tide, finally reaching friendly lines few days later. On 27 August he is awarded the Ritterkreuz and promoted to *SS-Oberscharführer.*

In "Wacht am Rhein", in the night from 24 to 25 December the I.Panzer-Abteilung and the grenadiers of regiment *Deutschland* are to attack Manhay. Barkmann on his own initiative decides to advance with his Panther Ausf.G in the direction of the enemy. Under cover of darkness he manages to approach a group of tanks setting on fire three of them; then mingling with the retreating American troops he crosses Manhay only to find himself right in the middle of the assembly area of hundreds of tanks and vehicles belonging to several enemy divisions. He runs over a jeep and collides with a Sherman; using smoke candles he

48

manages to escape, then he turns and fires back knocking out a number of Shermans and other vehicles; finally from the opposite side the rest of the panzer company attacks and the enemy is routed: countless vehicles and equipments are captured.

In March 1945 in the aftermath of the ill-fated "Frühlingserwachen" he destroys four T-34s in the area of Stuhlweißenburg, bringing the total score of *Das Reich* for the war so far to 3,000 enemy tanks. By April he is in action south of Vienna, where he is wounded by mistake by friendly fire. Later his Panther becomes disabled in a huge bomb crater and is destroyed by the crew. Barkmann was able to reach the Allied zone of operation and surrender to the British. After the war he settled in his hometown, where he served as fire brigade chief and as mayor. He passed away on 27 June 2009.

Notes. At the end of the war he was allegedly credited with destroying no less than 82 tanks, 43 AT guns and 136 other combat vehicles. However prior to Normandy his highest decoration was the EK I, so the number of his tank kills in the east could not have exceeded 40. In Normandy his claims at the "Coutances crossroad" do not completely match with the American reports and are most probably exaggerated. It should also be noted that, both in France and in the Ardennes, some of the "Shermans" knocked out by Barkmann were in fact M5 Stuarts light tanks.

Bath Carl, born on 15 June 1914 in the hamlet of Sanderahm (eight kilometers south of Wilhelmshaven). He entered the war as *Jägerführer* in the newly formed Panzerabwehr-Abteilung (mot.) 654; the unit fought with towed anti-tank guns through Poland, Holland and France. He took part in the invasion of the Soviet Union as a gun commander, receiving the EK II on 12 January 1942 and the EK I on 29 December 1942; he then became panzer gunner. On the Invasion front he was commander in the 2nd company, schwere Panzerjäger-Abteilung 654, and in August 1944 was promoted to *Unteroffizier.* On November 27 in the region of Belfort he destroys 2 out of 4 Shermans. In late January 1945 during the battle for the Colmar pocket, US forces managed to enter Jebsheim after days of fighting; the Germans however were still around the village. On the 28 Bath was credited with one tank "kill"; on the 30 he was securing the eastern outskirts with three Jagdpanthers, however in the afternoon French and US forces started a pincer movement and two of the German vehicles were quickly knocked out. Bath holds the position and destroys 5 Shermans; his gun fire attracts the Allied artillery and the Jagdpanther is hit and disabled, nevertheless he takes the on board machine-gun, fixes it on top of the hull and begins to spray the attackers forcing the French infantry to retreat. For this action and for reaching a total of 23 tank and several AT-gun "kills", he was awarded the Deutsches Kreuz in Gold on 9 March 1945.

Notes. In April 1940 the unit was redesignated Panzerjäger-Abteilung 654; in March 1943 the abteilung was transferred to France, equipped with Ferdinand tank destroyers and given the "schwere" designation. In "Zitadelle" it was deployed as II./Panzerjäger-Regiment 656. In early 1944 it was the first unit to be entirely re-equipped with Jagdpanthers.

Jagdpanthers of schwere PzJägAbt 654 in Normandy.

Baurmann Heinz, born on 11 November 1919 in Aachen. He took part in the French campaign receiving the EK II on July 1st 1940; then in the invasion of the Soviet Union receiving the EK I on 11 September 1941. In 1942 and early 1943 he fought in the central sector of the eastern front, and was awarded the Deutsches Kreuz in Gold on 16 April 1943 as *Oberleutnant* in the 3rd company, Sturmgeschütz-Abteilung 667. Promoted to *Hauptmann*, from December 1944 to 31 January 1945 he led the entire Sturmgeschütz-Brigade 322 in action in the area of Brody-Tarnopol and in southern Poland. On 28 March 1945 he was put in command of the Sturmgeschütz-Brigade 300 and immediately ordered to the sector of the 208.Infanterie-Division, west of Breslau. Here, along with Grenadier-Regiment 337, he launches a successful attack to envelop Striegau (today Strzegom) from the north. The Soviets are repelled by the handful of available sturmgeschütze; they take heavy losses (including over 50 tanks) and have to completely halt their offensive action in this sector. Baurmann and his men would distinguish themselves again in the counterattack to retake Bautzen. For these achievements and for a personal total of 38 enemy tank "kills", he was awarded the Ritterkreuz on 4 May. From 1956 to 1971 he served in the Bundeswehr reaching the rank of *Oberstleutnant*. He passed away on 7 December 1996.

Notes. No evidence regarding the presentation of the Ritterkreuz can be found in the Bundesarchiv files. Most probably it was made by *Feldmarschall* Schörner by teleprinter message, in compliance with the empowerment for autonomous presentations dated 3 May 1945.

Bausch Dr.jur. Albert, born on 2 July 1904 in Orken (a suburb of Grevenbroich, twenty-five kilometers southwest of Düsseldorf). A Doctor of Law, he joined the Wehrmacht in 1937. He took part in the Battle of France receiving the EK II on 13 July 1940. On the eastern front he fought with the Sturmgeschütz-Abteilung 226 in the central sector of "Barbarossa", then in 1942 in the battle of Voronezh. After a period of refitting, in late 1942 the abteilung was transferred back to the eastern front in the area of Leningrad. Here *Oberleutnant* Bausch led the 2nd battery, receiving the EK I on 9 October 1942. Promoted to *Hauptmann der Reserve*, on 4 July 1943 he was awarded the Deutsches Kreuz in Gold. In October 1943 he took command of the newly formed Sturmgeschütz-Abteilung 286.

In mid-December 1943 the Germans launched a corps-sized counterattack southeast of Kirovograd to close a frontline gap near Novhorodka, with the "286" attached to the 2.Fallschirmjäger-Division. After 8 days the old frontline was restored, however at this point the division, with a combat strenght of only 3200 men, was ordered to take over the sector of two panzer divisions that were being withdrawn; this section of frontline amounted to 21 km. On 5 January 1944 the Soviets attacked westwards from Novhorodka and Znamianka in order to envelop and capture Kirovograd. Against the southern arm Bausch launches a counterthrust with 3 sturmgeschütze and the remaining 40 men of the 9./Fallschirmjäger-Regiment 2: an enemy battalion is thrown back and many tanks eliminated (on this day alone, 61 tanks are destroyed by the Flak-Regiment, 60 by the sturmgeschütze, 12 by the divisional artillery, 3 by the light infantry gun Zug, 34 by the divisional Panzerjäger-Abteilung, 9 by close combat weaponry). In 4 days of combat the German frontline is pushed back but does not break. For these successes and for having personally destroyed 29 tanks by this time, Bausch was awarded the Ritterkreuz on 10 February. Promoted to *Major* he went on to lead his unit, by then upgraded to Brigade. He was killed on 29 August near Piatra Neamţ, Romania.

Bayer Franz, born on 3 February 1920 in the village of Langau (eighty-five kilometers northwest of Wien). After joining the Wehrmacht in 1938, he was posted to the Panzer-Regiment 33 of the 9.Panzer-Division. In 1940 in command of his own tank he took part in the battle of France; he was then selected for an officer candidate course in Wünsdorf. Promoted to *Leutnant*, with the Panzer-Regiment 39 of the 17.Panzer-Division he took part in the invasion of the Soviet Union as platoon leader in the 6th company. He received the EK II on October 1st 1941 and the EK I on the 20 of the same month. Promoted to *Oberleutnant*, in September 1942 in the area north of Orel (the division was positioned to the west of Belëv) he led an attack which inflicted heavy losses to the enemy; he was thus awarded the Deutsches Kreuz in Gold on 7 October. In August he had destroyed a tank in close combat. In 1943 after recovering from his fifth wound of the war he was given command of a company in the III.Abteilung, Panzer-Regiment "Großdeutschland". In late 1943 the battalion covered the withdrawal movements of the front; on 16 November, in the area of Lyubymivka, Bayer destroyed 10 tanks.

Promoted to *Hauptmann*, he achieved major successes in central Hungary in command of the I.Abteilung, Panzer-Regiment 26. On 22 December 1944 he was ordered to capture with his Panthers the village of Pázmánd from the north, with the support of an SPW company and a Sturmhaubitze battery. In a swift advance two hills located south of Vereb were captured and the enemy lost 7 tanks and 9 AT guns; a hundred prisoners were also brought in. At that point any further advance was stopped by a defensive front of anti-tank guns and dug-in tanks northeast of Pázmánd, and a withdrawal order was therefore issued. However Bayer had identified significant enemy armour assemblies on both side of the village; also it was no longer possible to transmit to the Regiment as the radio had been smashed. He thus decided to hold the captured ground in order to intercept the imminent enemy attack (aimed northwards to Komárom) against the withdrawing 271.Volksgrenadier-Division and elements of the 6.Panzer-Division. At around 10:30 the enemy launched its attack with about 40 tanks, partially enveloping the hills as it did so. After fierce

combat 21 tanks and 4 trucks with limbered AT guns are eliminated. In total, in the time period 22-24 December, with only 17 friendly panzers Bayer destroyed 73 tanks, 26 AT guns and 17 trucks for the loss of only one of his own vehicles. The "271" was also given time to set up a new defensive line further to the north along the line Vértesacsa-Vál. For his bold leadership he was proposed in January 1945 for the Ritterkreuz (he would be awarded on 9 May 1945 in accordance with the Dönitz-decree). Already in April 1944 he had received the third level of the Panzerkampfabzeichen for the participation in over fifty separate armoured engagements. In the last month of the war he was deployed with the Panzer-Grenadier-Division *Feldherrnhalle* as a company commander. He managed to surrender to American forces. He passed away on 28 April 2014 in Wien.

Notes. On January 1944 the I.Abteilung, Panzer-Regiment 26, equipped with the Panther was sent on the eastern front (while the rest of the 26.Panzer-Division stayed in Italy) and on November 1944 was assigned to Panzerkorps "Großdeutschland" (becoming, at the beginning of 1945, the I./Panzer-Regiment "Brandenburg"). Meanwhile the 26.Panzer-Division had received the I.Abteilung (Panther) from Panzer-Regiment 4 as its new I.Abteilung. - His nomination for the RK was written on 1 January 1945 and approved by the III.Panzerkorps. *Feldherrnhalle* had also submitted a nomination in January. Both were sent to the 6.Armee and approved in April.

Becker Heinrich, born on 23 January 1914 in the village of Gretesch (five kilometers east of Osnabrück). In service from April 1934, he volunteered to join the Legion Condor. He fought in the Polish campaign receiving the EK II on 9 October 1939; he then took part in the invasion of the Soviet Union and on 25 December 1941 was awarded the EK I. *Oberfeldwebel* and platoon leader in the 8th company, Panzer-Regiment 31, 5.Panzer-Division, he distinguished himself during the defensive combat northwest of Orel in the winter of 1942/43. Over the course of two consecutive days he destroyed 23 Soviet tanks and significantly contributed to crushing a strong enemy breakthrough attempt. He was thus awarded the Ritterkreuz on 15 March 1943. By the end of the war he had been promoted to *Leutnant*. He was captured by British troops and released in 1947. He passed away on 17 February 1960 in Osnabrück.

Beginen Josef, born on 5 December 1914 in the small town of Kaldenkirchen (forty-five kilometers west of Düsseldorf). In service from October 1934. After the Polish campaign he received the EK II on 16 November 1939; he then took part in the invasion of the Soviet Union and received the EK I on 23 August 1941. He particularly distinguished himself in early 1944 as *Oberfeldwebel* and platoon leader in the 4th company, Panzer-Regiment 35. On 8 January, north of the town of Kalinkaviču (in German reports: Kalinkowitschi) in the Gomel region, the Soviets attacked the sector of the 4.Panzer-Division with 7 rifle divisions and 1 tank corps. In the fighting which followed a force of around 40 tanks passed through a gap in the frontline (which consisted of a chain of strongpoints) and headed southwest towards the only available retreat road. Facing the danger of envelopment the division decided to pull back to a rearward position on the night. Deployed just to the south of this break-in point, "Jupp" Beginen on his own initiative leads his zug against the overwehlming enemy tank formation. Under strong AT gun fire he himself eliminates 6 tanks. His own Panther received severe damage and the turret jammed, meaning that he had to pivot turn the entire vehicle for every shot; nonetheless he held out until reinforcements arrived. Later that evening enemy tanks were again spotted just 3 km away from the road of the planned withdrawal. Despite the unfixed damage to his own panzer, he held off the Soviets for the entire night alongside two other friendly vehicles that were also barely operational, personally destroying another 3 tanks. He only disengaged around midday on the day after, when was informed of the successful completion of the withdrawal. For this action and for bringing his total of tank "kills" in the last six months to 25 he was awarded the Ritterkreuz on 23 February 1944. He was killed in the night of 16-17 April 1945 when the transport *Goya* was torpedoed by a Soviet submarine while leaving Danzig bay to Kiel.

Notes. Among the over 6000 people aboard the *Goya*, there were 200 men from Panzer-Regiment 35, mainly fathers or only surviving sons. 193 died out of 200.

Biermeier Fritz, born on 19 May 1913 in Augsburg. In 1933 he joined the NSDAP and simultaneously volunteered for the Waffen-SS. In 1938 he graduated from the SS-Junkerschule Braunschweig with the rank of *Untersturmführer* and platoon commander in *Totenkopf*. He took part in the French campaign receiving the EK II on 22 June 1940. For the invasion of the Soviet Union he was transferred to *Reich* as a tank company commander; on 7 October 1941 he received the EK I. When SS-Panzer-Regiment 3 was formed in 1942 he returned to *Totenkopf*; he was promoted to *SS-Hauptsturmführer* and put in command of the II.Abteilung. On 14 November 1943 north of Krivoy Rog, he leads a small armoured group (1 Tiger, 7 Panzer IVs, 3 Panzer IIIs) with the mission of advancing from the village of Chervono Kostyantynivka (in German reports: Krasno Konstantinovka) towards a number of high points in order to enable the grenadiers to occupy the old frontline for the neighboring unit on the right. As the Germans are standing by at Point 173.1, a strong enemy tank formation launches a southward thrust against the firing position of the I./SS-Panzer-Artillerie-Regiment 3. On his own initiative Biermeier attacks this hostile group near Luhanka: 38 enemy tanks are destroyed without any total losses on the German side; he then smashes another advancing force: of about 800 Soviet infantrymen only a few survivors manage to pull back to the east. On this day he personally destroys 6 T-34s, reaching a total of 31 enemy tanks since March 1943. On 10 (or 14) December he is awarded the Ritterkreuz.

In 1944 he repeatedly distinguished himself during the battles to the east and north of Warsaw. On 3 August 1944 at around 10:30 the 9./SS-Panzergrenadier-Regiment "Theodor Eicke" is ejected from its positions by much larger enemy infantry forces advancing from the south towards Grębków. Biermeier resolves to launch an immediate counterthrust with the still available pionieers and messengers supported by 2 sturmgeschütze. At 12:45 the old frontline is once again restored, thus preventing a rolling up of the division's left wing; the enemy infantry has been wiped out, 5 self-propelled guns and 2 artillery pieces eliminated. On 19 August the enemy commenced a major assault to the east and northeast of Sitki with overwhelming artillery and ground-attack aircraft support. In this situation

Biermeier immediately gathers up the available panzers and some grenadiers of the Aufklärungs-Abteilung in the Michałów-Klembów area. The enemy is thrown back suffering the following losses on this day: 11 lend-lease Shermans, 1 KV-85, 1 T-34, 3 artillery pieces, 2 AT guns, 1 infantry gun. On 26 August the pressure against the division's left flank reached its apex; the grenadiers and the panzers pulled back, but the enemy nevertheless thrusted into the rear with armoured forces. At the same time the enemy moved out of the forest northeast of Rasztów heading southwards in an attempt to prevent German forces from crossing over the Rządza. Biermeier once again sets out towards the Soviets with 2 panzers. In total twelve tanks are eliminated: 5-T34s, 5 Shermans and also 2 KV-85s personally destroyed by him from very close range; in addition 5 artillery pieces and 8 AT guns. During the morning hours of the 2 September, the enemy commenced a westward attack with 40 tanks from the area north of Duża. Biermeier launches a counterthrust with 4 Panzer IVs and restores contact with those friendly forces still fighting in the western part of Nadma. Over the course of ferocious combat the following is destroyed: 11 T-34s, 7 IS-2s, 2 KV-85s, 1 Sherman, 6 artillery pieces. On 13 September in a night attack the enemy tried to thrust from the southeast against Marki so as to interdict the Struga-Praga road. Five attacks are repulsed by the 5th company led by Biermeier, and he only orders his panzers to conduct a fighting withdrawal after the grenadiers had occupied their position during the evening. Destroyed: 8 KV-85s, 7 T-34s, 1 IS-2, 4 AT guns, 1 armoured car. He is killed in action on 11 October 1944 in the area of Modlin (40 km northwest of Warsaw). Posthumously awarded the Eichenlaub on 26 December, as *SS-Sturmbannführer* and commander of the II.Abteilung, SS-Panzer-Regiment 3.

Panzer IV Ausf.H from 3.SS-Panzer-Division "Totenkopf".

Bix Hermann, born on 10 October 1914 in the small town of Strehlitz (today Strzelce Opolskie, one hundred and ten kilometers southeast of Breslau). He attended vocational school as a mechanic, then in 1935 joined the Wehrmacht; he started the war as *Gefreiter* in Panzer-Regiment 35, 4.Panzer-Division. During the Battle of France he was promoted to *Unteroffizier* and awarded the EK II on 30 May 1940. In "Barbarossa" he was in command of a Panzer III in Kampfgruppe Eberbach. In early September on his own initiative he attacks the village of Baturyn (200 kilometers northeast of Kiev) throwing the enemy into disarray and leading to the capture of an entire Soviet motorized battalion. On October 1st, Panzer-Regiment 35 moved out to the northeast, towards Orel and Moscow. In the evening *Feldwebel* Bix is the lead tank. Moving far ahead of the company, under cover of darkness he crosses Dmitrovsk amidst a vast concentration of Soviet troops, then he turns and starts shelling the enemy; the other panzers come forward and the town is rapidly taken. The day after he is again at the point and after 20 kilometers manages to secure a fuel dump: the company can resume the advance and the bridge at Kromy is taken intact; the enemy can't believe that the Germans are already there and also this second town is immediately taken by surprise. On 3 October he is with the small group of panzers which charge at full speed into Orel, along the main street and across the gigantic viaduct over the Oka. On 6 October during the advance in the direction of Mtsensk the Germans meet the new T-34s and KV-1s; Bix fires at several tanks but even the best-placed hits ricochet off the armor! On 20 October he is awarded the EK I. On 21 November during the flanking manoeuvre east of Tula he is again the lead

tank; he manages to approach a KV-1 at 30 meters and fires three tungsten-cored rounds at the turret without result; then with a few more hits he disables the barrel: the Soviet crew fires and is killed by the internal explosion of his own round. On the 24 during the attack on Venyov (fifty kilometers east of Tula), Bix is at the point once again. In the town a KV-1 is going to ram in the side of the small Panzer III, the driver jumps back just in time and the Soviet tank crashes into a wall; at a distance of ten meters Bix places several rounds into the turret and the running gear of the colossus which is finally abandoned by the crew.

The KV-1 destroyed by Bix and his crew.

In the spring of 1942 with his company he was transferred to Panzer-Regiment 15 equipped with the new long barreled Panzer IV. In the middle of August, in the area west of Voronezh he leads a night attack against an important river crossing, destroying many AT guns. Wounded twice, on 5 November 1942 he was awarded the Deutsches Kreuz in Gold. He was then trained on the new Panther and in June 1944 sent back to the East, in the area of Baranavichy, as platoon commander in the 1st company of his old Panzer-Regiment 35. On 4 November he is severely wounded by a salvo of mortar rounds. During the second battle of Courland in the night of 27-28 October he rescues two Panthers which were struck in a ravine, destroying an enemy infantry unit in the process. The same day he eliminates a heavy IS-2 and a T-34, then in a following action several more T-34s. On October 29 he eliminates 8 enemy tanks; on November 2 another 12; two days later his Panther takes a direct hit from a Katyusha rocket. In January 1945 the regiment was transferred from Courland to the area of Danzig; the crews did not receive the promised Panzer Vs, but were issued instead the Jagdpanther. On the 7 March, east of Preußisch Stargard (today Starogard Gdański) the Soviets succeeded in breaking through the sector of the 35.Infanterie-Division; in response the armoured group of the 4.Panzer-Division was deployed to the area. The first enemy armoured spearhead was shot up, however four of the five jagdpanthers soon ran out of ammunition and so it was down to Bix to screen all on his own the withdrawal of the grenadiers. As the fog starts to lift he manages to destroy with the powerful 8.8-cm-PaK 43 two enemy tanks of American type at a distance of 1,200 meters; half an hour later two more lend-lease tanks at the same location.

After pulling back behind a slope, with only 25 rounds of ammunition left he takes on an entire enemy column, setting on fire eleven T-34s in ten minutes.

South of Danzig, near Kleschkau (today Kleszczewo), with three other panzers he crashes into an enemy occupied hamlet, personally knocking out another eleven tanks and rescuing a trapped battalion of Volkssturm. On 22 March he was awarded the Ritterkreuz as *Oberfeldwebel* and platoon commander in the 3rd company; at the same time he received the fifth level of the Panzerkampfabzeichen, for the participation in over 100 separate armoured engagements. Beginning of May in a blocking position at the Vistula lagoon he places his last hits of the war, but the three rounds only manage to penetrate half of the 20 centimeters of the enemy assault gun frontal armor and the Jagdpanther is hit in return and destroyed. He managed to escape across the Baltic reaching Kiel on May 14. During the war he destroyed 75 enemy tanks in 61 battle days. In 1956 he joined the Bundeswehr as instructor in the tank force, serving until 1970. He passed away on 31 July 1986.

Blaich Albert, born on 3 October 1913 in the village of Unterreichenbach (thirty kilometers southeast of Karlsruhe). Trained as machine fitter, at the age of twenty he joined the Reichswehr as driver in the Kraftfahr-Abteilung 5, then in the Kraftfahr-Lehrkommandos Zossen. In 1935 he was transferred to the newly formed Panzer-Regiment 5, then in October 1937 he volunteered for the Legion Condor and went to Spain. Again with his regiment, he took part in the Polish campaign as *Feldwebel* and platoon leader in the III.Abteilung (the former Panzer-Lehr-Abteilung of the Panzer-Lehr-Regiment 130) assigned to the 3.Panzer-Division. On 12 March 1940 he received the EK II. In February 1940 his battalion became the new I.Abteilung of Panzer-Regiment 33, 9.Panzer-Division. With this unit he fought in the battle of France until he was seriously injured by shrapnels to both legs and stomach. On 22 April 1941 he received the EK I. In March 1941 he was finally transferred to the Panzer-Regiment 6 of the 3.Panzer-Division, as *Oberfeldwebel* and leader of the point platoon of the 12th company. On 23 June 1941, the second day of "Barbarossa", he and his troops managed to capture the Yaselda (Jasiołda in Polish) bridge, then continued to pursue the Soviets and likewise seized a bridge over the Shchara (Szczara). During this bold drive Blaich personally destroys 26 enemy tanks, 16 artillery pieces and a few AT guns and is subsequently awarded the Ritterkreuz on 24 July 1941. In September his Panzer IV was knocked out and he was seriously injured. After recovering he was posted to various training units and in May 1942 he briefly joined the newly formed schwere Panzer-Abteilung 503. In the autumn he returned to his old

regiment in the southern sector of the eastern front, where he was again repeatedly wounded by shrapnels, to the right hand and to the head. After the battle of Kursk the I.Abteilung was converted to the Panther tank and incorporated in the Panzer-Lehr-Regiment 130 of the Panzer-Lehr-Division. With this unit Blaich fought on the Invasion front, where he received another artillery shrapnel to the left arm and an aircraft bullet in the left foot. On 15 December 1944 he was promoted to *Leutnant* and on the 19 he received the Panzerkampfabzeichen 2. Stufe for the participation in 25 armoured engagements. He was then given command of the 2nd company in his old Panzer-Regiment 6, which

in January 1945 was sent to Hungary. On 8 March he was awarded the Deutsches Kreuz in Gold. He was killed few days later, on 15 March 1945, in Öreghegy (near Székesfehérvár). He was posthumously promoted to *Oberleutnant*. The five brothers Blaich all fought to the front, only one survived.

Bölter Johannes, born on 29 February 1915 in the town of Mülheim (in the Ruhr industrial region). From 1921 to 1929 he attended primary school, then was hired by a local company as a plumber and apprentice roofer obtaining his craft certificate on March 1931. After a period of voluntary labor service, on 1 April 1933 he joined the 2nd squadron of the 10th (Prussian) cavalry regiment of the 2.Kavallerie-Division. Promoted to *Gefreiter* on 1 October 1934, on 9 October 1935 he was transferred to the 8th company of the 1st panzer regiment in the newly formed 1.Panzer-Division. *Unteroffizier* on 1 April 1936, then *Feldwebel* on 1 April 1938, in 1939 he was instructor in gunnery courses at Putlos. In the Poland campaign in command of a Panzer IV he destroys 4 enemy tanks and several AT guns and artillery positions, receiving the EK II on 30 September 1939. During the Battle of France he is in constant combat until he is wounded by a splinter in the left leg. He is awarded the EK I on 15 July 1940 for the destruction of no less than 7 tanks and a bunker; the first non-commissioned officer in the division to receive the decoration. On October 1st he was promoted to *Oberfeldwebel*.

In "Barbarossa" he destroys 10 tanks during the advance on Leningrad; here on 8 September his left hand is hit by a bullet. After recovery he became instructor in the replacement battalion of the 1.Panzer-Division in Erfurt, but on 3 December 1942 he volunteered to the schwere Panzer-Abteilung 502, first as leader of a Panzer III platoon, then with the Tiger. On 3 January during the second battle of lake Ladoga he was wounded by shrapnels in his left leg and in the stomach. He was awarded the Deutsches Kreuz in Gold on 29 March 1943, then on 31 July 1943 promoted to *Leutnant*. On 7 April 1944 in the area south of Pskov, he eliminates 15 tanks (his wing man another 7); after taking on additional ammunition he went on to destroy 2 artillery pieces and 2 AT guns. For this action (which prevented a penetration into the German frontline and the collapse of the 8.Jäger-Division) and for reaching a personal total of 89 tank "kills", he was awarded the Ritterkreuz on 16 April. On 22 June 1944 he became commander of the 1st company. On 24 July he is again wounded when a shrapnel penetrates his neck. Over the following days at the head of a

reduced kampfgruppe he is committed in continuous counterattacks in northern Lithuania allowing the withdrawal of several German divisions; here the five Tigers and the fifty grenadiers are able to contain a Soviet bridgehead on the Memel. On 12 August on his own initiative and without infantry support he thrusts into a Soviet tank assembly area: 4 tanks (his 92nd-95th kills in the east), 7 AT guns and a battalion of 300 infantry are wiped out. On the next day his panzer destroys an ex-German 8.8-centimeter PaK, but receives a direct hit from a second one. Severely burned, Bölter manages to bail out together with the driver. He is awarded the Eichenlaub by Himmler on 10 September 1944 and promoted to *Oberleutnant* on 20 September.

Promoted to *Hauptmann* on 1 January 1945, he was posted as instructor with the Panzer-Ersatz und Ausbildungs-Abteilung 500, then on 15 January he became company commander and instructor at the panzer school for non-commissioned officers in Eisenach. In March and April he was deployed with a combat group from the "500" in the area of Kassel. End of April in a last fight he may have destroyed 2 to 5 Shermans, however his tank received a hit in the turret which killed the gunner. He avoided capture and travelled on foot to Erfurt, to his wife and two children. In 1950 they escaped on a motorcycle to West Germany. He passed away on 16 September 1987 in his native town.

Notes. There is uncertainty over the number of Allied tanks he allegedly destroyed in 1945. Schneider (Tigers in Combat, vol. I) concisely writes that on April 1st, south of Paderborn a single Tiger belonging to the Abteilung 500 destroyed 2 lead tanks of an American task force, then was immobilized after being attacked by fighter-bombers. For Kurowski (Panzer Aces I), Bölter end of March led a kampfgruppe in a short fight in Kassel before pulling back into the Harz Mountains, then in April near the small town of Braunlage he knocked out the first and the last Shermans of an advancing American column, later he accepted battle again, setting on fire three more Shermans.

Tiger commander, summer 1943.

Awarded the Ritterkreuz.

Bohlken Erwin, born on 9 July 1919 in Osternburg (a suburb of Oldenburg). In service from November 1938, he fought on the eastern front with the 1.Panzer-Division. He received the EK II on 21 July 1941 and the EK I on 6 September 1942. He took part in the heavy fighting at Cherkassy (where he scored at least 2 "kills" with his Panther), and on May 1st 1944 he was awarded the Deutsches Kreuz in Gold as *Feldwebel* and zugführer in the 1st company, Panzer-Regiment 1. On 31 July his platoon (three vehicles) destroyed 22 tanks. He still greatly distinguished himself in Hungary in 1945. On 14 February he smashed through numerous Soviet anti-tank blocking positions during the northward attack of the 1.Panzer-Division against Csősz, and significantly contributed to the success of the German offensive battles south of Polgárdi which were concluded on the 15 February. As a result he was awarded the Ritterkreuz on 17 March and promoted to *Oberfeldwebel*. By the end of the war he had partecipated in over fifty separate armoured engagements and was credited with a total of 22 tank "kills". In 1951 he joined the Bundesgrenzschutz (the post-war federal police of West Germany). He passed away on 6 November 1954.

Bose Georg, born on 20 October 1921 in the town of Forst (twenty kilometers east of Cottbus). After service in the Reichsarbeitsdienst, he volunteered for the Wehrmacht being trained as gunner in an artillery unit. He took part in all early campaigns and in the invasion of the Soviet Union. In late 1942 he volunteered for the Sturmartillerie being posted to the refitted Sturmgeschütz-Abteilung 177. During "Zitadelle", in the northern sector he destroyed his first tanks and on 15 July 1943 was awarded the EK II. In October he destroyed a tank in close combat; on 10 January 1944 was awarded the EK I. On 23 July 1944 the remnants of the 292.Infanterie-Division became encircled near the village of Radziwiłłówka (about 60 km northwest of Brest-Litovsk). The 3.Kavallerie-Brigade, itself involved in heavy defensive combat, was only able to dispatch a small kampfgruppe that included three sturmgeschütze commanded by *Leutnant* Bose. During the march one vehicle threw a track and so only two were left to support the cavalrymen in their relief effort. On 28 July eleven T-34/85 tanks are eliminated, the village is recaptured and a breakthrough by the enemy into the flank of the whole 2.Armee is prevented. Bose, who led the attack on his own initiative and against the planning of the encircled division, personally destroyed 4 tanks. For this feat and for reaching a total of 19 "kills", he received the Ritterkreuz on 21 September, as platoon leader in the 1st battery. In August the Abteilung was re-equipped with the Jagdpanzer IV and renamed Panzerjäger-Abteilung 69. By March 1945 Bose had destroyed 44 enemy tanks. Captured by the Soviets, he was held captive until July 1948. He passed away on 26 September 2011.

Notes. The 3.Kavallerie-Division (formerly 3.Kavallerie-Brigade), to which the Panzerjäger-Abteilung 69 was attached, in 1945 fought in Hungary and Austria surrendering to American forces near Graz. Most probably its men were handed over to the Soviets on 11 May.

Bostell Wolfgang von, born on 25 February 1917 in the village of Heiningen (thirty-five kilometers east of Stuttgart). He joined the Wehrmacht in October 1935 being posted to the 2nd company, Artillerie-Regiment 48. One year later he joined the Panzerabwehr-Abteilung 12 of the 12.Infanterie-Division. With this same unit -which from April 1940 was renamed Panzerjäger-Abteilung 12- he fought in the Battle of France receiving the EK II on 11 June 1940 as *Unteroffizier* and platoon leader in the 3rd company. Promoted to *Feldwebel* he was awarded the EK I on 4 July 1941, but was severely wounded in action in Latvia and would return on the front line only in January 1942 as platoon leader in the 2nd company, until wounded again in April 1942 during the breakout from the Demyansk pocket. In early 1943 he fought as platoon leader in the 1st company, Panzerjäger-Abteilung 23. Promoted to *Leutnant* on March 1st 1944, from April he was again in combat in the Panzerjäger-Sturmgeschütz-Kompanie 1023, within the Panzerjäger-Abteilung of the 23.Infanterie-Division. In eastern Latvia, in the area around Madona (German: Modohn), on 11 and 12 August he destroys 11 enemy tanks and 2 self-propelled guns before being severely wounded. Two days later he is mentioned by name in the Wehrmachtbericht, and on 2 September 1944 he is awarded the Ritterkreuz. Promoted to *Oberleutnant* on January 1st, he fought in the Courland bridgehead as platoon leader in the 2nd company, Panzerjäger-Abteilung 205, 205.Infanterie-Division. On 26 March, near Skrunda (Schrunden), thirty kilometers west of Saldus (Frauenburg), he eliminates numerous enemy resistence nests and spearheads a counterattack after which an entire Soviet regiment is trapped in a pocket behind the frontline. For this feat he is awarded the Eichenlaub on 30 April 1945; by this time he had also reached a personal total of 28 enemy tank "kills". In the final weeks he was in command of the 2nd company, Panzerjäger-Abteilung 5. On 8 May he surrendered with his men to the Soviets, being released from captivity in October 1953. He passed away on 10 May 1991.

Notes. Structure and name of his unit in 1944 are not clear; could be also 2nd company "Sturmgeschütz-Abteilung 1023" attached to Panzerjäger-Abteilung 23.

Courland. Undefeated in battle, they were taken into captivity between 9 and 12 May.

Brandner Josef, born on the 1st of September 1915 in the village of Hohenberg (Austria, thirty kilometers south of Sankt Pölten). Already enrolled in the Austrian army, on 1 October 1938 he joined the Wehrmacht as *Obergefreiter*; he then took part in the Poland campaign in the 5.Batterie, Artillerie-Regiment 102. After an officer course, in January 1941 he joined the Sturmgeschütz-Abteilung 202. On 14 October 1941 he received the EK II and on 16 January 1942 the EK I. A few days later he was hit by a sniper (the bullet went through his neck) and only in February 1943 was again declared fit for the front. Promoted to *Hauptmann* he fought in the area of Kharkov as chief of the 2nd battery; on 14 September 1943 he was awarded the Deutsches Kreuz in Gold. In October 1944, for his support in over 100 separate infantry attacks, he received the grade V of the Sturmabzeichen. In November he assumed acting command of the Sturmgeschütz-Brigade 912. On 21 December 1944 -the first day of the third battle of Courland- Brandner leads his battery against a Soviet armoured spearhead aimed at the Tukums-Saldus (Frauenburg) road: within a short time 26 tanks are eliminated. He himself had reconnoitred the terrain on the day before and so was able to position his vehicles in ideal position to meet the enemy attack. In late January in the fourth battle of Courland he destroys his 57th tank (the whole battery a total of over 77 enemy AFVs). During the fifth battle with his unit he closes off a frontline gap preventing the collapse of the whole sector: in a single two-hours action 45 Soviet tanks are eliminated. On 17 March 1945, as brigade commander, he was finally awarded the Ritterkreuz. After the sixth battle he may have been awarded the Eichenlaub on 26 April, however no official confirmation is known. At the time, with the rank of *Major*, he had reached a personal total of no less than 61 enemy tank "kills" (possibly 66). He was released from Soviet captivity in 1948; he then served again in the Austrian army. He passed away on 6 June 1996 in Vienna.

Notes. According to his own account he received the Eichenlaub from the commanding general of the XXXVIII.Armeekorps, *General der Artillerie* Kurt Herzog.

Brandner and grenadiers in Courland.

Brandt Gerhard, born on 2 September 1919 in the town of Holzminden (sixty-five kilometers southwest of Hannover). He took part in the invasion of the Soviet Union receiving the EK II on 30 June 1941. On 16 February 1943 he was awarded the EK I. Promoted to *Oberleutnant*, in late 1944 he was in command of the 1st battery, Sturmgeschütz-Brigade 202. During the battle for the island of Ösel (Estonian: Saaremaa), during a nine-day period of combat on the Sworbe peninsula his sturmgeschütze destroy 54 Soviet tanks, relieve the encircled 9./Artillerie-Regiment 218 and eliminate numerous enemy penetrations at the cost of minimal friendly losses. By this time Brandt had reached a personal total of 35 enemy tank "kills" and was thus awarded the Ritterkreuz on 12 December 1944. He passed away on 25 November 1957.

Brandt Jürgen, born on 2 September 1921 in the town of Rendsburg (thirty kilometers west of Kiel). With the *LSSAH* he took part in the Battle of France. In "Barbarossa" he was StuG gunner in the SS-Sturm-Batterie, but one year later he was assigned to the Tiger company. After the battle of Kharkov he was awarded the EK II on 20 April 1943 and promoted to *SS-Unterscharführer*. In "Zitadelle" he destroys several tanks and is then promoted to *SS-Oberscharführer* receiving the EK I on 23 July. In mid-November during the advance on Brusilov, on his own initiative together with another Tiger he attacks in the flank and completely destroys a Soviet infantry battalion. Few days later with his lone Tiger he annihilates an entire enemy motorized column setting on fire countless trucks and other vehicles.

At Villers-Bocage, in the 2nd company under Wittmann, with his crew (Tiger 223) he destroys 3 Shermans and a number of tankettes, and brings in seventy British prisoners. On 14 August in the Falaise pocket he leads the remaining three Tigers of the company against a large concentration of enemy tanks, knocking out himself 5 Shermans; the day after, east of the Calais-Falaise road he breaks through the enemy encirclement running over an AT gun; later on, attacked by approximately one hundred and sixty (!) Canadian tanks, together with another Tiger he eliminates 12 of them; then under heavy artillery fire he withdraws taking under tow the second panzer. On 27 August he attacks the enemy bridgehead over the Seine at Vernon, knocking out two AT guns, one armored car and four munition carriers; the day after he attacks in the flank a battalion of enemy infantry. On 30 August he eliminates two tanks and damages one, the same day in the evening the two Tigers each destroy 3 tanks, then have to be blown up on account of lack of fuel and ammunition.

In the Ardennes, as platoon commander in the 1st company (Tiger 132) within Kampfgruppe Peiper, he is employed in screening missions around Stavelot; here on 20 December he helps an anti-tank unit repel an American assault group of forty tanks, personally knocking out one of them. He is killed on 25 December near the Petit-Spay bridge, when a single stray shell falls right in front of his vehicle. Awarded posthumously the Deutsches Kreuz in Gold on 13 January 1945 for having destroyed 47 enemy tanks.

Brandt (on the left) in Normandy, July 1944.

Brehme Gerhard, born on 7 September 1912 in the village of Reinswalde (today Złotnik), sixty kilometers east of Cottbus. He took part in the Battle of France with the 5.Panzer-Division receiving the EK II on 6 September 1940. In September 1940, Panzer-Regiment 15 was incorporated in the newly formed 11.Panzer-Division; with this unit he fought in "Barbarossa" receiving the EK I on 6 August 1941; then, in 1942, in the area of the Don. On 12 August 1942 he was awarded the Deutsches Kreuz in Gold as *Oberfeldwebel* in the 1st company. In January 1943 the entire I.Abteilung was employed in a failed relief attempt to save the Velikiye Luki garrison. During this action Brehme eliminates 8 tanks and 5 artillery pieces reaching a total of over 45 tank "kills". His unit was then sent to Germany for the conversion to the Panther and renamed Panzer-Abteilung 52. In view of "Zitadelle" the unit was incorporated in the 10.Panzer-Brigade of *Großdeutschland*. Although the Panthers were plagued with mechanical problems, Brehme, now platoon leader in the 1st company, repeatedly thrusts into Soviet assembly areas. He is critically wounded on 14 July west of Belgorod and dies three days later at the Kriegslazarett 610 in Kharkov. He had destroyed or captured a total of 51 enemy tanks and 44 guns, and on 23 August 1943 was posthumously awarded the Ritterkreuz.

Notes. In Velikiye Luki the I./Panzer-Regiment 15 had 37 Panzer III Ausf.L/M and three Panzer IV Ausf.G; Brehme was likely in command of a Panzer IV.

Brommann Karl, born on 20 July 1920 in the town of Neumünster (thirty kilometers south of Kiel). In 1937 he joined the SS and in the following years was posted to several different *Totenkopf* units. In 1940 having reached the rank of *SS-Unterscharführer* he was transferred to the 6.SS-Gebirgs-Division *Nord*, fighting in Finland as platoon leader in the 7th company, SS-Infanterie-Regiment 6. In September he was injured in both legs and hands. On 6 November he was shot through the right lung and the liver. Awarded the EK II, after a long stay in a reserve hospital, in May 1943 he was transferred to *Nordland*, in the SS-Panzer-Regiment 11. In October he volunteered to the newly formed schwere SS-Panzer-Abteilung 103 (later 503) and was trained on the Tiger I tank in Paderborn, then on the Tiger II in Senne.

On 28 January 1945 the abteilung is detrained in Kallies (100 kilometers east of Stettin). Brommann, now *SS-Untersturmführer*, leads an attack of the 1st company towards Deutsch Krone which covers several kilometers; he eliminates many AT guns and on February 1st is awarded the EK I. On 3 February few of the Tigers make their way to Arnswalde; for the next two weeks they manage to withstand the besieging enemy; then with the start of "Sonnenwende" the central corridor to Arnswalde is widened and the Tigers are able to eventually withdraw. During the night of February 17/18, parts of the battalion were loaded onto trains and moved to Danzig. On 7 March, Brommann leads a small kampfgruppe against a massive Soviet armored attack on Preußisch Stargard: out of eighty enemy tanks, fifty-seven are destroyed. Later that day with his lone panzer he relieves an encircled corps command post. Up to 18 March, despite having been wounded several times, he has eliminated 66 tanks, 44 AT guns and 15 trucks (gunner *Uscha* Emil Reichel). On 25 March he may have destroyed some more IS tanks, however the same day he is seriously wounded by the explosion of a shell. He is evacuated by way of Hela to Swinemünde and later admitted to a lazarett in Flensburg. On 10 April he is mentioned by name in the daily Wehrmachtbericht and on 29 April awarded the Ritterkreuz. Made POW by the British on 21 May, he was released in November 1947. After the war he trained as dental laboratory technician. He passed away on 30 June 2011.

Notes. On 25 or 26 March six IS tanks were destroyed by two Tigers in a blocking position on the edge of Oliva-Zoppot. Brommann was in command of one of the Tigers, but it is unclear whether he was put out of action before or after this last fight.

Buchner Heinz, born on 3 May 1924. During the counterattack of Kharkov he was gunner on a Panzer III Ausf.J of the Tiger company's light platoon. He was so successful that in view of "Zitadelle" he was quickly transferred to the Tiger tank. He was the gunner of Staudegger on 8 July 1943. Promoted to *Sturmmann*, he received both the EK II and EK I for the astonishing destruction of 51 tanks. He had just turned nineteen and at the time he may well have been second only to Knispel as gunner in the Panzerwaffe. In January 1944 he was promoted to *SS-Unterscharführer*, then in May 1944 he arrived at the SS-Junkerschule Klagenfurt where was promoted to *Standartenjunker* on 1 June. This was followed by a tank course in Fallingbostel and by the rank of *SS-Standartenoberjunker* on 1 July. On 20 October 1944 he was finally promoted to *SS-Untersturmführer* and put in command of the 2nd platoon, 1st company, schwere SS-Panzer-Abteilung 501. He briefly fought in the Ardennes, however for the remainder of the war he stayed in Schloß Holte.

Buckel Karl, born on 12 June 1920 in the village of Mörzheim (forty kilometers southeast of Kaiserlautern). At the beginning of the war he served in the RAD, then with the Sturmgeschütz-Abteilung 189 he took part in the invasion of the Soviet Union. On 16 December 1941, as *Unteroffizier* in the 2nd battery, he received the EK II. In 1942, already promoted to *Leutnant* he received the EK I on 15 October. He greatly distinguished himself in 1944, as *Oberleutnant der Reserve* in the Sturmgeschütz-Brigade 277. On 22 June the Soviets started their decisive operation "Bagration". Following the loss of Vitebsk the hard-pressed 212.Infanterie-Division, which had been sent as reinforcement, found itself defending a provisional position about a hundred km west of the city, on the 27. When the enemy succeeded in breaking through near the village of Kurilovichi (seventy km northwest of Lepel, in German reports "Durilowitschi"), Buckel's 3rd battery was deployed as the last reserve. The handful of vehicles were first able to bring the assault to a halt by knocking out numerous tanks, then with the help of hastily assembled stragglers, a counterthrust was launched that pushed the Soviets back across the original frontline in the direction of Ushachy. Kurilovichi, the cornerstone of the division, was retaken and held until the ordered withdrawal. The permanent loss of this village would have collapsed the entire front of the IX.Armeekorps, but this was averted due to Buckel's intervention.

For his achievements he was awarded consecutively the Deutsches Kreuz in Gold on 2 July 1944 and then the Ritterkreuz on the 15 of the same month, after the exceptionally high number of enemy tanks destroyed by the battery was confirmed. He personally had also destroyed two tanks in close combat. Further awards: the Nahkampfspange in Bronze (for 15 hand-to-hand combat actions) in March 1944, and the Panzerkampfabzeichen Stufe "75" on 31 October 1944. He was also promoted to *Hauptmann*. At the end of the war he was allegedly captured by French troop but escaped soon after. He served in the Bundeswehr retiring in 1976 with the rank of *Oberstleutnant*. He passed away on 2 September 1997.

80

Buhr Martin, born on 3 April 1913 in the village of Marienhafe (eighty kilometers northwest of Oldenburg); he joined the Wehrmacht in 1934. He took part in the Battle of France receiving the EK II on 5 July 1940, then he fought on the eastern front during the attack on Moscow and in the following battles in the central sector, receiving the EK I on 26 September 1942 as *Hauptmann* in the Sturmgeschütz-Abteilung 202. In March 1943 he was promoted to *Major* and put in command of the whole unit. On 17 August 1943, south of Sumy, the Soviets launched a decisive thrust with 6 rifle divisions and 2 tank corps against the position of the 68.Infanterie-Division. In response the German infantry on the right flank of the division pulled back to the railway embankment southeast of Nyzhnya Syrovatka; the supporting 1st and 3rd batteries suffered heavily in the process and both commanders became casualties. The main Soviet spearhead drove towards the village and the railway station; from there it was possible to turn south and roll up the entire defending position. At this point Buhr took control over the remaining sturmgeschütze and launched an attack on his own initiative despite the lack of escorting infantry. He breaks into a hostile tank assembly area, smashing it and ejecting the Soviets from the railway station; he then rushes northwards along the embankment with his remaining 3 operational vehicles into the main T-34 formation. Again he destroys several tanks and keeps the enemy force in check long enough for the German infantry withdrawal to be completed. On this day 48 Soviet tanks were eliminated by the sturmgeschütze, 14 of them by Buhr who raised his personal total to 29. On 11 September he was awarded the Ritterkreuz. Until October he led his unit in the battles around Kiev, then he was assigned as commander in chief to the Sturmgeschütz-Ersatz und Ausbildungs-Abteilung 500, by this time located in the Warthelager training area near Posen. Promoted to *Oberstleutnant*, in March 1945 he was put in command of Panzerartillerie-Regiment Müncheberg, a unit which fought near Küstrin and then in the Battle of Berlin. From 1955 he served in the Bundeswehr, retiring in 1971 as an *Oberst*. He passed away on 23 August 1988.

Bunzel Hans, born on 29 April 1915 in the small town of Haynau (today Chojnów), eighty km northwest of Breslau. With Panzer-Regiment 1 he served with a maintenance squad in the early campaigns, then as a panzer commander in the east (EK II on 19 September 1940 and EK I on 21 July 1941). In the defensive battles on the Don in January 1943, he was *Oberfeldwebel* and platoon leader in the 3rd company, Panzer-Abteilung 116, 16.Infanterie-Division (mot.). On the 14th of January his division received the mission of breaking out towards the west and taking the Manych dam at Spornyy. In a short fight elements of the Soviet 5th Motorized Division were destroyed, then advancing swiftly the unit secured the enemy-free area around Limanskiy and took up a hedgehog position there during the night; on the next morning it set out once again for the decisive thrust towards Spornyy. By this time the first enemy tanks had already begun probing the division's rearguard from the east and northeast; the village had to be taken as soon as possible, or else the unit would have been in danger of encirclement. Bunzel led the armoured spearhead. After driving forwards through several small settlements that were clear of the enemy, he carefully approached the village which covered the important dam with the bridge. Suddenly wild defensive fire erupted from an enemy that was clearly prepared. Under strong flanking fire Bunzel turned with his panzers and stormed both the dam and the bridge position; from here he thrust into the village itself, again far ahead of the by now dismounted friendly infantry. He destroyed one enemy tank, drove out a second, captured a third, overran an entire battery of 7,62 cm guns and cleared the way for the grenadiers. The Soviets, now cut off from their retreat route, defended bitterly: 140 enemy dead were later counted in the village. On 10 February 1943 he was awarded the Ritterkreuz, and on 30 April promoted to *Leutnant*. In May 1944 he was transferred to the newly formed Panzer-Regiment 16 in the west. On 17 December 1944 he destroyed his 55th tank; on 8 February 1945 was awarded the DKiG. Last rank *Oberleutnant*. After the war he settled in Bavaria; he passed away on 12 November 1995.

Notes. The battle in Spornyy, on the western Manych, is not to be confused with the battle of the Proletarskaya bridgehead, which took place in the same period on the eastern Manych (to the east of Rostov). - Bunzel may have partecipated in over 100 armoured engagements. He claimed 95 enemy tank "kills" by war's end.

Carius Otto, born on 27 May 1922 in the town of Zweibrücken (one hundred kilometers southwest of Mainz). The war broke out soon after he graduated from school; turned eighteen he applied to the Wehrmacht. He was drafted in the Infanterie-Ersatz-Bataillon 104, but then he volunteered for the panzer branch and joined the Panzer-Ersatz-Abteilung 7, a unit which in view of "Barbarossa" was integrated in the newly formed Panzer-Regiment 21 attached to the 20.Panzer-Division. He fought in Belarus and in the battle of Smolensk as loader in a Panzer 38(t). On 8 July 1941 the tank was hit by a round from a Soviet 45mm AT gun, he had to bail out suffering a shrapnel wound to the face and losing several teeth. On August 1st he was promoted to *Feldwebel*, then he left the front for a panzer driver course followed by an officer candidate course. He didn't obtain the certificate and was back to his unit in February 1942. During the defensive battles around Gzhatsk, from March through June, he was in command of a platoon of four light panzers. During a Soviet attack his tanks retreat without warning and disaster is averted only by the brave stand of the accompanying infantry. After this early setback Carius would shape his command style in dealing

with subordinates. On 15 September he was awarded the EK II and soon after promoted to *Leutnant*. At the beginning of 1943 he was transferred to the schwere Panzer-Abteilung 502 and after a period of training in Brittany he joined the Leningrad front in July 1943 as a section leader in the 2nd company. With his new gunner Kramer he started to accumulate a large number of "kills". For example, on 4 November screening between Lovec and Nevel he destroys 10 T-34s, three more the day after. On 23 November he was awarded the EK I. In February 1944 a kampfgruppe under his command (4 Tigers) is attached to *Nordland* and in the following months he would fight against Soviet tanks almost continuously. In an early engagement he destroys 4 SU-85s assault guns; during the time period 17-22 March he destroys many T-34s and a heavy KV-1 in the sector of Lembitu west of Narva. On 19 April he assumes acting command of the 2nd company; two days later escapes death when a projectile hits the turret the moment he bent down to have a cigarette light up. On 4 May while in hospital for an asthma crisis, he is awarded the Ritterkreuz; in July he officially took command of the 2nd company. On 22 July 1944 he is on reconnaissance with a Kübelwagen towards the village of Malinava, northeast of Daugavpils (Dünaburg); he finds the place already occupied by a Soviet assault column and rushes back to the company for briefing. As there is only one road leading to this village only two Tigers are going to attack while the remaining six are to stay behind in

covering position; speed is essential. He is at the point followed by Kerscher: over the next twenty minutes no less than 17 tanks are destroyed along with many support vehicles. Later that same day with the rest of his company he ambushes the main body of the Soviet brigade, 28 more tanks are eliminated with no friendly losses. On 24 July, on the road between Riga and Daugavpils, he is again on reconnaissance with a sidecar when a group of enemy soldiers and partisans start shooting at him from a nearby house. Wounded, he throws himself in a ditch where he is again shot several times at close range by a Soviet officer. Hit by bullets in the leg, arm, shoulder and neck, he is miraculously rescued by the Tigers rushing at full speed to the spot. What saved his life may have been his small build (he had been rejected twice for military service as unfit because of his slight weight). On 27 July he is awarded the Eichenlaub, which he received weeks later by Himmler once discharged from hospital.

Promoted to *Oberleutnant*, he is forbidden to return to the eastern front; instead, at the beginning of 1945 he is given command of the 2nd company of the schwere Panzerjäger-Abteilung 512. The company is equipped with 10 of the new Jagdtiger tank destroyers and is to be directed on the Rhine. Because of the insufficient training of the crews the employement of the 2nd company results in a complete failure; however in April, in a last fight, Carius with a single shot of the 12.8-cm-PjK that goes through all the walls of a house, manages to blow up an American Sherman. On 15 April he surrendered to the US forces with his men; he was released from captivity in June 1946. After studying medicine at the Freiburg im Breisgau University he became pharmacist in 1952. He would work in his pharmacy at Herschweiler-Pettersheim full time until 2011, later part time. He passed away on 24 January 2015, aged 92.

Notes. Destroyed in Malinava were a dozen T-34s from the 41st Tank Brigade and five IS-2s from the 48th Guards Heavy Tank Regiment (both from the 5th Tank Corps). In his book Carius claims there were 17 IS-2s and 5 T-34s destroyed in the village, but probably he is confusing with the after action report for the whole Abteilung, which listed a total of 17 T-34s and 6 IS-2s for the day. - Often credited with a total of 150+ tank "kills", Carius himself stated that the true figure was around 110.

Carpaneto Alfredo, born on 4 January 1915 in Rome, he studied in Vienna's Academy of Fine Arts. He decided to join the Wehrmacht when Italy chose to remain neutral at the outbreak of the war. Having an Austrian mother, he was accepted as a volunteer in the Panzer-Regiment 4 of the 2.Panzer-Division. He fought in the Battle of France and on 24 June 1940 received the EK II. With the same unit (in late September 1940 incorporated into the 13.Panzer-Division) he took part in the invasion of the Soviet Union in command of a Panzer III. In 1943 he was transferred to the 2nd company of the newly formed schwere Panzer-Abteilung 502. On 3 October 1944 he received the EK I. On 10 October a transport train with elements of the 2nd company made its way in darkness to the area of Memel. After unloading, the only two operational Tigers began their road march to the town, however the vehicle of the unit commander was soon knocked out by a hit from the flank. Carpaneto immediately recognized the danger: 13 Soviet tanks had exited their assembly area in the forest south of the village of Karlshof and were now beginning an attack against the I./Grenadier-Regiment 209. On his own initiative and even though he only has 6 armour-piercing rounds left he engages the enemy destroying 4 tanks and forcing the remainder to flee. He distinguished himself again in the Samland peninsula on 26 January 1945 through an extraordinary feat of arms. While in security position on the western entrance of the village of Kadgiehnen (along the road to Königsberg) he first eliminates at close range 2 T-34s; fully on his own he then maneuvers into a better firing position and engages another 18 tanks, destroying 4 of them; on the way back to his own lines, his Tiger breaks through the ice and sanks 1.2 meters deep in a pond. With the turret turned to the rear, he is able to fight off his pursuers and to destroy 2 more IS-2s; his vehicle is later recovered by means of a second Tiger. He is killed on the same day in the afternoon, near Schönwalde, by a round of anti-tank rifle. *Unteroffizier der Reserve* Carpaneto was posthumously awarded the Ritterkreuz on 28 March 1945.

Notes. He is usually credited with some 50 "kills"; the recommendation for the Ritterkreuz mentions 35 enemy tanks destroyed.

Chrzonsz Günter, born on 15 October 1914 in the small town of Meseritz (today Międzyrzecz), ninety kilometers west of Posen. He took part in the invasion of the Soviet Union receiving the EK II on 24 June 1941 and the EK I on 11 August. During October 1943 the 2nd battery of Sturmgeschütz-Abteilung 277, attached to the 9.Infanterie-Division, was deployed to help defend the Nikopol bridgehead. When the Soviets launched an attack in the area with one tank brigade and one rifle division, only two sturmgeschütze were in an operational state. One of the vehicles was quickly knocked out with the result that *Oberwachtmeister* and platoon leader Chrzonsz found himself alone against a force of about 50 T-34 tanks. He destroyed 10 before one of the tanks rammed his vehicle and lifted it up sideways. As the T-34 reversed it tore away the left track of the sturmgeschütz, however after pulling back to an approximately 30 meters range it fell into the gunsight of the German vehicle by chance and was promptly destroyed. Chrzonsz then, on his own initiative, advanced slowly into the contested village. Covered by the houses he proceeded to eliminate another 7 tanks. This combined with the close-combat kills by the nearby grenadiers forced the remaining Soviet armour to retreat. For this major local victory and for rising his personal total of tank "kills" to 23 he was awarded the Ritterkreuz on 12 November 1943 and was promoted to *Leutnant*. After the war he changed his name to Carsten. Between 1960 and 1967 he served in the Bundeswehr reaching the rank of *Hauptmann*. He settled in Bavaria and passed away on 31 October 2003.

Dallmeier Josef, born on 29 January 1911 in the village of Sünching (twenty-five kilometers southeast of Regensburg). Early in the war he received both the EK II and EK I. During February 1945 in the area west of Breslau he led his company of Hetzer tank destroyers in several successful combats. On the 10 the company supports an attack on Thomaswaldau knocking out 6 enemy tanks; on the 13 it supports the breakthrough of a grenadier battalion from Birkenbrück to Paritz; on the 17 the Soviets are thrown out of Siegersdorf; on the 20 and 21 Hennersdorf is recaptured. In another action, the two serviceable Hetzer take by surprise 14 enemy tanks that are advancing from Wünschendorf towards the south, knocking out half of them. In early March, Dallmeier would personally destroy several more tanks north of Lauban. He was awarded the Ritterkreuz on 28 March 1945, as *Leutnant* and commander of the Panzer-Jäger-Kompanie 1183. Promoted to *Oberleutnant*, by the end of the war he had been credited with about 50 "kills". He passed away on 4 July 1982.

Notes. Panzer-Jäger-Kompanie 1183 has nothing to do with the 183.Volksgrenadier-Division (a unit that was employed exclusively on the western front). The company fought in the east as an indipendent unit; in March 1945 was probably attached to the to the newly formed 6.Infanterie-Division (previously 6.Volksgrenadier-Division).

Jagdpanzer 38(t) "Hetzer", winter 1944-45.

Dath Friedrich, born on 26 April 1919 in the small town of Brackenheim (thirty-five kilometers north of Stuttgart). He took part in "Barbarossa", then in 1942 he joined the newly formed Sturmgeschütz-Abteilung 209. In late 1943 he transferred to the Sturmgeschütz-Abteilung 286, a unit that was then sent in combat in the area of Kirovograd. He received the EK II and the EK I. On 23 August 1944 the 3rd battery of the upgraded Sturmgeschütz-Brigade 286 had the mission of holding the village of Simioneşti, northwest of Roman, against strong armoured flanking attacks. Suddenly a group of 30 Soviet tanks tries to seize the village. *Oberwachtmeister* and platoon leader Dath deploys his sturmgeschütze with such skill that 14 tanks are eliminated, 6 by him and his crew. For this success as well as reaching a personal total of 25 "kills" he was awarded the Ritterkreuz on 9 December 1944. He was also recipient of the Hungarian Medal of Bravery [in both photos, just above the EK I]. He passed away on 3 December 2002 in his native town.

89

Dauser Hans, born on 31 July 1908 in München. He joined the NSDAP in 1930 and the Allgemeine SS in 1933. With the *LSSAH* he took part in the invasion of the Soviet Union; in mid-November 1943, at the beginning of the battles west of Kiev, he became Panther commander and on 5 December he received the EK II being promoted to platoon leader. On 28 December in a night attack near Chubarivka, southeast of Zhytomyr, he encounters a column of about 30 T-34s destroying 3 of them at very close range. On 26 January 1944, east of Vinnytsia, SS-Panzer-Regiment 1 had the mission of thrusting through to the Lypovets railway station in order to block the railroad and secure the area to the east; *SS-Oberscharführer* Dauser leads the point platoon and in the midst of heavy snowfall succeeds in breaking in the fortified village of Napadivka via a surprise flanking attack. At this time the enemy was retreating using a single bridge located atop a narrow dam that crossed the otherwise impassable creek. Advancing towards the bridge, Dauser is shot at by both an enemy assault gun as well as enemy infantry; despite this he manages to dismount his panzer and cut the demolition wires. After remounting he then clears the area around the bridge destroying the enemy assault gun. With this he forces the Soviets to leave behind the vast majority of their equipment, he also makes possible the continuation of the attack against the village of Rososha on the very next day. On 30 January he was awarded the EK I. In March 1944 he had reached a total of 34 destroyed enemy tanks since the start of operations in November, thus on 4 June 1944 was awarded the Ritterkreuz as *SS-Untersturmführer der Reserve* in the 2nd company, SS-Panzer-Regiment 1, 1.SS-Panzer-Division "Leibstandarte SS Adolf Hitler". By the end of the war he had been promoted to *SS-Obersturmführer*. He passed away on 20 November 2001 in his hometown.

Notes. His father, with the same name, was *SS-Brigadeführer* and Staatssekretär Hans Dauser (1877-1969).

Deutsch Heinz, born on 21 July 1920 in the small town of Mutterstadt (ten kilometers west of Mannheim). In January 1944 he joined the newly formed Fallschirm-Sturmgeschütz-Brigade 12, training as a StuG III commander. The unit was deployed south of Saint-Lô in support of the 3.Fallschirmjäger-Division. Deutsch received the EK II on 3 July 1944 as *Leutnant der Reserve* and commander of the 3rd battery; ten days later he destroys his first enemy tank. After reorganization, in the last months of war the brigade was employed in the defence of the lower Rhine region. On 25 February 1945 northwest of Weeze, Deutsch defeats a tank-supported enemy attack and on the same day is awarded the EK I for reaching a total of 13 tank "kills". On March 1st in the morning he leads a counterattack that restores the old frontline, 21 prisoners are taken; in the afternoon he prevents an enemy breakthrough destroying three tanks. On 2 March he defeats another armoured attack against Kevelaer destroying 3 more tanks. On 3 March he eliminates one tank and one armoured car. On 4 March he defeats yet another armoured attack with infantry support against the road to Sonsbeck destroying 1 Cromwell and 1 Sherman; due to his heavy infantry losses the enemy does not launch any more major attacks in this location. On 5 March he eliminates 1 Sherman northeast of Hamb in a tank duel after advancing forward in an exposed firing position; later that day he leads his sturmgeschütze in a counterattack that enables an encircled regiment to disengage, personally destroying a Churchill tank which had previously fired on him from an ambush position. On 6 March with his platoon he counterattacks the enemy that is advancing towards the Issum-Alpen road; under heavy enemy artillery fire he eliminates the two leading tanks, so that the front line can be held for the entire day. On 9 March after repairing his shot-up aiming device, he eliminates a Churchill tank at a range of 800 meters. On 31 March alone he eliminates 5 tanks. In the last days of combat he destroys another ten tanks, including a Sherman "Jumbo" at Edewecht (west of Bremen) on 24 April, finally reaching a total of 44 "kills". Promoted to *Oberleutnant*, he was awarded the Ritterkreuz on 28 April (his crew was awarded the Deutsches Kreuz in Gold), the only parachute assault gunner to be so decorated. On 8 May he surrendered with

his men to the British forces in the Cuxhaven pocket. He passed away on 15 October 1995.

Notes. On 5 March he was cited to receive the Deutsches Kreuz in Gold, changed to Ritterkreuz after his further successes. - His unit was formed in January 1944 as Sturmgeschütz-Abteilung 2; on 26 March was renamed Sturmgeschütz-Brigade 2 der Luftwaffe, then in Normandy gained the Fallschirm-Sturmgeschütz-Brigade 12 designation; finally on 28 March 1945 was renamed Fallschirm-Sturmgeschütz-Brigade 121. The unit was credited with destroying 240 Allied tanks in less than a year of combat.

Diddens Diddo, born on 22 April 1917 in the village of Bunderhammrich (in the Ems estuary, sixty-five kilometers west of Oldenburg), the son of a farmer. Already a NCO in the Allgemeine SS, he enlisted in the Wehrmacht in November 1938 being posted to the 2nd battery, Artillerie-Regiment 58, and later to the Artillerie-Abteilung 422. On September 1st 1940 he was promoted to *Leutnant der Reserve*, and in May 1941 he became platoon leader in the 2nd battery of the Sturmgeschütz-Abteilung 185, taking part in the invasion of the Soviet Union and receiving the EK II on 19 August 1941 and the EK I on 2 October. During the Battle of the Volkhov (the Red Army offensive to relieve the siege of Leningrad), in the time period 19 February-11 March 1942, in the area of Pogost'ye (seventy kilometers southeast of the city) his sturmgeschütze destroy the following enemy materiel: 12 heavy tanks, 4 medium tanks, 4 AT guns, 3 infantry guns, 1 heavy armoured car. By this time Diddens had personally destroyed 35 tanks, for a total along with his platoon of 57 enemy tanks over the course of nine months. He was thus awarded the Ritterkreuz on 18 March 1942; on 9 November he also received the SS-Ehrenring as a personal gift from Himmler. In the same

year he was transferred to the Sturmgeschütz-Abteilung "Großdeutschland". Promoted to *Oberleutnant*, he was involved with his 1st battery in the heavy fighting for Romania. On 25 April 1944 *Großdeutschland* commenced a limited counterattack with the goal of seizing the woods between Bărbăteşti and Vascani -north of Târgu Frumos- as well as the Dumbrăviţa heights. After the objectives are sized Diddens from the hilltop sees a strong enemy pakfront; on his own initiative he leads the sturmgeschütze against this position destroying 23 heavy AT guns. On the way back, alone with his vehicle he attacks an enemy battlegroup that is assembling at the edge of a forest, personally destroying 3 tanks and 2 guns; a few more AT guns are eliminated by his battery. For the tenacious resistence of his assault guns in the defensive battle north of Jassy, he was mentioned by name in the Wehrmachtbericht of 27 April 1944. Unselfishly he declared that each man in the unit had learned the same recognition, and he had all their name mentioned. On 23 May the sturmgeschütze, in cooperation with the Panzer-Aufklärungs-Abteilung, advanced towards Zahorna (ten kilometers northeast of Piatra Neamţ) against a massive Soviet attack supported by Il-2 Shturmoviks. The village was retaken for a short period before a renewed enemy attack thwarted the assault on point 181. In the process Diddens was severely wounded and his right leg had to be amputated. While in hospital he received the Eichenlaub on 15 June 1944. He spent the remainder of the war performing light duties with local defenses in his hometown. He passed away on 27 September 1997.

Diers Georg, born on 2 November 1921 in the municipality of Wiefelstede (fifty kilometers northwest of Bremen), the son of a farmer. In 1939 he volunteered for the Waffen-SS being posted to the SS-Standarte "Germania" on April 1st 1940; in June he was transferred to the SS-Regiment "Nordland" of the newly formed *Wiking*. In 1942 he fought in the Caucasus with the 3,7-cm-PaK 36, until he was badly wounded by mortars in late September near Grozny. On June 1st 1943 he was promoted to *SS-Unterscharführer*, he then spent the next several months training with the Tiger. In the summer of 1944 he got married. In late January 1945 schwere SS-Panzer-Abteilung 503 was finally transported to Pomerania; here the battalion was crucial in retaking Arnswalde.

During the battle of Berlin, Diers in command of Tiger II number 314, on 19 April in a blocking position on the hills northeast of Klosterdorf (three kilometers east of Straußberg), supported by another Tiger II, destroys thirteen enemy tanks; then he pulls back with the second vehicle in tow. From 26 April he is in action with the remnants of *Nordland* and with Kampfgruppe Charlemagne in the area of Neukölln. On 29 April he is awarded the EK I, later that day he moves to the Potsdamer Platz, where together with another Tiger destroys several tanks. On 30 April he is ordered by radio to the Tiergarten near the Reichstag; here he reportedly eliminates around 30 tanks (gunner Wolf-Dieter Kothe). On May 1st with his lone vehicle he leads a counterattack which temporarily recaptures the Kroll Opera House; on 2 May he takes part in the breaktrough attempt to the west.

After having his Tiger II blown up with mines, he escapes disguised as a civilian. Captured by the Soviets at the Elbe, he was sent to a forced labor camp in the region of Moscow. In December 1949 he was allowed to return to Germany.

Diers' Königstiger at the Marienkirche in Arnswalde.

Dressel Albert, born on 15 September 1914 in the village of Rebesgrün (twenty-five kilometers southwest of Zwickau). A locksmith, in October 1934 he joined the Wehrmacht being posted to the Kampfwagen-Regiment 2. This unit a year later was used to create the Panzer-Regiment 1 of the 1.Panzer-Division. He took part in the Polish campaign and in the Battle of France. In "Barbarossa" he fought in the northern sector and received the EK II on 9 July 1941 and the EK I on 20 November. In June 1942 he was transferred to the newly formed Panzer-Abteilung 160, as *Feldwebel* and platoon leader in the 3rd company. With this unit, which was subordinated to the 60.Infanterie-Division (mot.), he took part in the advance on Stalingrad in command of a Panzer IV. In September during a Soviet breakthrough attempt along the northern front of the city, he left his security position on his own initiative when he recognized the main direction of the enemy effort. He immediately attacks the far larger enemy force and personally eliminates 16 tanks (out of total of 37 by the whole platoon). For this feat he is awarded the Ritterkreuz on 13 October 1942. Following the disappearance of the division in Stalingrad, the battalion was reformed in early 1943 as Panzer-Abteilung "Feldherrnhalle". After a long period of training the battalion was employed in June 1944 in the area of Minsk where it was annihilated. Dressel, who on June 1st 1943 had been promoted to *Oberfeldwebel*, was transferred to the Panzer-Abteilung 2106 of the newly formed Panzer-Brigade 106 "Feldherrnhalle" (under the command of *Oberstleutnant* Bäke) as platoon leader in the 1st company. On 8 September 1944, near Briey, Lorraine, he is struck by shrapnel in the back of the head; his Panther (or possibly Jagdpanther) is then destroyed by a Sherman and the entire crew killed.

Eckardt Hermann (or Eckhardt), born on 4 October 1920 in the village of Lindach (fifty kilometers east of Stuttgart). In service from October 1940, he fought in North Africa with the Panzer-Regiment 8 of the 15.Panzer-Division. He was awarded the EK II on 6 February 1942 and the EK I on 20 February 1943 after a total of 26 "kills". In early May 1943 the German forces surrendered to the Allies in the sector of Tunis. Eckardt escaped the fate of his unit and in June 1944 was transferred to the eastern front, in northern Ukraine, as a StuG commander in the newly formed Panzer-Abteilung 8, 20.Panzergrenadier-Division. He was awarded the Deutsches Kreuz in Gold on 12 September 1944 as *Unteroffizier* in the 1st company. During the battles on the Vistula and in Slesia he may have transitioned to the Panzer IV. On 28 March 1945 he was awarded the Ritterkreuz as *Feldwebel* and platoon leader still in the 1st company. By the end of the war he was allegedly credited with 78 "kills". He passed away on 16 September 2010.

Notes. His kills in North Africa were likely tanks, vehicles and guns combined.

Egger Paul, born on 26 November 1916 in the village of Mautern (Styria, sixty kilometers northwest of Graz). Already a glider pilot, in 1938 he volunteered to join the Luftwaffe and started the war as a pilot in Kampfgeschwader 51, flying the Junkers Ju 87 "Stuka". After the Poland campaign he was transferred to Jagdgeschwader 27 and took part in the Battle of France and the Battle of Britain recording 2 (possibly 3) victories with the Messerschmitt Bf 109. In the last of his 112 missions he is shot down over the English Channel; with severe head wounds he is removed from flying and reassigned to ground staff duties. In May 1941 he volunteered for the Waffen-SS; he was trained as anti-tank gunner and posted to the motorcycle battalion of *Reich*. In the early stage of "Barbarossa" he was in command of a 3,7-cm-PaK. During the crossing of the Desna on 10 September he fends off an attack of Soviet tanks disabling an armoured train; the day after he provides antitank cover, then holds during four days in the bridgehead after the crossing. After this feat he is transferred to the 8th company, SS-Panzer-Regiment 2 in command of a StuG III, and in the battle of Kiev he is credited with the destruction of 28 enemy tanks, 14 AT guns, 40 other vehicles and 8 artillery batteries. In early 1943, now in command of a Tiger in the 8th company, he takes part in the Manstein's counterattack at Kharkov. On 20 and 21 February he spearheads the advance of *Das Reich* grenadiers, knocking out several AT guns and tanks. On March 1st he is taken

prisoner but manages to make his way back to the German lines, supposedly after killing his two guards. Promoted to *SS-Oberscharführer*, in "Zitadelle" and in the battles in southern Russia and Ukraine he is repeatedly wounded, however he would bring his total of "kills" to about 60. In October 1943 he was platoon leader in the 1st company.

In Normandy, during the fight for Hill 112 on 11 July, on his own initiative he leads a small group of panzers in a counterstroke in the flank of the enemy which eliminates several tanks and AT guns, he then pursues the enemy allowing the grenadiers to once again attain the old frontline. In this action he personally destroys 7 enemy tanks. On 30 December 1944 he is awarded the Deutsches Kreuz in Gold as platoon leader in the 1st company of the reconstituted schwere SS-Panzer-Abteilung 502. With the Tiger II, in March 1945 he destroys another 19 tanks in the battle around Stettin. In April he is directly promoted to *SS-Obersturmführer* and put in command of the company. On the 28 he is finally awarded the Ritterkreuz by the leader of the III.(germanisches) SS-Panzerkorps, *SS-Obergruppenführer* Felix Steiner. With one of the last operational Tiger II of the battalion he may have had his last "kills" in late April while escaping the Halbe pocket. He managed to evade the Soviets but was forced to surrender to the Americans on the Elbe after being shot in the arm, his ninth wound of the war. He was released from captivity in November 1947. After the war he became a sports reporter. He passed away on 12 July 2007 in Baden-Württemberg.

Notes. Prior to Normandy his highest decoration was the EK I, so at that time the number of his tank "kills" could hardly have exceeded 30 (to be added to the previous 28 StuG kills of the battle of Kiev; these were kills achieved in 1941 against an enemy in complete chaos, and so deemed of lesser value). - Most probably he didn't take part in the alleged destruction of 15 Shermans at Chenedollé. At the end of the Normandy campaign the total of his "kills" was around 68.

Eggers Johann, born on 26 April 1923 in the village of Sievern (sixty-five kilometers north of Bremen). In service from August 1940, he fought on the eastern front receiving the EK II on 20 February 1942 and the EK I on 14 July 1943. Gunner of the company commander's Panzer IV (*Oberleutnant* Arno Taulien, awarded the RK on 18 October 1943), from 7 to 9 August 1943 at Kharkov he wiped out more than 20 enemy tanks (out of a total of 30 by the company's five vehicles) reaching a personal total of 42 "kills". Later he also served as a panzer commander, and by August 21 he had a score of 46. On 14 December he was awarded the Ritterkreuz as *Unteroffizier* in the 7th company, Panzer-Regiment 6, 3.Panzer-Division. He passed away on 5 February 1974 in his native village.

Egghardt Alfred, born on 17 February 1920 in Wien. At the age of eighteen he became a member of the Allgemeine SS, however he joined the Wehrmacht in the Artillerie-Regiment 102. He took part in the Polish campaign as a gunner in the 4.leichte-Division. He was then transferred to the Artillerie-Regiment 74 of the 2.Panzer-Division, with which he fought in the Battle of France, in operation "Marita" and in the invasion of the Soviet Union. On 28 July 1941 he received the EK II. In 1942 he volunteered for the Sturmartillerie and was transferred to the Sturmgeschütz-Abteilung 912. On 26 December 1943 he received the EK I and on 4 September 1944 the Deutsches Kreuz in Gold as *Leutnant der Reserve* in the 2nd battery, Sturmgeschütz-Brigade 912.

During the sixth battle of the Courland bridgehead, on the morning of the 11 March 1945 the Soviets, with a strong armoured group, succedeed in capturing the homestead "Meiri", located east of Frauenburg. From this key position atop of a commanding height it was possible to dominate the railroad Frauenburg-Doblen as well as the road. Egghardt and another 5 sturmgeschütze had the mission of creating a blocking position north of "Meiri". However on his own initiative he decided to commence a counterattack leading his battery from the front. The enemy was pushed back off the hill, but the main gun of Egghardt's vehicle became inoperable due to a mechanical failure. To make matters worse, the command T-34 was firing from a very good position between two farm buildings, and from here the sturmgeschütze were unable to effectively combat it. He jumps out of his vehicle: armed with a panzerfaust and defying the machine-gun fire all around him, he destroys this enemy tank from a 20-metre range. On this day he eliminated 7 tanks (out of a total of 15 by his whole battery). With this action his personal total of tank "kills" had risen to over 30 (six of them in close combat); he was thus promoted to *Oberleutnant* and on 20 April 1945 awarded the Ritterkreuz. He passed away on 17 March 1996.

Eichert Robert, born on 14 June 1914 in the village of Pillupönen (today Nevskoye), one hundred and forty kilometers east of Königsberg. He joined the Wehrmacht in October 1935 being assigned to Panzer-Regiment 1. In November 1938 he was transferred to the newly formed Panzer-Regiment 36. He took part in the Polish campaign and in the Battle of France and received the EK II on 18 May 1940. Fighting on the eastern front he was awarded the EK I on 15 August 1941 and then the Deutsches Kreuz in Gold on 23 September 1942 as *Feldwebel* in the 8th company, Panzer-Regiment 36, 14.Panzer-Division. He escaped the fate of his division at Stalingrad. *Oberfeldwebel* and platoon leader, he was awarded the Ritterkreuz on 20 April 1943 and promoted to *Leutnant* on May 1st. Up to this time he had destroyed a total of 36 enemy tanks and 52 guns, over the course of 79 engagements in which he was wounded five times. In command of the 4th company, he was killed in action on 23 September 1944 during the battle for Riga.

Notes. In 1943 Panzer-Regiment 36 was rebuilt in France on 3 Abteilungen of 4 Kompanien each; the I.Abteilung was equipped with Panther tanks.

Eichler Wolfgang, born on 17 August 1914 in the naval base of Lüderitzbucht, in the then Deutsch-Südwestafrika. In service from November 1st 1935, he was awarded the EK II on 30 July 1941 and the EK I on November 1st 1942. He distinguished himself as *Leutnant der Reserve* and platoon leader in the 6./Panzer-Regiment 29, 12.Panzer-Division. On the 10 November 1943 the Soviets commenced a major offensive southwest of Gomel along a broad front with numerous rifle divisions and two full-strenght tank corps. At the start of the offensive, as he was marching with his zug towards the ordered assembly area, Eichler spotted an enemy tank column coming from the south. This force of at least twelve tanks had broken through the German lines and was now thrusting deep into the rear. Without esitation he attacks and with his three own panzers he destroys 9 Soviet tanks; the remainder are barely able to escape. Getting back to its original mission, for the entire morning the zug was locked in desperate combat -without any infantry support or other AT weapons- against continuously appearing new groups of enemy tanks. Ultimately five attack waves are smashed and 31 enemy tanks are eliminated (15 of them personally by Eichler), with another 10 so heavily damaged that they had to withdraw from the fighting. In the afternoon, with four panzers and acting in cooperation with a panzergrenadier battalion, he thrusts into an enemy assembly area: 4 T-34s and a truck column with infantry and cavalry are completely destroyed. The remainders of this group were only able to escape annihilation by scattering in a disordered flight, and a further intended enemy attack was smashed before it even got started. For this important local victory Eichler was awarded the Ritterkreuz on 20 December 1943. He died on 4 July 1944 west of Minsk.

Elsner Herbert, born on 9 February 1918. He joined the Wehrmacht in November 1937 serving in Panzer-Regiment 5. In January 1941 his 1st company was transferred to the newly formed Panzer-Abteilung 301, which in turn was incorporated in the Panzer-Regiment 201 assigned to the 23.Panzer-Division. In 1942, during the advance towards the Caucasus, Elsner received the EK II on 11 July, followed by the EK I on 15 November. In the summer of 1943 his unit converted to the Panther. In late 1943/early 1944 in command of an Ausf.D he fought in the area of Krivoy Rog and on 31 January 1944 was awarded the Deutsches Kreuz in Gold, as *Oberfeldwebel* in the 8th company, Panzer-Regiment 23. During the war he took part in 78 separate armored engagements and was credited with destroying 56 enemy tanks. He passed away on 10 May 2008.

Notes. In April 1945 he may have been promoted to *Leutnant*. He was also recommended for the Ritterkreuz, however the nomination was not forwarded or may have been lost.

Engelmann Richard, born on 30 December 1919 in the town of Limburg (sixty kilometers northwest of Frankfurt am Main). He received the EK II on 17 June 1940 and the EK I on 13 November 1941. Awarded the Deutsches Kreuz in Gold on 23 February 1944, as *Oberleutnant* in the Sturmgeschütz-Abteilung 912. At the start of July during the defensive battles in the Pskov-Opotschka area, his unit eliminates 53 tanks allowing the withdrawal of the 389.Infanterie-Division to a new blocking position. Of this total he was personally responsible for 17. He was thus awarded the Ritterkreuz on 27 July as *Hauptmann* and commander of the 1st battery, Sturmgeschütz-Brigade 912. He was mortally wounded on 19 October 1944 near the village of Jaunpils, (seventy-five kilometers west of Riga). At the time of his death he had been credited with destroying no less than 54 enemy tanks.

Ernst Albert, born on 15 November 1912 in Wolfsburg. In 1930 he joined the Reichswehr. He entered the war in the Panzerabwehr-Abteilung 24 of the 24.Infanterie-Division; during the battle of the Bzura with his 3,7-cm-PaK 36 he knocked out a Polish tankette, receiving the EK II. Transferred to the anti-tank unit of the 294.Infanterie-Division, he took part in operation "Marita". He then fought in the southern sector of "Barbarossa" and on February 1st 1942 was awarded the EK I. On 23 December 1943, southeast of Vitebsk in command of Hornisse "Büffel" he destroys 14 Soviet tanks using only 21 rounds of ammunition. On 8 January 1944 he leads his three vehicles in a surprise attack which eliminates an entire Soviet armored column. On 22 January 1944, as *Leutnant* and platoon leader in the 1st company, schwere Panzerjäger-Abteilung 519, he is awarded the Ritterkreuz for the destruction of 25 tanks and several AT guns. On one occasion, with the 8,8-cm-PaK 43 firing a tungsten carbide-cored round, his gunner reportedly succeeded in scoring a direct hit on a IS-2 at a distance of 4,800 meters. In continuous combat in the second battle of Vitebsk from 8 to 17 February, Ernst destroys tank after tank. Promoted to *Oberleutnant*, in the summer he was sent to a commander's course; later he may have briefly fought in a panzerjäger unit. Near Alytus (sixty kilometers south of Kaunas) his vehicle is hit and he himself is shot at close range.

After his recovery in Germany, on account of his knowledge of English he may have participated in operation "Greif" under Skorzeny. In early 1945, promoted to *Hauptmann* he was transferred to the schwere Panzerjäger-Abteilung 512, equipped with Jagdtigers, in command of the 1st company. After the failed assault on the enemy bridgehead at Remagen, he was tasked to cover the withdrawal of German forces. On 16 April at Iserlohn he formally surrendered his unit to the Americans. He was credited with destroying 55 enemy tanks during the war. Near Vitebsk he even shot down a ground-attack fighter. He passed away on 21 February 1986.

Notes. In July 1944, the "519" was almost completely destroyed, it was refitted in August with one Jagdpanther company and two StuG companies. - For Kurovski (Panzer Aces) Ernst became company commander in "Panzerjäger-Abteilung 1299" outfitted with Jagdpanthers. Such a unit never existed. There was a Panzerjägerkompanie 1299 equipped with StuG and attached to the 299.Infanterie-Division; this unit was then renamed Sturmgeschütz-Abteilung 1299.

Hornisse of schwere Panzerjäger-Abteilung 519 in action. Notice the observer, on the ground ahead of the vehicle.

Ertel Reinhold, born on 26 May 1918 in the village of Ebersheide (today Świniowice, Poland), forty kilometers northwest of Kattowitz (Katowice). He took part in "Barbarossa" fighting in the southern sector and receiving the EK II and the EK I. His unit may have been the Sturmgeschütz-Abteilung 190. Promoted to *Oberleutnant*, in mid-1943 he took command of the 1st battery of the newly formed Sturmgeschütz-Abteilung 276. In September/October 1943 during the heavy defensive battles in the Bryansk-Gomel area he personally destroys 27 enemy tanks in the space of a few days. Despite being wounded twice, he remained with his men at the head of his battery. On 31 January 1944 he was awarded the Ritterkreuz. Promoted to *Hauptmann*, on 20 December 1944 he was given command of the entire Sturmgeschütz-Brigade 341 which was in combat on the western front. He is killed by the explosion of an enemy mine on 22 January 1945 near Jülich.

StuG III Ausf.G in Russia, September 1943.

Eßlinger Willi, born on 2 June 1916 in the village of Markertshofen (sixty-five kilometers northeast of Stuttgart). He joined the Allgemeine SS in 1934 and, by the start of the war, the SS-Verfügungsdivision. He took part in the Polish campaign and in the Battle of France, receiving the EK II on 27 May 1940; he then fought in "Barbarossa", receiving the EK I on 13 July 1941. In early 1943 he was platoon leader in the 3rd company, SS-Panzerjäger-Abteilung 5, SS-Panzergrenadier-Division Wiking. At sometime during the fight, while en-route to refuel his Marder III he hears about a Soviet tank assault supported by infantry. He rushes to the scene and attacks the enemy quickly destroying 3 tanks. By constantly repositioning his gun he then eliminates other important targets, eventually bringing the enemy to a halt. He received the Ritterkreuz on 19 June as *SS-Hauptscharführer*. He is killed in action on 25 August 1944 near Radzymin, Poland. By the time of his death he had been credited with over 25 tank "kills".

Fey Wilhelm "Willi", born on 25 September 1918 in the small town of Lollar (sixty kilometers north of Frankfurt am Main). A pastry cook in civilian life, on 27 August 1939 he was drafted into the antitank battalion 152 of the 52.Infanterie-Division, at the time deployed in the Westwall. In "Barbarossa" he experienced heavy combat in the central sector, and on 20 December 1941 he was wounded west of Moscow and transferred to a reserve hospital in Vienna. In March 1943, during the retreat of the "52" from the Rzhev salient, he is again severely wounded. After being moved to a reserve hospital in Magdeburg, later that year he volunteered for the Waffen-SS in the schwere SS-Panzer-Abteilung 102 that was in the process of formation. In Normandy as *SS-Oberscharführer* and in command of Tiger 134 he is in continuous combat from July 10 until the end of August knocking out tank after tank, as well as countless AT guns, carriers and trucks. In his most successful day, August 7, to the north of the village of Chenedollé (southwest of Caen) despite an order to withdraw by the abteilung commander, he engages a British column allegedly destroying 15 Shermans. From 1 October 1944 he followed an officer cadet course and on December was promoted to *SS-Standartenjunker*. In the Battle of Berlin he was tasked with the leadership of a tank hunting group made up of soldiers from *Nordland*. From 22 to 29 April the group managed to destroy a number of tanks in close combat and Fey was allegedly presented the Ritterkreuz by *SS-Brigadeführer* Mohnke. From 1956 to 1972 he served in the Bundeswehr reaching the rank of *Hauptmann*. He passed away on 29 April 2002.

Notes. After the war he claimed the destruction of 68 (!) Allied tanks in Normandy (not to mention AT guns and light armored vehicles). This figure came from the logbook kept by his radio operator, who optimistically considered as "destroyed" all the targets engaged by Tiger 134. Leaving aside those claims that do not match with the Allied after-actions reports, it can be assumed that Fey's number of "kills" was about 30. This figure, still very impressive, is consistent with the fact that after the Normandy campaign Fey, who was already wearing the EK I, received no higher award. - The awarding of the Ritterkreuz was accepted by both the OdR and the Bundeswehr.

Fischer Franz, born on 13 December 1915 in the town of Schwabach (south of Nürnberg). In service from November 1937, from early 1942 he fought on the eastern front in the Führerbegleitbataillon, a sub-unit of *Großdeutschland*, receiving the EK II on 17 March 1942 and the EK I on 5 May 1943. In 1944 the unit was radically upgraded to Brigade and took part in the Ardennes counter-offensive, then from late January 1945 it was expanded to Division for its final deployment in Pomerania and Silesia.

In the time period 25 March-1 April 1945 in the area south of Leobschütz (today Głubczyce), Fischer, as platoon leader, personally destroyed 21 enemy tanks. On 29 March with his zug he is engaged in combat with 5 enemy tanks that are attacking from the hamlet of Poßnitz (Posucice) towards the south. As from the ordered position he can't achieve anything, on his own initiative he takes the enemy in the flank knocking out all 5 vehicles (including a heavy assault gun). The day after in the morning, with all other panzers unserviceable, he stood completely alone and without infantry support in a frontline gap. Ruthlessly applying himself to the fighting, he destroys 6 out of 11 attacking tanks and forces the remainder to retreat thus preventing an enemy breakthrough towards Branitz (Branice). For these successes and for reaching a total of 73 enemy tank "kills", he was awarded the Ritterkreuz on 30 april as *Feldwebel der Reserve* and platoon leader in the 2nd company of the Führer-Panzer-Regiment 1, Führer-Begleit-Division. During the course of the war he fought in all operations of his abteilung taking part in 105 engagements. He passed away on 6 November 1970.

Panther of the Führer-Begleit-Division in Langenöls (today Olszyna), mid-March 1945.

Fischer Gerhard, born on 4 December 1915 in the town of Görlitz (on the Neiße, ninety kilometers east of Dresden). He studied mechanical engineering, then joined the Wehrmacht in 1934. He was trained in the use of armored vehicles in Zossen, then sent to the Panzer-Regiment 5 of the 3.Panzer-Division. In the Poland campaign, platoon leader in the 1st company, he destroyed several AT guns and was awarded the EK II on 23 October 1939. In the Battle of France he was awarded the EK I on 23 June 1940. In 1942 he joined the newly formed 23.Panzer-Division on the eastern front, as *Leutnant* and platoon leader in Panzer-Regiment 201. During the advance towards the Caucasus he was in command of a Panzer III; on 6 August he attacks and stops two Soviet artillery columns; on 2 September during the crossing of the Terek, he attacks 4 T-34s destroying 2 of them. On 28 November he was awarded the Deutsches Kreuz in Gold. In March 1943 with the II.Abteilung he was sent to Germany for training on the Panther. In September he was back to the front and saw action during the defensive battles of the Dnieper as *Oberleutnant* and commander of the 8th company, Panzer-Regiment 23. During the first battle of Krivoy Rog, on 14 November he leads his Panthers in a successful counterattack at Nowo Ivanovka: 31 tanks and 12 guns are eliminated for the loss of only 2 panzers, hundreds of enemy soldiers are killed and 217 taken prisoners. For this feat he received the Ritterkreuz on 28 December 1943 and the promotion to *Hauptmann* soon after.

From January to early June 1944 the II.Abteilung was employed in northern Ukraine, before being reunited to the division in June in the Jassy area. Fischer is now in command of the battalion and would continue to lead his men aboard of his Panther for the rest of the war, even after his promotion to *Major* in October 1944. As a main striking force of the division, "Panzerkampfgruppe Fischer" would be constantly in action, first in the fighting against the Soviet bridgeheads on the Vistula and then again to the south: in Transylvania, in the battle of Debrecen, in the first battle for Stuhlweißenburg, in "Frühlingserwachen" and during the final retreat to Austria. On the evening of 8 May the

panzergruppe establishes contact with British forces and surrenders. Fischer was in combat from the first to the last day of the war, taking part in 138 separate armored engagements. After the war he became company manager, then from 1959 to 1972 served in the Bundeswehr reaching the rank of *Oberstleutnant*. He passed away on 9 August 2014, aged 98.

Notes. He is usually credited with 102 "kills". However this figure most probably includes not only tanks, but all armored vehicles and AT guns combined. If so, he may have personally destroyed around 50-60 tanks. This figure is consistent with the fact that, after the Ritterkreuz, in the remaining sixteen months of war he wasn't recommended for an higher degree of the award.

Panthers of the 23.Panzer-Division in Debrecen, October 1944.

Flügel Hans, born on 13 February 1919 in the small town of Arzberg (forty-five kilometers east of Bayreuth). At the age of sixteen (!) he was accepted in the SS-Totenkopfstandarte "Oberbayern"; two years later he also joined the NSDAP. After a short period in the RAD, in late 1938 with the rank of *SS-Unterscharführer der Reserve* he was transferred to the SS-Verfügungsdivision; in early 1940 he attended an officer course at the SS-Junkerschule Bad Tölz and was promoted to *Untersturmführer*. He took part in the Battle of France as platoon leader in the 4.(MG)/SS-Regiment "Deutschland", and received the EK II on 19 June 1940 soon followed by the EK I on July 1st. Promoted to *Obersturmführer* on 30 January 1942, in June he was transferred to the SS-Panzergrenadier-Division "Wiking", as platoon leader in the 2nd company (equipped with the Panzer III) of the newly formed panzer battalion. He was awarded the Deutsches Kreuz in Gold on 8 December 1942. In 1943 he helped form the schwere SS-Panzer-Abteilung 103; in mid 1944 he returned to *Wiking*.

On 9 August 1944, in the early morning hours, the Soviets penetrated into the extensive village of Stanisławów (thirty-five kilometers east of Warsaw) following a drumfire-like artillery preparation. They occupied the place with two strong infantry regiments supported by tanks, anti-tank guns and AA guns, ready to continue their advance in a general northward direction. *SS-Hauptsturmführer* Flügel, commander of the II.Abteilung, SS-Panzer-Regiment 5, received the order to retake the village. At 14:30 after a short artillery preparation he commenced the attack: while the weak 5. and 6. kompanien would tie down the enemy from the front, the 7. kompanie, along with a SPW group, would launch a wide strike from the east. However the northern and eastern edges were secured by strong forces and the attack stalled at close range. In this critical situation Flügel personally sets himself at the head of the company: with 6 Panthers he breaks into the commanding Stanisławów farm and destroys 19 heavy enemy AT guns. From this position he realizes that the village can only be captured from the west, thus he drives to the rest of the abteilung and reorganizes the companies. In hard combat the panzers thrust through the urban area coming up behind the strong enemy AT line, which is simultaneously suppressed by

a few panzers firing from the outside. At the cost of no friendly tank losses the following materiel is eliminated: 41 heavy AT guns, 5 AA guns, 6 tanks, 1 assault gun. Over 900 dead or prisoners are counted. On 16 October he was awarded the Ritterkreuz. By this time he had already partecipated in over 100 separate armoured engagements and had received a total of six wounds, some of which severe. In January 1945 he was promoted to *SS-Sturmbannführer der Reserve*. He passed away on March 1st 1989.

Notes. In February 1942 a new SS-Panzer-Abteilung with four companies was set up for SS-Division "Reich" (which was being transported to France for reorganization). This tank unit however was assigned to "Wiking" in view of the offensive to the Caucasus.

With his 2nd company outside of Alagir, late November 1942.

Gärtner Heinz, born on 21 December 1920 in the small town of Wittenburg (twenty-five kilometers southwest of Schwerin). Gunner in a Tiger I, in southern Russia and in Ukraine he destroyed some 70 enemy tanks. On 20 June 1944 he was awarded the Deutsches Kreuz in Gold as *Unteroffizier* in the 3rd company, schwere Panzer-Abteilung 503. When in September the battalion was reconstituted with 45 new Tiger II, he took command of his own panzer (turret 314). On December 1st he was promoted to *Feldwebel*. A very popular comrade, he was killed in action on 7 January 1945 during a feint attack on Zámoly in support of "Konrad II". By the time of his death he had been credited with a total of 103 enemy AFVs and guns.

Giese Horst, born on 13 October 1911 in the village of Hochstüblau (today Zblewo), fifty kilometers south of Danzig. He received the EK II on 21 May 1940, and the EK I on 6 September 1941. Until summer 1943 he was platoon leader in a panzerjäger unit. In 1944, as *Leutnant* and Panther commander in the 2nd company, Panzer-Abteilung 2101, he fought in the counterattack south of Riga that temporarily would reopen the land connection between Heeresgruppe Nord and Heeresgruppe Mitte, and on 20 September was awarded the Deutsches Kreuz in Gold. In February 1945 he was transferred to the Panzer-Abteilung 5 of the 25.Panzergrenadier-Division. On 22 March, during a counterattack on the Golzow train station, with his Panther he destroys 3 tanks. On the next day, early in the morning he observes an armoured formation that is about to attack. Under enemy artillery fire and changing position several times, from 06:30 to 10:00 he eliminates 15 tanks, preventing the Soviet breakthrough towards Seelow. On 24 March, with only 2 vehicles, he supports the night attack on Gorgast, then he covers the withdrawal as the rearguard panzer even though he has been badly wounded. In these actions he destroyed 19 enemy AFVs (2 assault guns SU-76, 4 IS-2s, 13 T-34s). By this time he had achieved a total of at least 58 tank "kills" and was thus awarded the Ritterkreuz on 17 April 1945 as commander of the 2nd company. He passed away on 13 July 1977.

Column of Panthers of the 25.Panzergrenadier-Division near Küstrin-Kietz, February 1945.

Göring Kurt, born on 30 October 1917 in the village of Großberndten (fifteen kilometers south of Nordhausen). He entered the war as *Unteroffizier* in the 7th company, Panzer-Regiment 4, 2.Panzer-Division. He took part in the Polish campaign and in the Battle of France receiving the EK II on 7 June 1940. In September his regiment was transferred to the 13.Panzer-Division; with this unit he fought in southern Ukraine and then, in 1942, in the Caucasus. On 8 December 1942, as *Feldwebel* and platoon leader, he was awarded the EK I. In December 1942 his 4th company was sent to Paderborn and incorporated into schwere Panzer-Abteilung 502. As Tiger commander, on 7 April 1944 near Ostrov (south of Pskov) he destroys seven tanks; on 11 April another thirteen. On 9 October he is awarded the Deutsches Kreuz in Gold, as *Oberfeldwebel* in the 2nd company. In late 1944 he fought in the Memel bridgehead, then in 1945 he would lead his small kampfgruppe in several counterattacks in the area of Königsberg. On 8 April 1945 his Tiger is knocked out; finally, on 22 April in Hela he is embarked on a ship to Copenhagen. He took part in over 100 separate armoured engagements and was credited with destroying 56 enemy tanks. He passed away on 9 October 2002.

Tigers of the 2nd company during the battle for Narva, January-February 1944.

Gransee Georg, born on 29 June 1917 in the village of Berkenbrügge (twenty kilometers east of Arnswalde, in the then Brandenburg). He entered the military in November 1938, being enlisted the following year in the 6th leichte-Panzer-Kompanie of the Panzer-Regiment 31. After the Battle of France he was promoted to *Obergefreiter* and transferred to the 2nd company as panzer gunner. With this unit he took part in the Balkan campaign receiving the EK II on 6 May 1941. Transferred to the 8th company, he fought in the battle of Moscow and on 23 December 1941 was awarded the EK I.

On 13 August 1943 in the region to the south of Vyazma, the 5.Panzer-Division had occupied a sector some thirty kilometers northeast of Spas-Demensk. On the right flank weak armored forces which included the zug of *Feldwebel* Gransee, had secured an important hill that dominated the entire area. Behind this hill were the firing positions of the artillery and the logistics net. On the evening of the 14, the enemy attacked with a tank brigade plus two battalions. When the loss of the hill threatened to take place, Gransee undertakes a bold thrust into the flank of the Soviets, destroying two tanks and the infantry. The next morning 10 tanks are eliminated by his zug (of this total he was responsible for 3 KV-1s), and five infantry attacks launched in battalion strenght are smashed; then when the enemy tried to bypass the hill through a depression he manages to prevent this envelopment by destroying another tank. Thereafter with his zug he was tasked with covering the retreat: additional enemy tanks are eliminated. He finally saved a light Flak gun that was still positioned east of the hill: the gun was hitched to the panzer, the crew mounted up on the panzer's hull and the new defensive front was reached in a swift drive. For these actions and for reaching a total of 21 tank "kills" he was awarded the Ritterkreuz on 19 September 1943 as platoon leader in the 7th company, Panzer-regiment 31. Few days earlier he had received multiple wounds (particularly to the left eye) and would stay in the hospital (Reserve-Lazarett IV, Regensburg) until mid-January 1944. Promoted to *Fahnenjunker-Oberfeldwebel*, he returned to his 7th company. He fell in combat on 23 January 1945 in the village of Ober-Stradam (today Stradomia Wierzchnia, 8 km southwest of Groß Wartenberg, today Syców), Silesia; his remains were never identified.

Großrock Alfred, born on 2 January 1918 in Ludwigsburg. He joined the Waffen-SS on November 1st 1936 and the NSDAP the following year on May 1st. With the 3rd company, SS-Standarte "Deutschland" of the Verfügungsdivision (renamed *Reich* January 1941, *Das Reich* October 1942) he took part in the Battle of France receiving the EK II on 2 June 1940. During "Barbarossa" he probably served in the Sturmgeschütz-Batterie (within the SS-Artillerie-Regiment); on 4 August 1941 he received the EK I. In 1942 after being promoted to *SS-Oberscharführer* he was assigned to the abteilung destined for *Wiking*. After the fight on the Caucasus and in southern Russia, on 9 June 1943 he was awarded the Deutsches Kreuz in Gold; later that year he was promoted to *SS-Untersturmführer* and, when SS-Panzer-Regiment 5 was formed, posted to the 6th company as platoon leader. During the battle west of Kovel, on 8 July 1944, his zug of 5 Panthers counterattacks an enemy armoured breakthrough destroying 26 T-34s in two hours without incurring any losses. For this success he was awarded the Ritterkreuz on 12 August; his tank crew all received the EK I or II. In mid-August he became company commander and on 30 January 1945 was promoted to *SS-Obersturmführer*. He was taken prisoner in early April 1945 in Hungary and most probably executed on 5 April in Kecskemét. By the time of his death he had been credited with personally destroying 29 enemy tanks.

Notes. According to some sources when awarded the DKiG he was still serving in *Das Reich*, in the StuG-Abteilung. To another source he had already been transferred to the "1st company, Panzer-Regiment 5". Both versions are not clear. In 1943 *Wiking* only possessed a Panzer-Abteilung and a Panzerjäger-Abteilung. SS-Panzer-Regiment 5 was formed in 1944 with the conversion to Panzer-Division.

Grünert Anton, born on 11 October 1917 in Neusattl (today Nové Sedlo) in the Sudetenland, ten kilometers west of Karlsbad, the son of a butcher. After the Anschluß, in June 1939 he joined the Wehrmacht in the schwere Artillerie-Abteilung 430; from May to August 1940 he attended an officer course in Burg near Magdeburg. On 21 September he was promoted to *Leutnant der Reserve* and in March 1941 was transferred to the newly formed Sturmgeschütz-Abteilung 201. He took part in the assault on the fortress of Brest and on 26 June 1941 received the EK II; then for his action in the battle of the Gomel pocket he received the EK I on 24 August. In 1942 during the advance on Voronezh his unit managed to eliminate two enemy bridgeheads south of the city; during this action he destroyed 15 enemy tanks and on 27 August was awarded the Deutsches Kreuz in Gold. Promoted to *Oberleutnant* and put in command of the whole 3rd battery, he distinguished himself in early 1943 during the battles along the southern wing of the 2.Armee. While serving with Gruppe Siebert (based around the 57.Infanterie-Division) he played a major role in spearheading a breakout by several thousand German soldiers using his 4 still operational sturmgeschütze. Three of these did not make it through and Grünert himself was wounded, but contact was finally made with the outside. On 15 March 1943 he was awarded the Ritterkreuz. He was then offered a post as instructor in Jüterbog, however he decided to return to the front, with his men in the upgraded Sturmgeschütz-Brigade 201. His wife married in March 1943 had died in childbirth in November. In Poland, on 8 August 1944 near the village of Żabiec, on the Vistula, the wireless aerial of his sturmgeschütz is shot away. He emerges from the hatch in order to manually send signals to the other vehicles and is killed by machine gun bullets to the chest. Posthumously promoted to *Hauptmann*, by the time of his death he had been credited with a personal total of no less than 21 enemy tanks.

Gsell Karl-Heinrich, born on 28 August 1922 in Kiel, the only son of a government official and his wife. He joined the Wehrmacht in September 1941 being assigned to Panzer-Regiment 35, 4.Panzer-Division. In 1943 he had been promoted to *Leutnant der Reserve* and put in charge of a platoon. In July during a counterattack he personally destroyed five Soviet tanks and was thus awarded the EK II; on the next day the Soviets repeated their breakthrough attempt with 50 tanks deployed in waves. Once again Gsell launched a counterthrust knocking out another 12 tanks with his zug. During this fighting, which earned him the EK I, he was wounded in the shoulder by a grenade splinter. In the middle of November, near Rechytsa (forty kilometers west of Gomel) he destroyed 11 tanks from a range of 80-100 metres (out of a total of 22 tanks by the whole zug); at that time, despite his young age he had already been given acting command of the entire 2nd company. At the start of January 1944 during the defensive battles near Kalinkaviču (south-western Belarus) he advanced at the head of his unit against a heavily occupied village without radio contact to the abteilung; when the gun of his Panzer IV jammed, he started tossing grenades out of his open hatch. Shortly afterwards a dangerous enemy penetration took place in the neightbouring village at the boundary between two German panzer divisions; Gsell eliminated the enemy garrison and held the village for days, along with panzergrenadiers, against a much numerically superior enemy. For his acts of bravery he was awarded the Ritterkreuz on 23 February 1944. In late January 1945 the 4.Panzer-Division was rushed from Courland to the area of Danzig. On 22 February 1945 in the course of fierce defensive battles north of Heiderode (today Czersk), near the village of Long he was hit in the head; he succumbed to his wounds three days later.

Günther Wilhelm, born on 17 May 1913 in the village of Grunau (today Jeżów Sudecki), ninety-five kilometers west of Breslau. With the 16.Panzer-Division he took part the invasion of the Soviet Union, in the southern sector, receiving the EK II and the EK I. During the combat in the Stalingrad area, within the space of just four weeks he was credited with destroying no less than 42 Soviet tanks, and on 18 December 1942 he was awarded the Ritterkreuz as *Feldwebel* and platoon leader in the 8th company, Panzer-Regiment 2. Promoted to *Oberfeldwebel*, he was killed on 8 April 1945 in Sondershausen, Thuringia, during a fighter-bomber attack.

Panzer IVs Ausf.G of the 16.Panzer-Division advancing towards Stalingrad, 1942.

Haen Rudolf, born on 12 March 1915 in Stuttgart. After graduation from the prestigious Military Academy in Potsdam, in 1938 he was promoted to *Leutnant* and assigned to the 2nd abteilung, Panzer-Regiment 4, 2.Panzer-Division. At that time he may also have joined the SS. He fought in the Polish campaign, receiving the EK II on 3 November 1939, then in the Battle of France. Promoted to *Oberleutnant*, he took part in the invasion of the Soviet Union in the II./Panzer-Regiment 18 of the 18.Panzer-Division operating in the central sector. On 10 July 1941 he received the EK I [according to another version he was in the Panzer-Abteilung 100, a unit assigned to the XXXXVII.Panzerkorps]. The following year he was transferred to the Panzer-Abtilung 103 of the 3.Infanterie-Division (mot.) and after the elimination of several enemy tanks he was awarded the Deutsches Kreuz in Gold on 15 august 1942, as *Hauptmann* in the first company. In one action on 18 September he knocked out 15 tanks. At the end of October, in the vicinity of Stalingrad, strong enemy forces penetrated into a strategically important village. *Hauptmann* Haen, even though he was sick and had a high fever, decided to act immediately. Under heavy enemy fire, with his company he broke into the village and threw the Soviets back; the small garrison then defended its ground refusing to give up the unequal battle after the village had been surrounded. After three days of hard defense he led his panzers in a counterthrust which obtained such total surprise that the enemy was completely defeated: in total 20 Soviet tanks were destroyed and numerous mortars, machine-guns and equipment captured. For this feat, on 18 December he was awarded the Ritterkreuz. Inside Stalingrad he was the commander of the hard-fought 29.Infanterie-Division (mot.). On 12 January 1943, with only six AFVs he prevented a furious breakthrough attempt by attacking Soviets rifle divisions and tank brigades northeast of Dmitrievka, one of which had the aim of cutting off the 3.Infanterie-Division (mot.) which was deployed at the western tip of the pocket. At the Kasatchi mound alone, he and his AFVs destroyed 19 of 35 attacking tanks, so that the division was able to pull back to its ordered position. During this fighting Haen was heavily wounded and evacuated from the pocket by air on the 15 January.

Promoted to *Major*, after a 3 months recovery period he was given command of the whole Panzer-Abteilung 103 of the reformed and upgraded 3.Panzergrenadier-Division which in July 1943 was deployed in Italy. Here he led his abteilung to successes in the Volturno valley which were decisive for the whole XIV.Panzerkorps. In mid-October near Faicchio, "Kampfgruppe Haen" held off the attacking enemy for two-and-half days, enough for the neighbouring units to occupy the vitally important hill positions: on multiple occasions, with his Sturmgeschütze and with courageous grenadiers, he countered the oncoming enemy inflicting heavy losses, especially at Fontanavecchia where 6 tanks were destroyed. In the course of the same battle heavy combat developed at Capriati on the 29 October. Here the enemy deployed an extremely powerful force (consisting of 3 regiments), wanting to outflank "Kampfgruppe Haen" to the west and cut it off from the crossing over the Volturno. However, after three days of ferocious combat the enemy was forced to call off its attack, and the kampfgruppe was able to pull back as ordered to pre-planned positions just north of Capriati on the night of the 31 October-1 November.

Haen further distinguished himself at the Anzio-Nettuno beachhead in early 1944. During the attack of the division against Aprilia on the night of the 8-9 February, as the infantry became bogged down, he decided on his own initiative to assemble the abteilung and then, personally leading at the spearhead, he captured the town in the morning hours. In the subsequent successful defence against all counterattacks the abteilung knocked out 14 Shermans. In total the abteilung succeeded in inflicting the following losses on the enemy in the bridgehead: 52 tanks knocked out, 12 heavy AT guns destroyed or captured, 240 prisoners brought in. On 21 September 1944 he was awarded the Eichenlaub; by May 1944 he had partecipated in over 100 separate armoured engagements. After attending the General Staff School in Berlin, in early 1945 he was ordered to return to the Italian front as a member of the command staff of the 14.Armee, being promoted (effective on 20 April) to *Oberstleutnant im Generalstab*. Haen never married; he died on 9 May 1945 at a POW camp just outside of Bad Kissingen, allegedly shot by US guards. After the war, veterans recovered and moved his remains to a military cemetery in St. Johann, Tyrol.

Hartelt Wolfgang, born on 28 November 1924 in Breslau. After the Reichsarbeitsdienst, in February 1943 he joined Panzer-Regiment 2. In December he was deployed with the I.Abteilung in southern Russia, where he fought as loader and gunner and received the EK II. From March to mid-September 1944 he attended the Fahnenjunkerschule der Panzertruppen Wischau (in Mähren); from there he was finally transferred to the Fallschirm-Panzer-Division 1 "Hermann Göring" as platoon leader in the 2nd company of the Fallschirm-Panzer-Regiment. On 12 January 1945 the Soviets began their general offensive on the Vistula. After the wounding of his company commander, *Oberfähnrich* Hartelt, just twenty years old, stepped in as acting commander of the unit. With his Panther he destroyed a number of tanks and on 21 January was awarded the EK I. On the 26 January the rearguard of the division was attacked by twenty-five T-34/85s near Benice (8 km northwest of Krotoszyn). Hartelt on his own initiative rushes to the scene with five vehicles: not a single enemy tank manages to escape. With this he raised the number of tanks eliminated by the company under his leadership to 59. Of this total he was personally responsible for 17, and on 23 February he was awarded the Ritterkreuz. On 20 March, while in combat with a group of IS heavy tanks, his Panther takes a direct hit. At the last moment his men manage to pull him out of the burning wreck. Severely wounded he would spend the remainder of the war in a lazarett. By this time he had been credited with over 25 tank "kills". In 1956 he joined the Bundeswehr as a *Leutnant*. With the rank of *Oberst* he retired in 1984, the last Ritterkreuzträger in active service in the army. He passed away on 18 January 2009.

Notes. Following the disappearance of the 16.Panzer-Division in Stalingrad, a new Panzer-Regiment 2 was created in February 1943; its I.Abteilung was equipped with the Panther.

Harth Helmut, born on 18 May 1917 in the small town of Berleburg (one-hundred kilometers east of Köln). He joined the Wehrmacht in October 1938, being posted to Panzer-Regiment 2 (attached to the 1.Panzer-Division, then from October 1940 to the 16.Panzer-Division). From the start of operation "Barbarossa" up until the 8 of January 1943 he eliminated 60 Soviet tanks first as gunner and then Panzer IV commander. He particularly distinguished himself during an attack of his abteilung that had the aim of closing a pocket southeast of Toropets. When the attack comes to a halt due to a heavy enemy artillery battery, he emerges from cover and destroys the enemy guns in a bitter firefight. He is awarded the Ritterkreuz on 22 January 1943 as *Unteroffizier* in the 12th company, Panzer-Regiment 21, 20.Panzer-Division. By the end of the war he had been promoted to *Oberfeldwebel der Reserve*. He passed away on 27 January 1992 in his native town.

Hein Willy, born on 26 April 1917 in the village of Hohenwestedt (forty kilometers southwest of Kiel). On April 1st 1936 he joined simultaneously the NSDAP and the SS, and on the 20 of the same month he entered the Kriminalpolizei. By the beginning of the war he had joined the regiment "Germania" of the SS-VT, however in May 1940 he was transferred to the SS-Standarte (Regiment) "Nordland" which was being formed at that time. In February 1942, with the rank of *Oberscharführer* he was posted to the SS-Division (mot.) "Wiking"; on 20 April 1942 was promoted to *SS-Untersturmführer der Reserve.* As leader of the Kradschützen platoon he received the EK II on 26 July and the EK I on 30 January 1943. On 31 August 1943 he took command of the 4th company (in the panzer abteilung) which was equipped with the Sturmgeschütz. In October he was complimented personally by Hitler for his outstanding defensive successes in the region of Kharkov; then in November he was promoted to *Obersturmführer* and was given command of the 2nd company in the newly formed SS-Sturmgeschütz-Abteilung 5 (in 1944 dissolved and incorporated into the panzer regiment). On 30 December he was awarded the Deutsches Kreuz in Gold.

He distinguished himself in the battle of the Korsun-Cherkassy pocket of January-February 1944. During the initial stages of the encirclement, near "Olschana" (actually the village of Vilshana, 25 km south of Korsun) *Wiking* was surprised by a Soviet attack from the south aimed at breaking into the very center of the German held area. In this situation Hein gathered two hastily repaired Sturmgeschütze and 25 grenadiers and launched a counterthrust which resulted in the destruction of three T-34s, 15 AT guns and the capture of 200 enemy soldiers. With his small unit he then held out against further attacks and mantained the German line until reinforcement arrived. For this critical action he was awarded the Ritterkreuz on 4 May 1944. In September he took command of the entire I./SS-Panzer-Regiment 5. Fighting with his Panzer IV (turret number 200) he was severely wounded in his lower leg on 5 January 1945 during "Konrad I", and would spend the remainder of the war in Lazarett Salzkammergut Bad Aussee, Austria. On 30 January he was promoted to *SS-Hauptsturmführer.* In November 1944 he had received the fourth level of the

Panzerkampfabzeichen, for the participation in over 75 separate armoured engagements. He passed away on 25 October 2000 in his native region.

Hendricks Heinrich, born on 4 April 1923 in Oppum (a district of Krefeld). *Unteroffizier* in the 9th company, Panzer-Regiment 33, 9.Panzer-Division, he was awarded the Ritterkreuz on 26 March 1943 for his successes as a tank gunner. In one action his lone panzer was in position in a German-held village against a Soviet force of 15 tanks; of the attacking tanks he destroys 5, the last from a range of just 5 meters. Two weeks later he was involved in a counterattack by Kampfgruppe Kohler (consisting of 4 panzers, 2 sturmgeschütze and about 80 infantry); while operating as security for the left flank his Panzer IV encountered a force of about 20 Soviet tanks in a depression; within 3 minutes he destroys 6 tanks and 3 AT guns (the village is retaken with the loss for the enemy of 20 tanks and over 1000 dead). By the end of October Hendricks had eliminated a total of 38 tanks. He was killed in action on 25 November 1943 in Dniepropetrovsk.

Notes. In the standard lists of Knight's Cross recipients he is referred to as panzer driver.

Henke Friedrich "Fritz", born on 6 January 1921 in the village of Welsede (forty kilometers southwest of Hannover). On 4 September 1939 he volunteered for the Waffen-SS being posted to the SS-Standarte "Germania". In 1940 he was transferred to the Sturmgeschütz battery of the *LSSAH* as radio operator and employed in operation "Marita"; he then took part in the invasion of the Soviet Union and received the EK II on 5 December 1941. On 13 July 1943 for his actions during "Zitadelle" he received the EK I. On 29 December 1943 as platoon leader in the 3rd battery, SS-Sturmgeschütz-Abteilung 1, in the area of Zhytomyr he is supporting a group of grenadiers when a small attack is launched. He eliminates two tanks, but this initial incursion is soon followed up by a much heavier assault. Without much support he engages the enemy in a merciless battle: when a Red Army officer escapes from his knocked out command tank, Henke shoots him with his pistol. By the end of the day he has destroyed a total of 21 tanks and 11 AT guns. On 12 February 1944 he was awarded the Ritterkreuz and promoted to *SS-Oberscharführer*; by this time he had reached a total of 38 Soviet tank "kills". By the end of the war he may have been promoted to *SS-Untersturmführer.* He passed away on 15 November 1999.

Notes. According to another version he was born in the village of Oldendorf (fifty kilometers west of Hamburg).

Heubeck Konrad, born on 22 April 1918 in the village of Alberndorf (thirty-five kilometers west of Nürnberg). As a member of the *LSSAH* he partecipated in both the occupation of the Sudetenland and the annexation of Bohemia and Moravia in March 1939. He then fought in the Battle of France receiving the EK II on 30 June 1940. He was awarded the EK I on September 1st 1942 and the Deutsches Kreuz in Gold on 4 June 1944 as *SS-Hauptscharführer* and platoon leader in the I.Abteilung, SS-Panzer-Regiment 1. Promoted to *SS-Untersturmführer*, he fought in the Ardennes (Panther 121). On 20-21 March 1945 during the defensive combat in the Hungarian town of Várpalota, in command of the 1st company with his Panther he destroys 11 Soviet IS-2s. In doing so he raised his total of "kills" to 52, and on 17 April 1945 was awarded the Ritterkreuz. He passed away on September 1st 1987.

Notes. Possibly near the end of the war he was badly wounded and lost a leg.

Heymann Otto, born on 17 January 1913 in the hamlet of Hopen (in the municipality of Sankt Michaelisdonn, seventy-five kilometers southwest of Kiel). He took part in the invasion of the Soviet Union in the Panzer-Regiment 31 of the 5.Panzer-Division. Already awarded with both classes of the EK, he received the DKiG on 6 May 1942 as *Hauptfeldwebel* in the 5th company for his actions during the winter defensive battles in the central sector of the front. Promoted to *Leutnant* and in command of the 8th company, he further distinguished himself in early 1945 in East Prussia. On the 17 January his abteilung was involved in cleaning up several enemy penetrations in the sector of the 549.Volksgrenadier-Division (northeast of Gumbinnen). During the fighting Heymann was deployed alone with his Panzer IV, with no infantry to cover the flanks of his retreat. In this situation he is attacked three times by 20-28 tanks, however he holds the line and is able to knock out 25 tanks. He only pulled back after he had run out of armour-piercing ammunition and the Soviet infantry had approached to within close-combat weapon range. For this feat he was awarded the Ritterkreuz on 17 March 1945. He passed away on 13 March 1974 in his birthplace.

Himmelskamp Bernhard, born on 21 December 1919 in the village of Grüppenbühren (twenty kilometers west of Bremen), the son of a farmer. He was *Obergefreiter* in the 4th company, Panzer-Regiment 35, 4.Panzer-Division. On 29 August 1943 during a counterattack at Sevsk, southwest of Orel, the company commander's Panzer IV (*Oberleutnant* Hans Müller, DKiG on 15 September, killed on 14 November 1943) is set on fire by several hits. Although repeatedly wounded by shrapnel, gunner Himmelskamp does not leave his position; he dies while being transported to the dressing station. Posthumously awarded the Ritterkreuz on 13 September 1943 for having destroyed a total of 40 enemy tanks.

Höhno Helmut, born on 15 December 1913 in the small town of Lübbenau (eighty kilometers southeast of Berlin). In 1931 he completed an apprenticeship as a pastry chef, however he applied for the Reichswehr being posted on October 1st to the Kraftfahr-Lehrkommando Zossen. When the first tank units were built in 1935, he joined the Panzer-Regiment 6 of the 3.Panzer-Division. In 1936 he volunteered together with other unmarried soldiers to join a special ground unit equipped with Panzer I tanks which was then sent to Spain with training roles. Back to his Panzer-Regiment 6 he took part in the Polish campaign, receiving the EK II on 28 September 1939. He then took part in the Battle of France and in operation "Barbarossa", in the central sector, receiving the EK I on 12 September 1941. In 1942 with his unit he advanced on Voronezh and then towards the Caucasus reaching the Terek. On June 1st 1943 he was promoted to *Fahnenjunker-Oberfeldwebel*; in the following months he fought in "Zitadelle", in the area of Kiev and in Kirovograd. Promoted to *Leutnant* on March 1st 1944, he was transferred to the schwere Panzer-Abteilung 510 as platoon leader in the 2nd company. He fought in Lithuania and in the first battles of Courland. At the start of October 1944 he had destroyed his 83rd enemy tank. Severely wounded he was evacuated to a military hospital in Germany where he was awarded the Ritterkreuz on 9 December 1944. In April 1945 he was transferred to the schwere Panzer-Abteilung 508, however as this unit could not be re-equipped with tanks, he never entered into combat again. After the war he served in the Bundeswehr reaching the rank of *Hauptmann*. He passed away on 17 March 1966.

Hönniger Theodor, born on 10 February 1915 in the small town of Betzdorf (fifty-five kilometers northeast of Koblenz). He received the Deutsches Kreuz in Gold on 7 December 1944 as *Oberfeldwebel* in the 5th company, Panzer-Regiment 25, 7.Panzer-Division. In the region to the southwest of Danzig, on 23 February 1945 as platoon leader he was ordered to attack Sawüst (today Czartołomie), 5 km north of Konitz (Chojnice) in cooperation with elements of Panzer-Aufklärungs-Abteilung 7. The village was occupied by enemy infantry with several AT guns and with artillery in support, so a frontal advance from the north offered no prospect of success. Hönniger, who had already proven himself in 65 armoured battles, made the decision to split up the zug. While two panzers were left behind providing covering fire from the north, with three panzers he made it to the west entrance unnoticed, he then charged into the village putting the enemy into total confusion. Without any friendly panzer losses, 5 Shermans, 11 AT-guns, 7 other artillery pieces, 12 trucks, were destroyed or captured, numerous enemy killed. On this day he personally destroyed his 59th and 60th tank. On 9 May 1945 he was awarded the Ritterkreuz. He passed away on 18 February 1974 in his native village.

Notes. The nomination for his Ritterkreuz was received by the *Heerespersonalamt* on 19 April. The award was approved by *Major* Joachim Domaschk and presented in accordance with the Dönitz-decree.

Panther and panzergrenadiers in East Prussia, February 1945.

Höper Ahrend, born on 26 November 1920 in the village of Heringsdorf (fifty-five kilometers north of Lübeck). He took part in the invasion of the Soviet Union; on 20 August 1942 he received the EK II and on 6 November 1943 the EK I. During the fighting in Courland, on 19 October 1944 he received the order to reach Ķekava (German: Keckau), just south of Riga. As all of his platoon's other vehicles are out of action, he departs with his own sturmgeschütz only. Suddenly from a hill he spotts a group of 28 Soviet tanks; he decides to attack, driving down the hill at full speed under strong enemy fire. Soon the gunner's optics are hit, the reserve sights was missing. In response Höper begins to direct his gunner by observing and correcting the shots from his commander's hatch. In this way 7 tanks are knocked out. Within the space of just one year he eliminated the following enemy materiel: 33 tanks, 10 heavy AT guns, 11 medium/light AT guns, 3 other guns, a large number of heavy infantry weapons. On 18 November during the Soviet attack on the Sõrve peninsula (the southernmost section of the Estonian island Saaremaa, dominating the sea route to Riga), Höper destroys 4 tanks, bringing his total to 47, however the day after he is severely wounded. Evacuated to Germany, he is awarded the Ritterkreuz on 26 November 1944 as *Leutnant der Reserve* and platoon leader in the 1st battery, Sturmgeschütz-Brigade 202, attached to the 205.Infanterie-Division. He passed away on 5 March 2013 in his native village, aged 92.

Holzinger Franz, born on 21 May 1919 in the village of Traunkirchen (sixty-five kilometers southwest of Linz), Upper Austria. *Leutnant der Reserve* and platoon leader in the 1./Gebirgs-Panzer-Jäger-Abteilung 95, he distinguished himself during the fighting of his 3.Gebirgs-Division in the Nikopol bridgehead in late 1943. On the 26 November the Soviets attacked the division with 4 rifle brigades and a unit of 70 brand-new T-34s. The German artillery positions east of the Bolshaya-Bilozerka-Dniprovka road (on the south bank of the great river, opposite Nikopol) were penetrated, with some of the enemy tanks getting as far as just south of Dniprovka. However 51 Soviet tanks were ultimately lost, 15 of them eliminated by Holzinger's sturmgeschütze. The same platoon would destroy a further 9 tanks in February 1944 near the villages of Mykolaivka and Maryinske (still on the Dnieper, some fifty km southwest of the previous location). In just three months his zug destroyed a total of 63 tanks and 34 AT guns. Holzinger was thus awarded the Ritterkreuz on 13 April 1944. Promoted to *Oberleutnant* and in command of the entire company, he further received the Deutsches Kreuz in Gold on 9 March 1945. He passed away on 9 June 1963.

Notes. The 1st company was the Sturmgeschütz-Kompanie of Abteilung 95 (it had received 14 StuG IIIs Ausf.G in August 1943). In June 1944 the company became the Pz.Jäg.StuG.Kp. 1095. In January 1945 it started to be equipped also with a number of Hetzers and was renamed Pz.Jäg.Kp. 1095, then in February Jgd.Pz.Kp. 1095.

StuG III Ausf.G (with some 13 kill rings) of Gebirgs-Panzer-Jäger-Abteilung 95 somewehre in Hungary, winter 1944/45.

Hurdelbrink Georg, born on 6 October 1919 in the village of Altenmelle (twenty-two kilometers southeast of Osnabrück). In November 1936 he volunteered for the SS being posted to the SS-Totenkopf-Standarte "Ostfriesland"; in May 1938 he joined the NSDAP. Transferred to the *LSSAH*, on 20 April 1942 he was promoted to *SS-Untersturmführer*; on 8 March 1943 he received the EK II. In the context of the formation of *Hitlerjugend*, on 9 November 1943 he was promoted to *Obersturmführer* and put in command of the 1st company, SS-Panzerjäger-Abteilung 12.

In Normandy, in mid-July the company was still being set up and had just received its new Jagdpanzer IVs. Against operation "Totalize", on 8 August it was attached to Kampfgruppe Prinz for a counterattack. At 11:50 the company launched a swift thrust around the Robert Mesnil homestead and penetrated into the village of Saint-Aignan from the east destroying 6 tanks. The enemy tanks which had moved into position about 1.5 km to the east are brought under fire: 18 of them are eliminated and the remaining flee the area. Hurdelbrink and one other vehicle then move over to the village, destroying a further 5 tanks from its northern edge. The positions are held until 22:00, then the company together with Waldmüller's I.Bataillon pulls back to Soignolles via Saint-Sylvain while taking along all wounded men. 11 tanks have been personally destroyed by Hurdelbrink out of a total of 29. The day after the company took up security position on the high ground south of the Renémesnil homestead under heavy enemy artillery, mortar and infantry fire. At 22:00 in the middle of the withdrawal movement Allied tanks advancing in the direction of Soignolles suddenly appeared. Hurdelbrink, together with another panzer, attacks in the flank: the enemy is annihilated except for two vehicles that manage to escape. 22 tanks have been destroyed on this day. On 10 August the company was attached to SS-Panzer-Regiment 12 with the order to relocate from its position at Maizières via Potigny to the road fork 1.5 km east of Fontaine-le-Pin during the morning, then to move into position at Hill 195 and provide security to the north. After reaching the road fork it was learned that the hill was already occupied by the enemy. *SS-Obersturmbannführer* Wünsche mounted an immediate attack, however it was not long before a strong artillery barrage

prevented any further advance. Hurdelbrink makes the following plan: while his attached 6 sturmgeschütze would tie down the enemy from the front, with 2 jagdpanzers he would try to continue forward swinging to the right. The two vehicles manage to get into the flank of the slowly retreating enemy and are able to eliminate all tanks. On this day he accounted for 10 tanks out of a total of 13 destroyed by the company. On 11 August he received the EK I, however for his outstanding leadership and for reaching a total of 36 tank "kills" in the time period 8-16 August (out of a total of 86 by his 1st company), he was awarded the Ritterkreuz on 16 October 1944. He passed away on 26 August 2002 in his native village.

Jagdpanzer IV L/48 of the 1st company, I./SS-Panzerjäger-Abteilung 12 in Normandy.

Jakwert Josef, born on 22 July 1914 in the small town of Namslau (today Namysłów), fifty kilometers east of Breslau. He took part in the Battle of France with the 76.Infanterie-Division receiving the EK II on 28 June 1940 and being promoted to *Unteroffizier*. On the eastern front, fighting in the divisional panzerabwehr-abteilung he was awarded the EK I on 12 March 1942. *Feldwebel*, he was seriously wounded during the battle of Stalingrad and evacuated to Germany. After attending a Fahnenjunker school he was promoted to *Oberfeldwebel* and in October 1943 was posted as platoon leader to the Panzerjäger-Kompanie 361.

In April 1944 near Brody his 361.Infanterie-Division had been encircled for over 14 days. In fierce attacks he destroys 7 enemy tanks with his panzerjäger and one more tank in close combat, enabling the division headquarters and the main body of the unit to finally fighting free the road from Brody to Olesko. Awarded the Ritterkreuz on 14 May 1944 and promoted to *Leutnant*, he was transferred to the Panzerjäger-Abteilung 1562, 562.Volks-Grenadier-Division, as platoon leader in the 2nd (sturmgeschütz) company. In February 1945 in East Prussia, while defending the Zinten (today Kornevo) airfield he destroys several tanks reaching a personal total of 51. He was thus awarded the Eichenlaub on 24 February. Promoted to *Oberleutnant*, in the final weeks of the war he commanded the Panzerjägerschule Milowitz (Milovice) near Prague. He passed away on 21 October 2003.

Kalss (or Kalls) **Alois**, born on 18 February 1920 in the village of Rußbach (Austria, forty kilometers southeast of Salzburg). In 1939 he volunteered to join the Waffen-SS, being posted to the SS-Verfügungstruppe in the SS-Standarte "Der Führer". He took part in the invasion of the Soviet Union as *SS-Unterscharführer* receiving the EK II on 10 July 1941 and the EK I on 17 September. On September 1st 1942 he was promoted to *SS-Untersturmführer* and transferred to the newly formed *Das Reich* Tiger company (8th company, II.Abteilung, SS-Panzer-Regiment 2) in command of the light platoon equipped with the Panzer III. Finally in command of a Tiger, in "Zitadelle" and during the following battles in southern Ukraine he destroys a large number of tanks, two of them in close combat, and on 16 September 1943 he is awarded the Deutsches Kreuz in Gold. In the early stages of the counterattack west of Kiev, on 18 November, he assumed command of the entire Tiger company (after Tensfeld was killed in action), however in December he was seriously wounded and evacuated to Germany. On 30 January 1944 he was promoted to *SS-Obersturmführer* and transferred to the schwere SS-Panzer-Abteilung 102, in command of the 1st company where most of the veterans were gathered.

In Normandy, on 11 July, after the English with the support of an artillery barrage and a smokescreen have sized Hill 112, he launches an immediate counterattack on his own initiative, leading his six Tigers through the tick smoke in a flanking maneuver: 7 enemy tanks and 8 heavy AT guns are eliminated and the old line of defense is reached. With this action Kalss raised his total of destroyed enemy tanks to 42. On 19 August the remnants of his company are ordered to break through the Falaise pocket. After a last counterattack on 21 August he withdraws with another Tiger in tow, however both tanks have to be blown up after running out of fuel. On 23 August 1944 he was awarded the Ritterkreuz. Promoted to *SS-Hauptsturmführer* on 9 November, he was put in command of the 2nd company, schwere SS-Panzer-Abteilung 502. In February and March thirty-one Tiger IIs were delivered in Sennelager and the battalion was sent to the Oder. On 23 March he leads his Tigers in a night attack from the west for the relief of Küstrin. Under incessant enemy artillery fire and AT fire, an anti-tank belt is penetrated and three tanks destroyed; several more are destroyed in the following days. End of March the Tigers were redeployed behind Seelow, with the 2nd company attached to *Kurmark*. On 27 April the remnants of the battalion assembled in the forest north of Halbe for the breakout attempt to the west, the seven Tigers of the 2nd company in the lead. On May 1st the forward elements of the 12.Armee were reached in the area south of Beelitz. Kalss was killed near Kummersdorf, most probably at the end of April, when his Tiger received a direct hit from an AT gun. By the time of his death he had partecipated in over one-hundred separate armoured engagements. His final total of tank "kills" is not known, but should exceed 50.

Notes. In September 1944, during the refitting in the area of Köln, Tiger 132 was symbolically painted with 51 kill rings. This was the total number of Allied tanks destroyed on the Invasion front by the 1st company (the total for the battalion was 227 tanks and 28 AT guns). - May 2 as date of his death seems unlikely; his Tiger II was disabled on 29 April (W. Schneider, Tigers in Combat II) and by the 2 the Germans had advanced more than 20 kilometers to the west of Kummersdorf.

144

Kaminski August, born on 9 August 1915 in the hamlet of Mertenheim (today Martiany) in the municipality of Lötzen (Giżycko), East Prussia. After finishing school he became an apprentice baker, however in 1934 he was drafted in the Reichsarbeitsdienst to perform six months of community work; in November he joined the Wehrmacht, being enlisted in the Panzerabwehr-Abteilung 1 of the 1.Infanterie-Division. In 1938 he partecipated in the occupation of Austria and the Sudetenland, then in the Polish campaign. By the start of the battle of France he had been transferred to the Panzerjäger-Abteilung 670, which was equipped with the Panzerjager I. Kaminski was one of the first soldiers to penetrate the perimeter of Dunkirk. In 1941 he fought in "Barbarossa", crossing the southern border to Odessa. In 1942 he followed the advance of the 6.Armee towards Stalingrad. In the city one of his crew was severely wounded; while escorting him to the Pitomnik airfield for evacuation, he too was wounded by shrapnel and embedded in a He 111 off the siege. By this time he had received both the EK II and the EK I. The destroyed "670" was reorganized in Germany in a single company which was then incorporated in the newly formed schwere Panzerjäger-Abteilung 655 equipped with the heavy 88 mm tank destroyer. In the battle of Kursk *Oberfeldwebel* Kaminski wiped out several T-34s showing a unique ability to command the Nashorn. With over 50 tank "kills" he was awarded the Deutsches Kreuz in Gold on 10 October 1943. Wounded in action several times, he continued his string of successes. Zugführer in the 3rd company, he was awarded the Ritterkreuz on 6 October 1944.

At the end of December 1944 he returned to the front in the schwere Panzerjäger-Abteilung 88 (attached to the 20.Panzer-Division). The Vistula-Oder offensive commenced on 12 January in the early morning, with an intense bombardment by the guns of the 1st Ukrainian Front. Protecting the city of Kielce, 17 Nashorns are ready for battle. Kaminski saw combat in Poland, Upper Silesia, on the Oder and across the Czechoslovakian border, and by May 1945 had reached the mark of 100 armoured vehicles destroyed; his company commander recommended him for the Eichenlaub, but the process was never completed due to the war's end. Taken prisoners by the Soviets he was sent to Siberia and only released in 1952. He married in 1957, working in the auto industry until retirement. An active member of the OdR, Kaminski attended the meetings annually. He passed away on 15 August 2012, one of the last soldiers who fought from the first to last day of the war. He left a wife and two daughters.

Notes. In September 1944 the s.Pz.Jäg.Abt. 655 was reorganized in two Jagdpanzer IV companies (the first and the third) and one Jagdpanther company, and later employed in the west. Kaminski however stayed in the east.

Kannenberg Kurt, born on 8 April 1912 in East Prussia. During the French campaign he may have been platoon leader in the 2nd company, Panzer-Regiment 6. On November 1st 1940 he received the EK II. In late 1943 he joined the newly formed schwere Panzer-Abteilung 506 and fought in southern Ukraine. For his accomplishments he would receive simultaneously the EK I and the Deutsches Kreuz in Gold on 12 September 1944. In August-September the battalion was refitted with 45 Tiger II tanks and immediatly employed in the Netherlands against the British near Arnhem. On 17 November 1944, in support of a counterattack of the 9.Panzer-Division near the village of Puffendorf, from his spot in the nearby village of Ederen he destroys 14 American Shermans firing at up to 4500 meters. He is then killed when his Tiger II (turret number 313) is struck by 105mm howitzer fire. Posthumously awarded the Ritterkreuz on 9 December 1944 as *Stabsfeldwebel* and platoon leader in the 3rd company.

Kannenberg, at far right with his right arm on the front hull of the Tiger I, with soldiers of his platoon.

Karl Josef, born on 26 December 1910 in Nürnberg. He took part in the Polish campaign in the Panzerabwehr-Abteilung 17 of the 17.Infanterie-Division. In 1940 for the Battle of France he was transferred to the Panzerjäger-Abteilung 49 (formerly Panzerabwehr-Abteilung 49) of the 4.Panzer-Division. He then took part in the invasion of the Soviet Union receiving the EK II on 26 February 1942.

During operation "Zitadelle" he was *Unteroffizier der Reserve* in the 2nd company; on 21 July 1943 he was awarded the EK I. On 22 July near the village of Slobodka (fifty kilometers south of Kromy, in the Orel oblast) with his self propelled anti-tank gun he destroys 11 Soviet tanks as well as two AT gun positions. For this action and for reaching a total of 20 tank "kills" he was awarded the Ritterkreuz on 26 August. He further distinguished himself in early 1944 during the fighting withdrawal of the 4.Panzer-Division in eastern Latvia. On 9 January to the west of the small town of Rēzekne (Reschiza in Russian), on his own initiative he counterattacks an assaulting Soviet infantry battalion. He crushes the attackers with HE rounds and with the mounted MG 42, throwing them back to their jump-off positions. He was wounded few hours later when his vehicle received a direct hit. By this time he had destroyed a total of 38 enemy tanks and on 16 February was awarded the Eichenlaub; subsequently he was also promoted to *Oberfeldwebel*. In the lazarett in Germany one of his leg had to be amputated and he never returned to the front again. He passed away on 31 March 1962.

Kerscher Albert, born on 29 March 1916 in the Bavarian village of Woppmannsdorf (thirty-five kilometers northeast of Regensburg). During the Poland campaign and the Battle of France he was in the supply column of the 2.Panzer-Division, then he was transferred to the 13.Panzer-Division, at first still in the supply column and then as panzer driver in Panzer-Regiment 4. At the end of 1943 he joined the schwere Panzer-Abteilung 502 as *Feldwebel* and Tiger commander in the 2nd company. He was the wing man of Carius in the Narva sector and during the retreat to Latvia. In Malinava when Carius' Tiger was about to enter the village, two T-34s were observed rotating their turrets: Kerscher fired in rapid succession and knocked them out (during the twenty minutes battle 10 tanks are eliminated by Carius, 4 by Kerscher and 3 by a nearby force of sturmgeschütze). On 26 July 1944 during an attack to the east bank of the Daugava (Düna), north of Daugavpils, his tank received a direct hit, 3 men dead. On 23 October he was awarded the Ritterkreuz and promoted to *Oberfeldwebel*.

In January 1945 the Abteilung (redesignated 511) was shipped from Memel to Pillau. On 13 April 1945 near the hamlet of Norgau (today Medvedevo), in the Samland peninsula, in cooperation with another Tiger Kerscher demolishes a Soviet armored column of about fifty tanks (with him claiming 32). On 21 and 22 April at the edge of the Neuhäusel Forest he holds the enemy advance destroying dozens of tanks. The next day, fighting back, he withdraws to Pillau where finally he has to blow up his panzer. Most of the men are ferried to the Frische Nehrung where the battalion is disbanded. Allegedly he was recommended to the Eichenlaub on 20 April. He managed to escape to the west and surrender to the British. In two years of combat he destroyed more than 100 -possibly 107- Soviet tanks in the course of 97 armoured engagements. From 1956 to 1969 he served with the Bundeswehr, reaching the rank of *Oberstabsfeldwebel*. He passed away on 12 June 2011, aged 95.

Ketterer Karl, born on 8 October 1912 in the village of Niedermorschweier (six kilometers west of Kolmar, Alsace). With Panzer-Regiment 35 he took part in the advance on Moscow. In June 1942 his abteilung was transferred to the Panzer-Regiment 15 of the 11.Panzer-Division as III.Abteilung. With this unit Ketterer fought in the area of the Don, being awarded the Deutsches Kreuz in Gold on 8 August 1942, and the Ritterkreuz on 24 March 1943 as *Oberfeldwebel* and platoon leader in the 7th company. In late 1943 the unit returned to its old Panzer-Regiment 35, 4.Panzer-Division, to become again the II.Abteilung, entirely equipped with Panther tanks. Ketterer promoted to *Leutnant* served as platoon leader in the 2nd company. He died on 13 April 1945 in the Bavarian village of Memmelsdorf/Untermerzbach. He was credited with a total of 96 "kills".

Notes. The circumstances of his death are not known. - The figure of 96 is likely to be tanks and guns combined.

Kirchner Kurt, born on 19 March 1911 in Berlin. He took part in the invasion of the Soviet Union receiving the EK II on 23 July 1941. As a StuG commander in the Sturmgeschütz-Batterie 667, in the time period 19-27 August 1941 he helped defeat a number of major Soviet infantry attacks northwest of Luga, receiving the EK I on 16 September. In mid-December his unit -a small battery of 4 vehicles directly subordinated to the Armeekorps- was rushed to the Volkhov front. Here, in the time period 11-13 February 1942 during fierce fighting in the area around Pogost'ye (seventy kilometers southeast of Leningrad), *Wachtmeister* Kirchner destroyed at least 18 enemy tanks including several heavy ones. Having raised his total of tank "kills" to 30, he was awarded the Ritterkreuz on 20 February 1942. His victories were all the more exceptional because achieved with the low-velocity and short-barreled early version of the gun. Promoted to *Oberwachtmeister*, in early 1944 he was platoon leader in the 1st battery of the newly formed Sturmgeschütz-Brigade 341, a unit which entered combat in Normandy on 31 July 1944. He was killed on that same day near Avranches. The number of tanks he destroyed in the east could be as high as 42.

Kling Heinrich, born on 10 September 1913 in Kassel. On August 1st 1932 he joined both the NSDAP and the Waffen-SS with the rank of *SS-Anwärter*. In 1938 he attended the Junkerschule at Bad Tölz and on 9 November was promoted to *SS-Untersturmführer* and made platoon leader in the 9th company, SS-Standarte "Germania". After the Poland campaign he was posted to the SS-Totenkopf Standarte 12. In the Battle of France he led the 3rd company, being promoted to *Obersturmführer* and receiving the EK II on 20 August 1940. In "Barbarossa" he led the 18th company of the *LSSAH*; he was awarded the EK I on 16 July 1941 and promoted to *Hauptsturmführer* in November. Repeatedly wounded, in July 1942 he was sent to a training course for panzer company commanders. In late 1942, when the *LSSAH* was upgraded to the status of a Panzergrenadier-Division, he took command of the new heavy company equipped with the Tiger. In March 1943 during the counterstroke at Kharkov, with Warmbrunn at the gunner's position, he eliminates several tanks and AT guns. In "Zitadelle", on the second day, with his three serviceable Tigers he takes the fortified Hill 243.2; on 8 July he advances with his mixed panzergruppe into the rear of a strong enemy front of AT guns and dug-in tanks causing the enemy to flee in panic. On 11 July west of Prokhorovka he is severely wounded and is then evacuated to Germany. In autumn 1943 he resumed command of the reinforced 13th company which was organized into five (!) platoons, each with five Tigers. On 16 November, with a small kampfgruppe he attacks the village of Lisovka: eighty heavy AT guns and the bulk of a Soviet battalion are destroyed. On 22 November the few serviceable Tigers overrun several anti-tank strongpoints and break into the fortified village of Yastrebenka. On

20 December 1943 during the attack on Chepovichi station Kling destroys his 46th tank and on 30 December he is awarded the Deutsches Kreuz in Gold. In total, at Kharkov, in "Zitadelle" and in the battles west of Kiev the *LSSAH* Tiger company has destroyed 343 tanks, 8 assault guns, 255 heavy AT guns and 20 other guns. Twenty-four Tigers have been lost in these actions (four more evacuated for depot-level maintenance). On 23 February 1944 he was awarded the Ritterkreuz, despite the fact that he had already handed the company over to Wittmann in December. Promoted to *SS-Sturmbannführer*, he assumed

152

command of the 2nd battalion, SS-Panzer-Regiment LSSAH.

On 20 March 1945 in Hungary he was appointed as the new commander of the whole SS-Panzer-Abteilung 501. In the final weeks he led a mixed battlegroup formed with the few remaining Tigers and the tank-less crews employed as infantry. In the Traisen valley (south of Sankt Pölten) they take back Sankt Georgen; on 17 April they drive the Soviets out of Wilhelmsburg: eleven Soviet tanks are wiped out; on 21 April they take back the village of Eschenau. The battalion surrenders to the Americans on 8 May near Steyr. During the war Kling was wounded eleven times; he was credited with destroying 51 enemy tanks. On 30 September 1951 he drowned in the Bodensee, near Radolfzell.

With his crew prior to the battle of Kursk (on the left, gunner Warmbrunn).

Kloskowski Karl, born on 9 February 1917 in the village of Lankow (a western suburb of Schwerin). He joined the Waffen-SS in 1936 being posted to the 3./SS-Standarte 2 "Germania". He took part in the French campaign as *SS-Scharführer*, then in 1941 he fought in operation "Barbarossa" receiving the EK II on 19 July and the EK I on 2 October. In mid-October he set out towards Mozhaysk with a recon troop; he entered the small town (located just 110 kilometers to the west of the Kremlin) and then through skillful leadership gave impression of stronger forces in such a way that the enemy gave up completely.

Platoon leader in the 4th company, SS-Panzer-Regiment 2 "Das Reich", on 10 January 1943 he was promoted to *SS-Hauptscharführer*. During the initial defensive fights west of Kharkov, often employed as the point zugführer he was credited with 9 heavy/medium Pak, 8 heavy mortars, 1 artillery piece and several AT rifles. In the subsequent attack on Pavlograd, leading the point zug ten minutes ahead of the abteilung along the only negotiable road embankment, he destroyed 4 AT guns, 1 armoured car and 8 trucks up until reaching the town's western edge. On his own initiative he carried on across the large bridge over the Vovcha against a pakfront and abundant enemy infantry, destroying three AT guns. Here he stalked 3 defending T-34s forcing them to retreat and later knocking out another one; he then fought his way further through the 8 km built-up area knocking out the aforementioned enemy tanks as well as 4 AT-guns, 1 Katyusha rocket launcher and 12 occupied trucks. For this swift advance that led to the capture of a Soviet brigade with minimal friendly losses, Kloskowski was promoted to *SS-Untersturmführer* on April 20 and awarded the Ritterkreuz on 11 July 1943. In June he was given command of the 7th company (Panzer III), however during operation "Zitadelle" he was severely wounded. In November he was promoted to *SS-Obersturmführer*; he was further awarded the DKiG on 23 May 1944.

He further distinguished himself on the Invasion front. In early July with his company he was deployed to support the depleted Kampfgruppe Wahl (composed of the remnants of *Götz von Berlichingen*'s SS-Panzergrenadier-Regiment 38). In very dense terrain where visibility was mostly restricted to 50 metres distance, the panzers stood in the foremost line. The crews would launch counterthrusts on foot against enemy infantry with success on a couple of occasions. On the 10, against the weary grenadiers the enemy succeeded in achieving two deep penetrations from the north and east. Kloskowski commenced a counterthrust with only 4 friendly panzers: 12 enemy tanks are destroyed. Two days later the order to pull back was given, but in the evening the enemy threatened to overtake the kampfgruppe in its withdrawal movement to the bridge and thereby cut its only escape route. Amidst heavy artillery fire and the onset of darkness, Kloskowski made the indipendent decision to attack, and with only a few infantry as support he managed to overrun an entire enemy battalion. In total, during the desperate combat in the time period 09-12 July, the company had captured or destroyed the following enemy materiel: 17 tanks, 8 AT guns, 21 bazookas, 5 trucks, innumerable light infantry weapons. 700 dead or severely wounded enemy soldiers were counted. On 11 August he was awarded the Eichenlaub to the Ritterkreuz and on 9 November was promoted to *SS-Hauptsturmführer*. In 1945 was reassigned to the SS-Brigade Westfalen. He was killed on 23 April 1945, after being captured by American troops near Orken in the Harz.

Knauth Wilhelm, born on 29 January 1916, in the village of Salchendorf (ninety kilometers east of Cologne). In 1936 he volunteered in the Wehrmacht and served until 1938. At the start of the war he was once again enlisted taking part in the Battle of France as *Unteroffizier* in the 6th company of Panzer-Regiment 5, 3.Panzer-Division. He was awarded the EK II on 25 May 1940, followed by the EK I on 11 November. On June 1st 1942 he was promoted to *Leutnant der Reserve*; on 12 February 1943 he joined the newly formed schwere Panzer-Abteilung 505. In "Zitadelle" the battalion was employed in the northern sector. On the first day, the attack of the Tigers reaches as far as Butyrki -where 42 T-34s are eliminated- and leads to the collapse of an entire Soviet infantry division. In the two following days all panzers receive heavy multiple hits and the battalion is withdrawn; then in the last days of the offensive it is employed in a last breakthrough attempt beyond Teploje. During the retreat in the direction of Smolensk, the battalion was attached in turn to several units. In covering missions and in counterattacks Knauth destroyed tank after tank; on 4 August alone, 14 enemy tanks are eliminated by his 3rd company in an attack against Kolki on the Kroma river; another 5 on 10 August. On 23 September together with another Tiger he destroys 8 T-34s; another 4 the following day. He is awarded the Ritterkreuz on 14 November 1943 as *Oberleutnant der Reserve*. On 31 January 1944 the battalion was mentioned in the daily Wehrmachtbericht for having eliminated 446 tanks since 5 July 1943 (68 by Knauth alone). He led Kampfgruppe Knauth in the battles west of Vitebsk and on March 1st 1944 was promoted to *Hauptmann*. In the course of 1944 he was repeatedly wounded and on 20 January 1945 was awarded the Deutsches Kreuz in Gold. In February 1945 he was ordered to take command of the 1st battalion of the envisaged "Panzer-Regiment Brandenburg" and on April 1 he was sent to a battalion commander's course; but the course was cancelled and he was sent into the Berlin area in command of a panzer unit. He is killed during the battle of Halbe, somewhere between 20 and 30 April.

Notes. The number of his "kills" could be much higher. It is entirely possible that the "68" enemy tanks were credited to him already in the Wehrmachtbericht of 31 January 1944. Then on 22 October of the same year he could have reached a total of 101. This figure was confirmed by his son in a private correspondence. - On 2 February the I.Abteilung of the PzRgt "Brandenburg" was assigned to the Panzergrenadier-Division Kurmark. During the Battle of Halbe Knauth may have been in command of that battalion.

Knispel Kurt, born on 20 September 1921 in the village of Salisfeld (today Salisov), in the municipality of Zuckmantel (Zlaté Hory), one hundred kilometers south of Breslau. A Sudeten German, very young he left his parents' farm and went to work in a car factory at Niklasdorf (Mikulovice). In April 1940 he volunteered in the Wehrmacht. After a period as infantryman he applied for a transfer in the Panzerwaffe and was trained as a tank loader at Sagan and Putlos until early June 1941. At the beginning of "Barbarossa" he was loader in a short barreled Panzer IV in the Panzer-Regiment 29 of the 12.Panzer-Division. At the end of August, while temporarily serving as a gunner, he destroys his first tank. In early 1942 his III.Abteilung was transferred to the Panzer-Regiment 4 of the 13.Panzer-Division for the advance on the Caucasus. In January 1943, already credited with a dozen confirmed victories (7 near Leningrad, 5 in southern Russia with the longer 75mm cannon), Knispel was selected to join the newly formed schwere Panzer-Abteilung 503.

Gunner in a Tiger I, he takes part in the battles which would allow the German retreat from the lower Don. He then fights in the southern sector of "Zitadelle", where he destroys 27 tanks in twelve days of combat, and in the battles of the Korsun-Cherkassy pocket and Kamenets-Podolsky pocket. In October 1943, he blows up a T-34 at 3,000 meters, possibly the longest recorded tank shot from World War II. He is mentioned by name in the Wehrmachtbericht of 25 April 1944 for the elimination of 101 tanks in the timeframe July 1942-March 1944. He is still a gunner and *Unteroffizier* when on 20 May 1944 is awarded the Deutsches Kreuz in Gold after the elimination of 126 enemy tanks. In September the battalion received 45 new Tiger II and was hurried to Hungary where it was redesignated as schwere Panzer-Abteilung "Feldherrnhalle". In Hungary and Slovakia Knispel, as Tiger II commander, would destroy 42 tanks bringing his total to 168.

He was a "character". Dressed with a customized uniform, rarely shaved, he had multiple conflicts with authorities. He was very modest and whenever there was a dispute over a kill, he always allowed the other party to get the credit; as a result it has been assumed that the number of his "kills" could be as high as 195. He is critically wounded on 28 April near Wostitz (today Vlasatice, thirty kilometers south of Brno) by shrapnel to the head and abdomen when his Tiger II is hit in battle with a group of Soviet tanks, and dies two hours later in a German field hospital at Urbau (today Vrbovec).

Notes. He wasn't among the Tiger commanders in Normandy. Pictures show him near some Tiger II during detraining in France, and according to some rumors in August he was gunner in a Tiger II (Porsche turret) and may have destroyed some enemy tanks. But given the lack of evidence, one must assume in August he remained in Mailly-le-Camp and did not see any combat. - After the war some of his comrades reported 29 or 30 April as dates of injury and death.

Kochanowski Johannes, born on 9 May 1910 in Bochum (in the Ruhr industrial region). He took part in the invasion of the Soviet Union receiving the EK II on 14 July 1941 and the EK I on 12 July 1942. On the morning of 14 August 1942, twenty kilometers east of Voronezh, a kampfgruppe of the 75.Infanterie-Division supported by assault guns, began an attack with the aim of retaking the village of Podkletnoye and the small forest nearby. Kochanowski, a StuG III commander, notices some 20 tanks at the forest edge on the flank of the friendly forces, and decides to take on this enemy group alone. He destroys two of them, but he has to exit the StuG among heavy enemy small arms fire to make the jammed gun operational again. He then continues the fight eliminating a total of 12 tanks. For this feat, as well as raising his total of destroyed armour to 31, he is decorated with the Ritterkreuz on 15 October 1942, as *Oberwachtmeister* and platoon leader in the 2nd battery, Sturmgeschütz-Abteilung 201. In late 1942 the "201" managed to avoid the encirclement at Stalingrad reaching in continuous combat the area west of Rostov. After a period of refitting in Greece, in 1944 the unit, now Sturmgeschütz-Brigade 201, fought in the Balkans, then in Poland and on the Oder. Kochanowski last rank was *Leutnant*. By the end of the war he had been credited with 55 tank "kills". He passed away on 4 April 1993.

Köhler Heinrich, born on 3 July 1922 in the town of Hameln (forty kilometers southwest of Hannover). After a period of training in the schwere Artillerie-Ersatz-Abteilung 49, in November 1942 he was transferred to the 19.Panzer-Division in the Artillerie-Regiment. In late 1943 he volunteered for the Sturmartillerie and joined the newly formed Sturmgeschütz-Abteilung 322 (soon renamed Brigade 322), taking part in the battles in the area of Kovel and Brody in March 1944. Here he destroyed a number of tanks and on 25 March received the EK II. On August 1st he received the EK I; during the first two days of that month the sturmgeschütze had managed to push back repeated Soviet attempts to break out of the bridgehead at Baranów (23 enemy tanks knocked out).

In March 1945 the Heeres-Sturmgeschütz-Brigade 210 was deployed at the Stettin bridgehead in support of the 1.Marine-Infanterie-Division. On the 16, *Leutnant der Reserve* Köhler, platoon leader in the 3rd battery, was sent with his vehicles on Hill 42, located at the seam between the division and the Panzer-Division Schlesien. On this day the Soviets attacked three times with about 20 Shermans, but they were unable to take the hill and lost 15 tanks in the process; 6 of these were eliminated personally by Köhler. With this the enemy attempt to break through to the road bridge over the Oder failed, and the refugee columns which were still crossing were allowed to pass over unhindered; the German units in turn followed them and the bridge was blown at dawn on the 17 March. For his role in ensuring this successful outcome, as well for raising his total of tank "kills" to 21 he was awarded the Ritterkreuz on 20 April 1945. With his unit he surrendered to the British forces. He passed away on 25 June 2009.

Notes. The Sturmgeschütz-Brigade 210 was created in February 1944 from the reorganization of the Sturmgeschütz-Abteilung 210. After being destroyed in January 1945 at Kielce, it was re-created with the remains of the Sturmgeschütz-Brigaden 201 and 322.

Körner Karl, born on 19 April 1920 in the village of Hoym (forty-five kilometers southwest of Magdeburg). Early in the war he volunteered to join the Waffen-SS. On 27 March 1940 he was in the 4th company, SS-Ersatzbataillon "Germania" of the SS-VT in Hamburg; one month later he was transferred to Klagenfurt to the SS-Panzergrenadier-Regiment "Nordland" of *Wiking*. Till the beginning of 1943 he was active as a *schwere MG-Schütze* in the 4th company. After his second wound he came in the SS-Feldersatzbataillon 11 of the newly formed *Nordland* in Croatia, then by the end of the year he was transferred to the schwere SS-Panzer-Abteilung 103 which was in training at the time. The battalion, equipped with Tiger II and renamed 503, was finally sent to the eastern front on 27 January 1945, attached to the III.(germanisches) SS-Panzerkorps. He was now an *SS-Oberscharführer* and platoon leader in the 2nd company. In February the battalion is deployed in Pomerania in the area of Neustettin and then in "Sonnenwende". In March, under the command of Körner, ten of the remaining Königstigers are loaded on the flatcars and sent to the rear for reorganization (while other elements would be employed around Danzig).

On 16 April the Königstigers are ordered into the area thirty kilometers to the east of Berlin. On 19 April Körner, acting in support of an infantry attack on the high ground near Bollersdorf, locates two IS-2 tanks; he destroys the first while the second drives in a ditch and is then abandoned by the crew; advancing further along the road to Strausberg he observes a Soviet tank brigade consisting of another eleven IS-2s lined up on the road, followed by around 120 T-34/85s being refueled and rearmed; he opens fire and knocks out the IS-2 tanks, then attacks the T-34s together with the other two panzers of his platoon which have arrived in the meantime; some of the fuel and ammunition trucks explode causing further panic amongst the Soviets. After he has expended all the ammunition supply -39 rounds for 39 hits, gunner Herbertz- he withdraws back to the German lines. We are facing a historical event: the highest number of AFVs ever eliminated by a single tank in a single action. Inside Berlin in the following days he would be credited with another 17 enemy tanks. On 23 April in Köpenick he

destroys a IS-2; the Tiger II then receives a hit by another IS (with the death of the gunner) and is moved to Grunewald to be repaired. Promoted to *SS-Hauptscharführer*, on 29 April he was awarded the Ritterkreuz by *SS-Brigadeführer* Mohnke for the elimination of 102 enemy tanks and 26 AT guns in a 3 months period. On May 1st he "takes possession" of an abandoned Panther; the day after he moves via Staaken towards Döberitz. There he destroys a IS that is blocking the Reichsstraße 5, then two more enemy assault guns. During the night the Panther suffers alternator damage and is set on fire. Körner survived the battle of Berlin and passed away on 8 August 1997.

Notes. Körner's files for 19 April report 11 destroyed tanks and more than 30 other "hit"; in the same action the Tiger of *SS-Hauptscharführer* Harrer claimed 25 kills. - On the 19, Hgr. Weichsel credited a total of 226 enemy tanks/SPGs, of which around 100 to s.PzAbt 503 (out of 200 claimed by the unit). The 1st Belorussian Front admitted the loss of 189 tanks for this day; the rest are losses of the 2nd Belorussian Front also opposing Hgr. Weichsel.

Krämer Richard, born on 15 September 1915 in the village of Bacharach (on the Rhine, forty kilometers west of Mainz). He took part in the invasion of the Soviet Union and, in 1943, in the battles in the area of the Don, receiving the EK II and the EK I. As *Leutnant* and platoon leader in the 1st battery, Sturmgeschütz-Brigade 232, he particularly distinguished himself on 5 August 1944 during the defensive battles fought astride the Dubysa river, near Juodaičiai, in central Lithuania. In the subsequent general counterattack (operation Greif), while attached to a kampfgruppe of the 252.Infanterie-Division, he leads his zug against the high ground northeast of the small town of Raseiniai (in German: Raseinen) and in the conquest of the town itself. Over the course of this operation, which was supported by elements of the 7.Panzer-Division, the enemy lost 63 tanks and 16 guns. Krämer raised his personal total of enemy tanks destroyed to 35 and was awarded the Ritterkreuz on 30 September 1944. His last rank was *Oberleutnant*. He passed away on 26 March 1992.

StuG III Ausf.G (fitted with the *Topfblende* pot mantlet), eastern front, 1944.

Kramer Heinz, born on 6 February 1921 in the hamlet of Michelsdorf (today Miszkowice), ninety kilometers southwest of Breslau. He was the gunner of Carius in schwere Panzer-Abteilung 502. On 16 December 1943 he reportedly achieved the singular feat of shooting down a Soviet aircarft in mid-flight with the Tiger's main gun! Awarded the Ritterkreuz on 6 October 1944, as *Unteroffizier* in the 2nd company, for a personal total of 50 tank "kills". In late 1944 he was given command of his own panzer. On 27 January 1945 during a counterattack of the 2nd company on the village of Prawten (Samland peninsula, north of Königsberg) that eliminates many enemy AT guns and assault guns, he is critically wounded after a direct hit on his Tiger. He is killed when the ambulance that is taking him away is also destroyed.

Notes. The episode of the aircraft is mentioned by Carius in his book. - Maybe by the time of his death he had reached the rank of *Oberleutnant.*

Kretschmer Franz, born on 5 October 1918 in the small town of Eulau (today Jílové, Czech Republic), forty kilometers southeast of Dresden. In 1932 he joined the Hitlerjugend. For his political activism he was detained sixteen months in two different Czech prisons. After the annexion of the Sudetenland he became *Jungbannführer* in Eger. In 1939 he joined the Wehrmacht in the I.Abteilung, Artillerie-Regiment 115 of the 46.Infanterie-Division, with which he took part in the Polish campaign and in the Battle of France. Still with the same unit he fought in operation "Marita" and in the southern sector of "Barbarossa". He was promoted to *Unteroffizier* and on 25 August 1941 received the EK II. He then volunteered for the Sturmartillerie and in September was sent to an officer's course in Jüterbog. In early 1942 he was promoted to *Leutnant* and transferred to the Sturmgeschütz-Abteilung 197. In January 1943 the battalion began its reorganization as a Brigade, however from April it was re-equipped with 45 Ferdinands and designated as schwere Panzerjäger-Abteilung 653.

At the Nikopol bridgehead, on 25 November 1943, the Ferdinands were employed against a Soviet armoured group that had broken through. In the battle Kretschmer eliminates 21 enemy tanks (out of a total of 54 by the whole kampfgruppe). The next day he is mentioned by name in the Wehrmachtbericht, and on 17 December awarded the Ritterkreuz as platoon leader in the 3rd company. On February 1st 1944 he was promoted to *Oberleutnant* and was given command of the whole company. With his unit he fought in the area of Tarnopol (with Elefant 301). From September 1944 the abteilung was re-equipped with the Jagdtiger heavy tank destroyer. In January 1945 two operational vehicles of his 3rd company, were attached to *Götz von Berlichingen* and briefly employed in operation "Nordwind". Kretschmer surrendered to US forces in Austria. He passed away on 28 May 1987.

Kretschmer reporting on his action in Nikopol to *General der Panzertruppe* Sigfrid Henrici.

Kühn Hans-Jochen, born on 28 September 1922 in the town of
Waldenburg (today Wałbrzych), seventy kilometers southwest of Breslau.
He probably took part in the Battle of France and in the invasion of the
Soviet Union, being awarded both classes of the EK. In 1943 he joined the
newly formed III.Abteilung, Panzer-Regiment 36, which was equipped with
sturmgeschütze. He fought in the area of Cherkassy and on 12 January 1944
was awarded the Ritterkreuz as *Leutnant der Reserve* and commander of the
9th company. On 15 January the daily Wehrmachtbericht mentioned his
50th "kill" near Kirovograd. In August the whole 14.Panzer-Division was
transferred to Heeresgruppe Nord, retreating in the Courland bridgehead and
ending the war in Libau. He was awarded the Deutsches Kreuz in Gold on 9
March 1945 as *Oberleutnant* in the 5th company; he may also have been
promoted to *Hauptmann*. He passed away on 15 August 1985.

Kujacinski Norbert, born on 11 July 1920 in Berlin. Called up to the army in August 1939, he took part in the French campaign before being posted to the 23.Panzer-Division on the eastern front. He fought in the soutern sector and, as *Leutnant* in the I./Panzer-Regiment 23, received the EK I on 28 December 1942 and the Deutsches Kreuz in Gold on 11 November 1943. Promoted to *Hauptmann der Reserve* and in command of the 4th company, he distinguished himself during the fighting in Transylvania in late 1944. On the morning of the 3 October, he and his company while advancing towards the Pankota farmstead (10 km southwest of Großwardein) encountered a formation of T-34/43s, KV-85s and heavy ISU-122 assault guns. In the ensuing battle the Panthers destroyed 16 tanks and 3 AT guns without loss; five of them by Kujacinski and his crew. In the course of that day PR 23 knocked out its 1200th enemy tank; that record was praised in numerous articles in the press. For the elimination of the Soviet armoured group and for reaching a personal total of 51 enemy tank "kills" he was awarded the Ritterkreuz on 18 November 1944. By the end of the war he had partecipated in over 75 separate armoured engagements; last rank: *Major der Reserve*. He joined the Bundeswehr retiring as an *Oberstleutnant*. He passed away on 2 May 2009.

Larsen Rudolf, born on 2 May 1921 in Marienburg (today Malbork), East Prussia. He fought in "Zitadelle" and in the battles in southern Ukraine and Romania becoming one of the most experienced and successful *Großdeutschland* tank commander. He had already received the Deutsches Kreuz in Gold on 29 September 1943, but he distinguished himself again in East Prussia, in the battles of the I./Panzer-Regiment "Großdeutschland" (which at the time was subordinated to the 6.Panzer-Division) at the Różan bridgehead. On the 6 October 1944 he is instrumental in preventing the Soviets from breaking through to the Różan-Ostenburg road. On the 9 October he stalks a heavy assault gun and destroys it from a range of 100 meters. In total during the time period 4-15 October, in command of his Panther he eliminated 14 enemy AFVs, increasing his number of "kills" to 66. He was thus awarded the Ritterkreuz on 23 October 1944 as *Unteroffizier* in the 2nd company. His last rank was *Feldwebel*. He passed away on 19 April 1998.

Panthers Ausf.D of *Großdeutschland*.

Laubmeier Ludwig, born on 30 January 1919 in München. Early in the war he received both classes of the EK. During the German evacuation of Crimea, on 12 May 1944 the Soviets achieved a dangerous penetration near the fort "Maxim Gorky" in Sevastopol. *Oberleutnant der Reserve* Laubmeier in command of the 1st battery, Sturmgeschütz-Brigade 191, hastily gathers up some grenadiers and the last sturmgeschütze on hand and with this force launches a counterthrust which succeeds in preventing an enemy breakthrough from developing. For this action, in which he is heavily wounded, as well as reaching a personal total of 38 enemy tanks destroyed, he is awarded the Ritterkreuz on 4 October 1944 and also promoted to *Hauptmann*. He passed away on 9 December 2010.

Litzke Erich, born on 6 July 1914 in the village of Benndorf (sixty kilometers south of Magdeburg). In 1943 he joined the newly formed schwere Panzer-Abteilung 509 and with this unit he entered combat in November in the counterattack west of Kiev. On 29 December south of Berdichev while in covering position he destroys 10 T-34s in half an hour. In early 1944 the battalion was in action in southern Ukraine within Kampfgruppe Bäke; then in August it was employed in southern Poland. In these battles Litzke destroys large numbers of tanks, and on 20 October 1944 is awarded the Ritterkreuz as *Oberfeldwebel* and platoon commander in the 2nd company.

Beginning of 1945 the battalion, after being refitted with 45 new Tiger II, was transported to Hungary where it was employed notably during "Konrad III" in the area of Stuhlweißenburg and Pettend. Litzke was credited with a total of no less than 76 enemy tank "kills". He passed away on 25 November 1997.

Notes. Allegedly the notification of his Ritterkreuz reported the destruction of 76 enemy tanks. If that's true, then his final total would be probably higher because for sure he was also in combat in 1945, in Hungary (see photo below).

Lubich von Milovan Berndt, born on 7 December 1913 in Riga, Latvia. His father had a brewery in Moscow but after the October Revolution moved to Riga. He joined the Waffen-SS in june 1940 and with *Totenkopf* took part in the invasion of the Soviet Union; in November 1941 with the rank of *SS-Standartenoberjunker* he may have been already in command of a StuG III. He fought at Demyansk and received both classes of the EK.

As *SS-Obersturmführer* and leader of the 1st battery, SS-Sturmgeschütz-Abteilung 3 "Totenkopf" he particularly distinguished himself on 5 September 1943 in the area north of the village of Slobidka (ninety kilometers west of Kharkov). Here he was deployed with his 4 vehicles as security, when in the midday hours the enemy began a breakthrough attempt with about 1400 men supported by 33 tanks. They attacked out of the forest in a southerly direction towards the village. Without waiting for further orders Lubich decides to launch a counterattack. Despite losing two sturmgeschütze right way due to engine failure, he continues to proceed against the overwhelming enemy force and in the shortest time he destroys 11 T-34s (the other vehicle destroys a further two). The rest of the tanks turned around to exit the battlefield and the enemy infantry too, under heavy fire from German artillery, fled back to the jump-off positions. With this the enemy attempt to encircle the elements of the division in the area of Kolontaiv, as well as the vital bridges on the Merla, was prevented. Since the start of March Lubich with his crew had eliminated 31 enemy tanks and on 14 October 1943 he was awarded the Ritterkreuz. When in late 1943 the

unit was disbanded and then incorporated into SS-Panzerjäger-Abteilung 3, Lubich was transferred to the 3rd company. On 26 August 1944 he was severely wounded east of Warsaw; by this time he had been credited with a personal total of 46 tanks, 45 AT guns and 29 other guns. On 9 October 1944 he further received the Deutsches Kreuz in Gold. After recovery he returned to the division serving until the end with the rank of *SS-Hauptsturmführer.* After the war he lived abroad and passed away on 17 April 2006 in Norway.

Mixed panzerkampfgruppe of *Totenkopf* in Szomor, Hungary. "Konrad I", early January 1945.

Lutz Waldemar, born on 24 May 1913 in the small town of Maikammer (eighty kilometers south of Mainz). Early in the war he received both classes of the EK. In mid 1942, during the advance on Stalingrad, he was *Hauptmann* and commander of the 1st battery, Sturmgeschütz-Abteilung 245. In the time period 06-08 September his group of 7 sturmgeschütze eliminates the following enemy materiel: 37 AFVs (including one KV-2, eight KV-1s and twenty-two T-34s), 2 heavy flak batteries, 5 heavy and 15 light gun batteries, 17 bunkers. During an attack against a fortified village he personally destroys 7 heavy AT guns within the space of just 15 minutes. He is killed in action on 15 September 1942 two kilometers west of the city. By the time of his death he had been credited with 47 tank "kills". He was posthumously awarded the Ritterkreuz on 2 October.

Magold Hanns, born on 16 November 1918 in the village of Untereßfeld (seventy kilometers northeast of Würzburg). He joined the army in 1937, serving in all early campaigns. On 2 January 1942, as *Oberleutnant* in the II.Abteilung, Artillerie-Regiment 74, 2.Panzer-Division, he was awarded the DKiG. On 5 August he was hit by machine gun bullets in the left thigh and was sent back to Germany for a five months convalescence. Around this time he was transferred to the Sturmgeschütz-Abteilung of the Infanterie-Division (mot.) "Großdeutschland", in command of the 1st battery. In February 1943, during the initial retreat from the Kharkov area, Magold and his unit had already played a key role in holding open the route for the rearguard of the division. In early March the Germans in turn began their counterattack to retake the city. On the 7 the kampfgruppe advanced through "Grigorovka" (unknown, possibly Grajvoron), eliminated several enemy horse-drawn columns at Hill 188 and reached Oleksandrivka; here it was halted by an enemy blocking position with AT guns and tanks. Magold led his sturmgeschütze in an attack that inflicted the following losses to the Soviets: 4 heavy AT guns, 21 medium and 16 light AT guns, 7 tanks (of which he personally accounted for 5). One week later during the final assault on Belgorod, at Stanovoye (a rural locality to the west of the town) he achieved the remarkable feat of personally destroying 14 out of 15 enemy tanks that his battery encountered. For these actions, on 3 April 1943 he was awarded the Ritterkreuz and soon afterwards promoted to *Hauptmann*. In mid-January 1944 he was placed at the head of the entire Abteilung, however in July 1944 with the rank of *Major* he took command of the Sturmgeschütz-Brigade 311. He fell in combat at the Dukla Pass, Poland, on 15 September 1944.

Malachowski Wilhelm von, born on 6 June 1914 in Rostock. He joined the Wehrmacht in 1935 being posted to Infanterie-Regiment 27, then in 1937 he served in the Artillerie-Regiment 48 and was promoted to *Leutnant*. Promoted to *Oberleutnant* on September 1st 1939, he fought in the Polish campaign and in the Battle of France as platoon commander in the 7th battery, Artillerie-Regiment 68, receiving the EK II on 9 July 1940. Later that year he volunteered for the Sturmartillerie and in 1941 he may have partecipated in the invasion of Yugoslavia, receiving the EK I on 26 May. In view of "Barbarossa" he was given command of the 2nd battery in the newly formed Sturmgeschütz-Abteilung 189. In late January 1942, in the Rzhev area he leads his sturmgeschütze in assisting the breakout of the XXIII.Armeekorps; on 23 January alone 18 enemy AT guns are destroyed near the village of Bachmatowo. During this battle he raised his personal total of destroyed enemy tanks since the start of "Barbarossa" to 35, and on 30 January was awarded the Ritterkreuz. On March 1st 1942 he was promoted to *Hauptmann* and on 30 November was given command of the entire Sturmgeschütz-Abteilung 228. During the defensive battles in the area of the lower Don, on 14 January 1943 he leads a group consisting of seven vehicles, two 2cm anti-aircraft guns and 50 grenadiers, in an attack along the Reka Bystraya river. After heavy combat against enemy tanks the village of Novopavlovka is taken; then the small kampfgruppe moves forward to the area of Ignatenko capturing the village of Maslov in a flanking manoeuvre: 18 T-34s and one KV-1 are eliminated, von Malachowski personally accounting for four T-34s and the heavy tank. On 6 March 1944 he was awarded the Eichenlaub and on 30 April promoted to *Major*; however he had been severely wounded and one arm had to be amputated. After a period as instructor in the Sturmgeschütz-Schule in Burg, in April 1944 he was posted to the Kriegsakademie in Hirschberg (today Jelenia Góra), then on September 1st transferred to the Generalstab des Heeres. He passed away on 28 October 1980.

Malkomes Hans, born on 15 November 1913 in Bremen, the son of a machinist. In September 1933 he joined the NSDAP. On April 1st 1934 he was accepted in the *Leibstandarte SS Adolf Hitler* and in 1936 he become platoon leader in the Panzerabwehr-Sturm. As *SS-Oberscharführer* he took part in the Polish campaign and the Battle of France, receiving the EK II on 8 June 1940. During "Barbarossa" he was promoted to *SS-Untersturmführer der Reserve* on September 1st 1941, receiving the EK I on 30 December. In November 1942 he was promoted to *Obersturmführer* and transferred to the 4th company, Pionier-Bataillon LSSAH. Finally in 1943 he was transferred to the 2nd company, I.Abteilung, SS-Panzer-Regiment 1. While in command of this unit he was awarded the Deutsches Kreuz in Gold on June 1st 1944 for his action in the battles west of Kiev, and the Ritterkreuz on 30 October 1944 for his leadership on the Invasion front and for reaching a personal total of 24 enemy tanks and 31 AT guns destroyed (as well as 12 other guns and 17 light armoured vehicles). By this time his panzer company had destroyed: 188 tanks, 52 AT guns and 43 other guns. After his promotion to *SS-Hauptsturmführer*, in November he temporarily left his command, taking it back for the deployment in Hungary. In the night of 20-21 March 1945, in Várpalota the Soviets attacked with around 20 tanks. Malkomes reports the destruction by the Germans of thirteen T-34s, soon after he is shot to the head while in the turret of his Panther.

Notes. The tank battle in Várpalota began just before midnight. The Germans had fired flares to avoid being shot at by their own side, this may have given enough light for a sniper to center on Malkomes.

178

Mausberg Heinrich. With the schwere Panzer-Abteilung 505 he fought in "Zitadelle" and in the central sector of the eastern front, for most of the time as *Feldwebel* in the the 3rd company under Knauth. In February 1945 during the counterattacks in the Königsberg area he eliminates a great number of tanks, he is then awarded the Deutsches Kreuz in Gold on 9 March 1945 and promoted to *Oberfeldwebel*. Still in combat around the villages of Tenkitten (today Beregovoye) and Bludau (Kostrovo), on 15 April he leads the two remaining Tigers II to the coast at Fischhausen (Primorsk); in the process the heavily damaged panzers have to be blown up by their own crews. With few of the men he reaches a ship sailing to Pillau (Baltiysk). In the town he is unjustly accused of desertion (!) and sentenced to deportation to Stutthof. Somehow he manages to escape and is finally captured by the Red Army; in 1948 was allowed to return to Germany. Mausberg was credited with destroying over 50 (possibly 53) Soviet tanks. He passed away on 17 May 2010, aged 89.

Meißner Herbert, born on 27 April 1913 in Allenstein (today Olsztyn), East Prussia. In 1941-42 on the eastern front he destroyed 12 enemy tanks (four of them near Stalingrad), thus receiving the EK I on 2 October 1942. Promoted to *Oberwachtmeister* and zugführer in the 3./Sturmgeschütz-Abteilung 244, in the time period 5 July-1 August 1943 he was credited with the elimination of 18 tanks. In particular he distinguished himself on the 17 of July. On this day the abteilung, without the 2.Batterie, was to provide security against armoured attacks south of Buzuluk (a village along the railway line Orel-Kursk). By evening the Soviets succeeded in breaking-in with strong tank forces, however Meißner lone sturmgeschütz and soldiers of the heavily depleted Grenadier-Regiment 184, despite being encircled and almost running out of ammunition, held their ground for several hours until they were finally relieved in a counterattack. In this action he destroyed 7 tanks. Having reached a personal total of 30 tank "kills" he was awarded the Ritterkreuz on 8 August 1943. He was killed on 28 June 1944 in Bobruisk.

Metzger Eugen, born on August 1st 1914 in Stuttgart-Feuerbach. In the thirties he joined both the NSDAP and the Allgemeine SS. Promoted to *Leutnant der Reserve* in April 1940, he took part in the Battle of France and on 20 July 1940 received the EK II. He then volunteered for the Sturmartillerie and by the time of the invasion of the Soviet Union he was in the Sturmgeschütz-Abteilung 203; on 5 August 1941 he received the EK I. On the morning of the 30 August the Soviets launched a major attack on the 23.Infanterie-Division and managed to break with several tanks into the position of the II.Bataillon, Infanterie-Regiment 68. In this critical situation Metzger leads his platoon of sturmgeschütze in a counterattack which destroys the bulk of the enemy forces. The next day he is deployed around the village of Budka (sixty kilometers southwest of Gomel) and together with another vehicle he eliminates 18 tanks preventing a breakthrough here; over the next two days the Germans were then able to retake the ground they had lost. For his role in defeating the Soviet armoured attacks and for a personal total of 17 "kills" he was awarded the Ritterkreuz on 29 September 1941 as platoon leader in the 1st battery. On 15 December 1941 he reached the rank of *Oberleutnant*, and in parallel on 9 November 1942 the rank of *SS-Obersturmführer*. Promoted to *Hauptmann* on 10 June 1943, from July 1944 until the end of the war he commanded the Sturmgeschütz-Brigade "Großdeutschland". He was credited with a total of 23 enemy tanks. He passed away on 6 February 2004.

Montag Alfred, born on 15 June 1918 in the village of Reitendorf (today Rapotín), ninety-five kilometers west of Ostrau (Ostrava), the son of a landowner. He entered service with the Wehrmacht in January 1939, serving in the Artillerie-Regiment 2, 2.Infanterie-Division (mot.). After the Poland campaign he was transferred to the Artillerie-Regiment 116. Promoted to *Leutnant der Reserve* in November 1940, he took part in the invasion of the Soviet Union, being awarded the EK II on 30 July 1941 and the EK I on 11 February 1942. Promoted to *Oberleutnant* in November, in January 1943 he was transferred to the Sturmgeschütz-Abteilung 909 in command of the Stabsbatterie. For his achievements during the battle in the northern sector of Kursk and the fighting retreat on the Dnieper he was awarded the Deutsches Kreuz in Gold on 3 August 1943. From 7 to 27 July he had personally destroyed 24 tanks (in total, from 5.7.43 to 5.8.43 2nd battery under his command was credited with 115 tank kills with 8 own losses). In the same period he also received the wound badge in gold and the rare Anerkennungsurkunde des Oberbefehlshabers des Heeres. Promoted to *Hauptmann* on July 1, in November-December he fought to the west of Gomel as battery commander in his old Pz.Art.Rgt. 116.

Back to the 2nd battery, he distinguished himself in early 1944 in southern Belarus. On the 30 January the Soviets launched a major attack supported by armour in the sector of the 110.Infanterie-Division, some fifty kilometers south of Bobruisk, and succeeded in breaking into German lines at several locations. However the battery, along with the infantry, managed to retake the old positions after heavy fighting during which numerous enemy tanks were destroyed. On the 19 February the enemy, after an hour-long artillery barrage, attacked the sector of the Füsilier-Bataillon 110. The German unit was forced to pull back 2 km to the second defensive line, however with the support of Montag's Sturmgeschütze and of Grenadier-Regiment 255, by around midday it was able to launch a counterattack that succeeded in recapturing the previous main battle line. For this successes, as leader of the 2nd battery, Sturmgeschütz-Brigade 909, Montag was awarded the Ritterkreuz on 21 April 1944. On 20 May he received the Sturmabzeichen III.Stufe for the participation in 50 separate armoured engagements.

On 27 January 1945 he took command of the whole Sturmgeschütz-Brigade 341 on the western front (after the death of *Hauptmann* Ertel). In late February in the area to the northeast of Aachen, the enemy had taken the village of Katzem in an overwehlming attack from the south while continuing to penetrate to the north and northeast. On the 25, Montag launched a lightning-fast counterstroke with just 4 Sturmgeschütze into the deep flank of this force: the enemy was stopped and a decisive breakthrough between the XII.SS-Armeekorps and the LXXXI.Armeekorps was prevented. The day after the enemy, with overwehlming strenght, attempted to encircle and take Holzweiler. Montag with 6 vehicles launched a counterthrust into the midst of this formation and prevented the premature loss of the village. This extraordinarily brave operation was executed despite the enemy having 60 tanks at his disposal. On the 27 he launched with his Sturmgeschütz a personal reconnaissance of enemy occupied terrain near Borschemich and Keyenberg which delivered vital information to the higher command; during this bold action he also shot up a number of enemy trucks. The first of March, with 6 sturmgeschütze he penetrated through the blocking position of the US 83rd Infantry Division at the river Erft, driving into the flank of the US 2nd and 5th armored divisions (which were moving towards the north). Despite heavy fire from the M10 tank destroyers as well as an enemy infantry company equipped with close combat weapons, and in the face of constant fighter-bomber attacks, the Germans were able to destroy the following materiel: 10 tanks (including at least one heavy M36), an artillery battery, 17 trucks. The day after, the Sturmgeschütze led by Montag, supported by an infantry company, once again punched through the enemy blocking position. They recaptured the village of Kapellen (6 km northeast of Grevenbroich) and continued to thrust an additional kilometre to the northwest. In the course of this attack, despite heavy enemy fighter-bomber activity, 15 enemy tanks and numerous trucks were destroyed, 45 prisoners taken. On 9 May 1945 he was awarded the Eichenlaub (the nomination was approved but left unfinished). During the war he was wounded no less than 13 times. In 1957 he joined the Bundeswehr with the rank of *Hauptmann*. From 1959 acting commander of PzBtl 74, he retired in 1974 with the rank of *Oberstleutnant*. He passed away on 18 November 1990.

Müller (later Müller-Reinders) **Eduard**, born on 27 March 1916 in the village of Rodenkirchen (forty-five kilometers north of Bremen). He took part in the invasion of the Soviet Union and received the EK II on 22 February 1942. During the offensive towards Stalingrad he was in command of a Sturm-Infanteriegeschütz 33B (a heavy assault gun built on the chassis of the StuG III and produced in only 24 exemplars) in the Sturmgeschütz-Abteilung 244. On a single day, 17 May 1942, while fighting in the sector of the Infanterie-Regiment 261 he eliminates 11 tanks. His unit was annihilated in the city with the rest of the 6.Armee, however Müller was evacuated in time. He was awarded the Ritterkreuz on 25 January 1943 as *Oberwachtmeister* and platoon leader in the 2nd battery for a total of 46 tank "kills". By the end of the war he had been promoted to *Oberleutnant*. He served in the Bundeswehr reaching the rank of *Hauptmann*. He passed away on 13 July 1982.

The StuIG 33B mounted the 15 cm s.IG 33 L/11. Here in a rare picture before Stalingrad.

Müller Johann, born on 16 June 1922 in Linz, Austria, the son of a train conductor. Unfortunately little is known about him. At seventeen he volunteered for the Wehrmacht taking part in the battle of France and in the Balkan campaign. He then fought on the eastern front receiving the EK II on 24 December 1941 and the EK I on 10 July 1942. During the battles of Lake Ladoga in January-March 1943 as Tiger commander he accounted for some 25 enemy tanks. On 23 October 1944 he was awarded the Ritterkreuz as *Feldwebel* in the 3rd company, schwere Panzer-Abteilung 502. Allegedly he died the following day, 24 October, in Laugaliai, Lithuania. He was credited with destroying over 50 (the total could be as high as 60) enemy tanks.

Notes. In Schneider, Tigers in Combat, vol. I, there is a *Leutnant* Müller still fighting in the 2nd company, schwere PzAbt 502 in the Samland peninsula in mid-April 1945.

Naumann Horst, born on 23 December 1921 in Berlin. He took part in operation "Barbarossa", then in 1942 he fought in the northern sector, at Kholm and Demyansk, receiving the EK II on 13 February and the EK I on November 1st. On January 1st 1943, in the narrow corridor to Demyansk, just after 09:30 the Soviets launched an armoured attack in the sector of the 225.Infanterie-Division. Naumann was positioned with his sturmgeschütz 800 meters east of the village of Sofronkovo (unknown, probably near Staraya Russa) in support of III./Jäger-Regiment 75. Alone he manages to eliminate 6 enemy tanks, preventing a breakthrough in the sector of the battalion. For this action as well as raising his total of destroyed Soviet tanks to 26, he was awarded the Ritterkreuz on 4 January as *Unteroffizier* in the 3rd battery, Sturmgeschütz-Abteilung 184. By the end of the war he had been promoted to *Leutnant*. In 1956 he joined the Bundeswehr, retiring in 1979 with the rank of *Oberstleutnant*. He passed away on 27 November 2000.

Neigl Ludwig, born on 5 August 1921 in Augsburg. In 1943 he became Hornisse commander in the newly formed schwere Panzerjäger-Abteilung 519, to be employed with Heeresgruppe Mitte. Near the village of Osinniki he eliminates his first enemy tank; at the Slabodka lake with his lone vehicle he attacks and destroys four tanks. By the summer of 1944 he had been promoted to *Feldwebel* and, with a total of 10 confirmed tank "kills", had already received both classes of the EK. By this time, however, two of his brothers had been killed in action and a third one was reported missing in Stalingrad, so as the last surviving son he was to be removed from front line duties and returned to his mother. On 22 June the Soviets started in the area of Vitebsk their decisive operation "Bagration"; soon entire German units were faced with the danger of encirclement. Neigl, about to take a train for immediate evacuation, refuses to leave his battalion. On the 24, with three serviceable vehicles of the Stabskompanie (033, 034, his 035) and gathering some newly arrived soldiers, he moves along the Daugava towards the Soviet armoured group which is trying to seize the bridge of Beshankovichy (fifty kilometers west of Vitebsk), the only supply and escape road for the Germans. Near the village of Bondarevo the first three T-34s are destroyed, then at 18.00h seven more (six by Neigl in just 8 minutes, gunner *Obergefreiter* Schwarz); the enemy infantry is repelled and two boats sunk. The day after in Mamoiki, Neigl eliminates another seven T-34s but his vehicle is destroyed with the death of the driver. Another Hornisse after scoring two kills is also hit and has to withdraw. With the last vehicle Neigl, though wounded himself and with an infantryman as loader, manages to reach Beshankovichy and to wipe out a last T-34, forcing the enemy to retreat. On 27 July he was awarded the Ritterkreuz. In November he was transferred to the supply company, and yet in March 1945 he was wounded by a low-flying aircraft. Credited with a total of over 26 tank "kills" (out of a total of 63 by the whole platoon under his command). He passed away on 23 September 2003 in his hometown.

Niemeck Gerhard, born on 10 June 1916 in the small town of Zerbst (forty kilometers southeast of Magdeburg). He fought in the Balkan campaign and in the central sector of the eastern front, receiving the EK II on 5 May 1941 and the EK I on 22 July 1942. During the first part of the war he was probably in command of a Panzer III. In defensive battles from 22 February to 7 March 1943 the 5.Panzer-Division succeeded in holding its front, knocking out 55 enemy tanks in the process. Of these, Niemeck alone in command of a long-barreled Panzer IV destroyed 15. He was awarded the Ritterkreuz on 14 March 1943 as *Feldwebel* and platoon leader in the 8th company, Panzer-Regiment 31. By the end of the war he had been credited with 32 enemy tank "kills"; his last rank was *Fahnenjunker-Oberfeldwebel*. He passed away on 19 July 1983.

Nökel Friedrich-Karl, born on 2 June 1917 in the village of Langenberg (fifty kilometers southeast of Münster). He fought throughout the war in the Panzer-Regiment 31 of the 5.Panzer-Division. In the battle of France he was platoon leader in command of a Panzer III. On 15 May 1940 his company scored 19 tank kills, then he also destroyed two tanks in a following action, and on 26 May received the EK II. In the east he received the EK I on 25 February 1942. On 7 April near Belyj (halfway between Smolensk and Rzhev) he was the leading scorer of the stabskompanie; he had some more kills on his credit also on 7 July and on 29 November. Promoted to *Leutnant der Reserve*, during the battles in the Orel salient, between 23 and 25 February 1943 with the 5th company under his command he was successful in inflicting on the enemy a loss of 58 tanks (of this total he was personally responsible for at least 3 tanks). In recognition of this important defensive victory he was promoted to *Oberleutnant* and, on 2 April 1943, awarded the Deutsches Kreuz in Gold. By early 1944 he had been promoted to *Hauptmann* and given command of the 2nd (Panther) company.

On 22 June 1944 the enemy started operation "Bagration". The 5.Panzer-Division which at that time was being reorganized in the area of Kovel, was loaded aboard trains and on July 1-2 counterattacked the Soviet 5th Guards Tank Army north of Minsk. In this fighting Nökel destroyed 11 tanks (the company a total of 22 tanks and 30 AT guns). For his leadership he was given command of the entire II.Abteilung and on 17 September 1944 he was awarded the Ritterkreuz being simultaneously promoted to *Major*. On 4 December he got the fourth level of the Panzerkampfabzeichen for the participation in over 75 separate armoured engagements. He was still in action in early 1945 in East Prussia being promoted to *Oberst*. From Pillau he managed to reach Denmark and surrender to western forces. With the same rank of *Oberst* he served in the Bundeswehr from 1956 to 1975. He passed away on 17 October 1998.

Oberloskamp Walther, born on 27 January 1920 in the village of Friedeberg (today Mirsk), one hundred and twenty kilometers west of Breslau. He received simultaneously both classes of the EK on 13 September 1942. During March 1943 while acting in support of the 98.Infanterie-Division in the south-eastern corner of the Rzhev salient, in just a few days he destroys 40 enemy tanks. On 10 May he was awarded the Ritterkreuz as *Leutnant der Reserve* and platoon leader in the 3rd battery, Sturmgeschütz-Abteilung 667. Promoted to *Oberleutnant* and in command of the 2nd company, Heeres-Sturmgeschütz-Brigade 667, he was killed in action east of Minsk on 26 June 1944.

Olin Ulf-Ola, born on 18 July 1917 in Helsinki. An ethnic-Swede, during the Winter War he served as a reserve officer in a Finnish infantry regiment. In 1941 he joined the Waffen-SS and at the start of "Barbarossa" he was in the 4th company of the Finnisches Freiwilligen-Bataillon. In 1942 he married a German woman and chose to remain even after the departure of the Finnish volunteers. As *SS-Obersturmführer* and platoon leader in the 7th company, SS-Panzer-Regiment 5 "Wiking", he received the EK II on 24 April 1944 and the EK I on 8 August. During the fighting around Warsaw on 10 August he and his crew destroyed 11 AT-guns and two T-34s. He also destroyed five tanks on the 20 October. From August through October his Panther zug was credited with 24 tanks and 11 heavy AT guns. After further successes he was finally awarded the Deutsches Kreuz in Gold on 28 February 1945. In early April, 150 men of *Wiking* were sent to Germany to pick up new tanks at Paderborn. On the 6 they managed to acquire thirteen Sd.Kfz.250 and 251 from a Heer depot, and two days later seven brand new Jagdpanthers in the factory yard of the MNH assembly facility at Hannover-Laatzen. In the following days, under the command of *SS-Hauptsturmführer* Nicolussi-Leck, "Kampfgruppe Wiking" would be in constant combat against US forces, first in defensive battles around Hannover and later in its march towards the Elbe. Several Shermans and countless other vehicles were eliminated; Olin was in command of one of the Jagdpanthers. When the kampfgruppe surrendered on April 16 in Hohne, Olin had the remaining equipment sabotaged and with few other men managed to reach southern Germany in a captured jeep. By the end of the war he may have been credited with 34 tank "kills"; in battle he never lost his panzer. A decorator in civilian life, he passed away on 11 January 1995 in Kassel.

Paul Roland, born on 30 September 1920 in the village of Dümmlinghausen (fifty kilometers east of Köln). As of September 1941 he was *SS-Unterscharführer* in the 13rd company, SS-Infanterie-Regiment 11, and as of July 1942 he had been promoted to *Untersturmführer*. In 1943 in a six months period, as a platoon leader in the 1st battery, SS-Sturmgeschütz-Abteilung "Das Reich" he eliminates 37 Soviet tanks. In Normandy in July he destroys a further three tanks. On 28 August 1944 he was awarded the Deutsches Kreuz in Gold as an *SS-Obersturmführer* in the 3rd company, SS-Panzerjäger-Abteilung 2, which at the time was equipped with the Jagdpanzer IV. By the end of the war he had partecipated in over fifty separate armoured engagements and was credited with no less than 45 enemy tank "kills".

Sturmgeschütz Ausf.G of *Das Reich*, summer 1943 (on the rear of the vehicle, in white, the temporary divisional insignia in use during the battle of Kursk).

Pfreundtner (or Pfreudtner) **Karl**, born on 15 April 1912 in München. He took part in the invasion of the Soviet Union, receiving the EK II on 28 July 1941 and the EK I on 20 May 1942. During the attack on the Don, in command of a StuG III Ausf.F in the Sturmgeschütz-Abteilung 244, he contributed significantly to the creation of the first 6.Armee bridgehead over the river by the 384.Infanterie-Division. In one action he launches a thrust on his own initiative destroying 9 enemy tanks within the space of twenty minutes. On 10 September he was awarded the Ritterkreuz as *Oberwachtmeister* and platoon leader in the 2nd battery, then in October he was seriously wounded in Stalingrad. Allegedly he was killed in action on 26 June 1944 at the Rogachov bridgehead. By the time of his death he had been credited with destroying 43 enemy tanks.

Notes. According to another version, he may have been captured and killed while in Soviet custody on 3 July 1944 in Stolbtsy, near Minsk.

Pieper Heinz, born on 25 July 1916 in Hannover. Little is known about this soldier. On the eastern front he received both classes of the EK. He had 6 tank kills as a gunner at least. After the failure of "Zitadelle" the 19.Panzer-Division retreated towards the Dnieper. Panzer commander Pieper died of wounds on 7 September 1943 in Gadjač. In recognition of his total of 28 enemy tanks destroyed he was posthumously awarded the Ritterkreuz on 17 September as *Unteroffizier* in the 1st company, Panzerjäger-Abteilung 19.

Pietsch Werner, born on 21 August 1912 in Berlin. Until July 1942 he may have belonged to the Panzer-Regiment 11. He received the EK II and EK I. Transferred to the 17.Panzer-Division he took part in late 1942 in the offensive and defensive actions near Orel, in the operation "Wintergewitter" towards Stalingrad, and then in the counterattacks between the Donets and the Mius. On 3 February 1943 he was awarded the Deutsches Kreuz in Gold as *Oberleutnant der Reserve* in the 6th company, Panzer-Regiment 39.

Promoted to *Hauptmann* and in command of the entire company, he distinguished himself during the 11 days of the second battle of Izyum (also known as the Izyum-Barvenkovo offensive, 17 July-27 July 1943), when his Bavarian Panzer-Kompanie destroyed 77 enemy tanks. Of this total he was personally responsible for 20 tanks and 3 assault guns. In another action, on 22 August, he spotted 40 advancing AFVs as he was reconnoitring an assembly area. Without esitation he launched an attack and in a short fight his 10 panzers destroyed 14 of the enemy vehicles. For these achievements he was awarded the Ritterkreuz on 16 November 1943. He passed away on 8 February 1956.

Primozic Hubert "Hugo", born on 16 February 1914, to a Slovenian father and German mother, in the town of Backnang (thirty kilometers northeast of Stuttgart). In 1933 he enlisted in the Reichswehr being posted to the artillery. He fought in the Battle of France as a field artillery gunner. In 1942 he joined the newly formed Sturmgeschütz-Abteilung 667, which in July was transferred to the central sector of the eastern front. He was awarded the EK II on 18 August 1942 as *Wachtmeister* and platoon leader in the 2nd battery. On 15 September 1942, he leads his lone platoon against a main Soviet assault on the Rzhev salient and eliminates, together with his two wingmen, 24 enemy tanks; after firing his last shell he has to retreat, but there is another StuG immobilized; amidst the advancing Soviet infantry he cames out to connect the other vehicle, then he breaks through and drives back to the German lines. For this action he is awarded the EK I. In the following days he brings his total of "kills" to 45 and is awarded the Ritterkreuz on 19 September. From 25 November onwards he was committed against operation "Mars", a renewed Soviet offensive on Rzhev which included an entire brigade of IS tanks. On 11 December alone, he eliminates 7 tanks, and by the end of the month he has raised his total to 60 destroyed enemy AFVs. On 25 January 1943 he received, as the first non-commissioned officer in the Wehrmacht, the Eichenlaub; his entire crew was awarded the Deutsches Kreuz in Gold. Promoted to *Leutnant*, he was reassigned to a training unit where he would spend the remainder of the war. Primozic destroyed 68 tanks within a time span of just five months. He passed away on 18 March 1996.

Przedwojewski Felix, born on 7 December 1920 in the village of Meyenburg (one hundred and twenty kilometers northwest of Berlin). He took part in the invasion of the Soviet Union and was awarded the EK II and the EK I. In mid-November 1943 in the area of Krivoy Rog *Totenkopf* had to hold a frontage that stretched for around 40 km despite having only about 60% of its authorized number of troops. The six StuGs on hand were in position in the rear of the main battle line supporting SS-Panzergrenadier-Regiment "Thule". The enemy breaks through approximately 3 km to the left with a massive infantry attack supported by around 50 T-34s. Under explicit instructions of the divisional commander *SS-Brigadeführer* Prieß, Przedwojewski moves forward together with the other two StuGs of his platoon, hiding behind a hill. The first tank, a KV type, is destroyed only 200 meters away. Firing shot after shot he uses up all of his ammunition, then instead of retreating back he traverses the enemy formation, links up with friendly forces and stocks up with more ammunition. At the end of this engagement 34 enemy tanks lie destroyed on the ground in front of the three StuGs, Przedwojewski being credited with 13 of them. On a following day, ruthlessly committing himself to the battle, he engages a further strong enemy force: another 10 tanks are wiped out. He is awarded the Ritterkreuz on 16 December 1943 as *SS-Unterscharführer* in the 2nd battery, SS-Sturmgeschütz-Abteilung 3 "Totenkopf". By the end of the war he had been credited with 45 enemy tank "kills". He passed away on 15 June 1986.

Rahlenbeck Robert, born on 12 April 1923 in the town of Arnsberg (ninety kilometers northeast of Köln). In April 1942 he enlisted in the Wehrmacht serving as a gunner in the 16th company, Jäger-Regiment 38. In the Demyansk area, in the sector of the 8.Jäger-Division a number of German soldiers including Rahlenbeck had managed on their own initiative to turn an abandoned T-34 into an ad-hoc pillbox. The tank had been left behind from the fighting in 1942 and was immobilized, but still possessed an intact turret and gun; ammunition was also available for it. The pillbox was christened "Panther" and manned by five men. When on 21 August 1943 the Soviets launched their big offensive, at the time of the initial barrage only Rahlenbeck was present in the tank, with the remaining crew being in a bunker nearby. He thus operated the turret and cannon on his own when the first enemy tanks came up: he destroys three of them, and in doing so compels the rest to withdraw. The next day he and his loader were once again present when the Soviets renewed their attack. He destroys another 2 tanks and is then awarded the EK I. On the third day the entire crew was present when the enemy launched a particularly heavy attack at noon. The gun commander, who was standing close by outside the tank, observed the field with binoculars and assigned targets to gunner Rahlenbeck. In the course of this battle the pillbox was hit a few times and the optics were knocked out; he was thus forced to target the Soviets by sighting through the gun barrel with the help of binoculars; he didn't abandon the fight even after being wounded twice. At some point the gun jammed. He ran to the bunker, retrieved the cleaning device and worked to get the gun back in order again. In the nick of time he is able to re-engage the last tanks, right as they are about to reach the main German defense line. In 90 minutes he has wiped out no less than 10 tanks (5 more were destroyed by a 5-cm-PaK nearby). On 23 August 1943 *Gefreiter* Rahlenbeck was awarded the Ritterkreuz. He passed away on 2 December 2008.

Rakowitz (or Rakowitsch) **Andreas von**, born on 11 January 1920 in Rome, Italy. His father was an officer of the Tsar's guard who after the victory of the Bolsheviks emigrated to Germany. In 1939 he volunteered for the Luftwaffe, being posted to a heavy flak unit and taking part in the Battle of France. Promoted to *Wachtmeister* he fought in the central sector of operation Barbarossa. In 1942 he was promoted to *Leutnant* and transferred to the assault gun arm; in February 1943 he was given command of a battery: the 4.(Stug)/Pz.Jg.Abt 15 of the 15.Luftwaffen-Felddivision. After a number of successes on the Mius front, he was awarded the Deutsches Kreuz in Gold on 9 August 1943. Despite extensive wounds (14 shell splinters) he further distinguished himself few days later against the Soviet Donbas strategic operation. On 18 August the battery was used to support a friendly attack on an enemy-held height, but before the Germans had reached the height, 19 enemy heavy tanks came towards them. In just six minutes 16 are wiped out by the three Sturmgeschütze on hand (eight personally by Rakowitz); then about one hour later, at the same place seven more heavy tanks (three by Rakowitz). On 19 August the battery commander destroys two assault guns. On 20 August in a night attack the Germans, despite extraordinarily strong enemy artillery fire, manage to take back the lost ground, with the loss for the Soviets of nine tanks (the battery commander accounting for three of them). Throughout the day *Leutnant* Rakowitz with his single Sturmgeschütz, despite engine trouble keeps protecting the height against about twenty infantry and tank assaults, knocking out in the process two more tanks. For this feat and for reaching a personal total of 30 "kills" (out of a total of 96 tanks eliminated by the battery under his command) he would receive the Ritterkreuz on 24 June 1944. By this time he had been posted to the Feldersatz-Bataillon of the 4.Felddivision (L) (formerly 4.Luftwaffen-Felddivision). He passed away on 22 November 1981 in Brasil.

Rampel Josef, born on 5 April 1915 in the Bavarian village of Witzmannsberg (fifteen kilometers north of Passau). In 1941-42 he may have fought in the east with the 18.Panzer-Division; in this early part of the war he also received the EK II and the EK I. He was awarded the Deutsches Kreuz in Gold in February 1943 as *Feldwebel* in the 1./Panzer-Abteilung 18 (which was equipped with the Panzer IV Ausf.F). He was then transferred to the III./Panzer-Regiment "Großdeutschland" in command of a Tiger I. As Halbzugführer in the 11th company, he distinguished himself in late 1943 during the defensive battles northeast of Krivoy Rog. On the 18 October, near the hamlet of Tarasivka, fifty kilometers east of the city (in German reports: "Taranzoff"), the Soviets managed to penetrate the German positions. At the time Rampel was in a workshop waiting for his Tiger's transmission being repaired; however when he heard of the breakthrough he indipendently decided to engage the enemy. He was able to prepare the vehicle (turret number C33) for action by taking ammunition from another damaged panzer and also borrowing a loader from the same tank. After a friendly 8,8-cm-Flak had pulled back, Rampel found himself all alone against some 40 enemy tanks. He started engaging the enemy at a range of 1200-1500 metres and after 90 minutes he and his crew had managed to wipe out 17 enemy tanks; in the meantime two other barely operational Tigers had joined the battle knocking out an additional dozen tanks. The remaining enemy vehicles were forced to retreat and the Tiger pulled back to friendly positions with a panzer in tow. *Oberfeldwebel* Rampel was killed in action about one month later, on 16 (or 17) November in Lyubymivka. He was posthumously awarded the Ritterkreuz on 14 December 1943.

Notes. In May 1942 the Panzer-Regiment 18 of the 18.Panzer-Division was disbanded; however its III.Abteilung survived as Panzer-Abteilung 18, an indipendent unit but still assigned to the division. In December 1943, the abteilung was employed in the reconstitution of the s.PzAbt 504. Already in June 1943, the 3rd company (that had not been sent to Tunisia) of the s.PzAbt 504 had been transferred to Panzer-Regiment "Großdeutschland" becoming its 11th company.

Rappholz Walter, born on 4 June 1912 in Olvenstedt (a suburb of Magdeburg), the son of a carpenter. In 1935 he joined the Panzerabwehr-Abteilung 13; in 1938 he was *Unteroffizier* in the 1st company. After the annexation of the Sudetenland, he took part in the Polish campaign and in the Battle of France receiving the EK II on 30 May 1940. Promoted to *Oberfeldwebel*, in October 1940 he was transferred to the Panzerjäger-Abteilung 616 as platoon leader in the 1st battery. He would fight in this unit, in the central sector of the eastern front, until the end of the war. During the invasion of the Soviet Union he was involved in heavy combat, being repeatedly wounded and receiving the EK I. For his successes as commander of a self-propelled Panzerjäger I, he was awarded the Deutsches Kreuz in Gold on 5 May 1943. In December he obtained the Verwundetenabzeichen in Gold.

In October 1944, during the fighting for the Dukla Pass, west of Sanok, he had to defend against a massive Soviet armoured assault with his Marder II tank destroyer and with only 90 men. Despite the odds he was able to wipe out 16 enemy tanks. He was thus awarded the Ritterkreuz on 3 November 1944. Severely wounded in Silesia, in May 1945 he was captured by US forces while in hospital; he was released later that month. He then returned to Magdeburg where he started a business of furniture manufacturing. He passed away on 30 September 1991.

Rettlinger Karl, born on 8 February 1913 in the town of Gunzenhausen (twenty-five kilometers southwest of Nürnberg). As *SS-Untersturmführer* he took part in the invasion of the Soviet Union and received both classes of the EK. On 28 March 1943 he was awarded the Deutsches Kreuz in Gold as *SS-Hauptsturmführer* in the 3rd battery, SS-Sturmgeschütz-Abteilung 1. During operation "Zitadelle", on 10 July, now in command of the whole battery, Rettlinger was given the order to attack on the left of the railway Belgorod-Kursk together with the I./SS-Panzergrenadier-Regiment 2. Advancing at full speed through a minefield the kampfgruppe manages to breach the enemy defenses; the sturmgeschütze destroy several AT guns positions and the important ground is occupied.

During the counterattack west of Kiev, on 17 November 1943 an armoured group of the *LSSAH* was advancing north of Bila Cerkva with the mission of breaking through as far as the Kiev-Zhytomyr road and set up a blocking position. The forward elements of SS-Panzer-Regiment 1 had reached a small river near the village of Vil'nya, however in the forest north of the river was a strong enemy defensive front with AT guns and dug-in tanks; crossing the bridge would only have been possible with substantial losses to the kampfgruppe. Rettlinger with his batterie was tasked with reconnoitering to the northeast. He succeeds in winning ground to the south of Kocheriv (in German reports: Kotscherowo), a village that lies on this important main road and where approximately thirty enemy tanks were standing in security positions. In a surprise attack the enemy lines are penetrated; 6 T-34s are destroyed and the area can be entirely occupied.

Under his leadership the 3rd battery had so far eliminated altogether: 65 tanks (sixty T-34s, three T-70s and two KV-1s), 124 heavy AT guns (of which 33 personally by him) and 12 medium AT guns. On 20 December 1943 he was awarded the Ritterkreuz. In Normandy he led the entire Sturmgeschütz battalion, later he went on to command the SS-Panzerjäger-Abteilung 1 in the Ardennes and in Hungary. By the end of the war he had been promoted to *SS-Sturmbannführer*. Seriously wounded five times, he was credited with destroying over 30 enemy tanks. He passed away in his native town, 14 June 1990.

Rettlinger (at right, with *SS-Hauptsturmführer* Hans Becker) at Kursk.

Riedel Franz, born on 2 December 1921 in the town of Teschen, Sudetenland (today Český Těšín, Czech Republic). In October 1939 he volunteered to join the Waffen-SS; he was promoted to *Sturmmann* on December 1st 1940 and posted as a gunner in the 3rd battery of the Panzerjäger-Abteilung, SS-Division *Reich*. Fighting in the Soviet Union he received the EK II on 29 July and in August he was given command of his own vehicle; in November he was promoted to *SS-Rottenführer*. In January 1942 he was temporarily assigned to the 2nd battery of the SS-Panzerjäger-Abteilung "Nord", then from June to December he attended the SS-Junkerschule in Braunschweig. In March 1943 he was promoted to *SS-Untersturmführer* and in May he became platoon leader in the 3rd battery, SS-Panzerjäger-Abteilung 10. After a panzer course at Sagan, in February 1944 he was transferred to the 7th company, II.Abteilung, SS-Panzer-Regiment 10 "Langemarck". Now in command of a Panzer IV he fought with *Frundsberg* in the relief of the Kamenets-Podolsky pocket and received the EK I on 20 April.

In Normandy near Gavrus, twelve kilometers southwest of Caen, the enemy attempted to thrust into the flank of the advancing Germans with 16 Shermans. Riedel, despite a lack of orders, at the head of his company manages to get around the enemy: for the loss of just one panzer, 11 enemy tanks are wiped out (5 personally by him). He was promoted to *SS-Obersturmführer* on 21 June and awarded the Deutsches Kreuz in Gold on 19 August.

In 1945 *Frundsberg* was deployed to Pomerania, and in "Sonnenwende" was tasked with advancing along the right flank. On 17 February a divisional armoured group has to attack out of the Blumberg bridgehead in order to capture the village of Muscherin and, beyond that, Sallenthin. From here it would be possible to strike out and seize the entire area between the Plönesee and the Madüsee. Without any artillery support Riedel leads his company forwards followed by the infantry; two panzers are swiftly knocked out and the attack bogs down under heavy fire. Despite being wounded in the head and shoulder by shell splinters, he pushes ahead with two panzers destroying 6 enemy tanks; this action gives courage to the grenadiers and Sallenthin is completely cleared. Only then, at the end of his strenght due to blood loss, he allows himself to be taken to the main dressing station. On 28 March he was awarded the Ritterkreuz. By the end of the war he had been credited with the elimination of more than 40 enemy tanks. He passed away on 17 May 2001.

Notes. A "SS-Panzerjäger-Abteilung Nord" was formed in January 1941. This unit (later renamed SS-Panzerjäger-Abteilung 6) was intended to be a company with nine self-propelled vehicles with Soviet 7,62 AT guns. These vehicles never arrived in Finland and the company was removed from the inventory of *Nord* during the end of 1942.

Panzer IV Ausf.H of *Frundsberg* in Pomerania, March 1945.

Röhder Dr. Wolfgang, born on 17 August 1911 in Wuppertal. In 1940 he attended an officer course at the SS-Junkerschule Braunschweig and on 30 January 1941 was promoted to *Untersturmführer*; he was then posted to *Reich* as platoon leader in the 2nd company, SS-Regiment (mot.) "Deutschland". Promoted to *SS-Obersturmführer der Reserve*, in February 1943 he was transferred to the SS-Sturmgeschütz-Abteilung 2 "Das Reich". On 20 September 1943, during the fight out of the Poltava bridgehead enemy elements advanced ahead of the Germans and then approached the last bridge on the Vorskla (a tributary of the Dnieper), located just east of the town. Röhder with the two platoons of sturmgeschütze of his 3rd battery had the order to secure the bridge so the division could pull back over it. At 14:00 hours friendly units, among them tanks, began the crossing. At about 17:00 hours *SS-Obersturmbannführer* Stadler come from the southeast with the rearguard; the two sturmgeschütze positioned in that direction followed him safely. Now also the other platoon, positioned a few hundred metres to the northeast, had completed its mission and could cross back; however one of the vehicles after had thrown off its camouflage and was about to turn back was hit by an enemy AT gun that had gone unnoticed; only the other vehicle was able to retreat together with a last Panther. At this point Röhder and another soldier set out across the bridge on a motorcycle to check out the situation in the direction of the knocked out sturmgeschütz. After a while fire erupted from the gardens and side roads: the Soviets had pursued at great speed, obviously in order to gain control of the bridge and keep it for their planned attack route later. Röhder, armed with only a pistol, decided to resist together with two (!) remaining men from SS-Panzer-Pionier-Bataillon 2 equipped with flamethrowers. He sent the dispatch rider to retrieve the batterie, and also ordered a 3.7 cm anti-aircraft gun positioned on the opposite bank to support the almost hopeless defense. The enemy attacked violently from the northeast with mortars and machine-guns and with houses for protection, and soon was at a distance of just 70 m. Suddenly the sturmgeschütze arrived and deployed in a semicircle on the eastern bank; with concentrated fire they neutralized the enemy infantry in all directions. After fifteen minutes, four demolition squads of the pioneer kompanie under *SS-Hauptsturmführer* Fleischer came from the direction of the town. Röhder covered them while they set their charges, after which he withdrew the batterie. As soon as the last sturmgeschütz had crossed, the bridge was blown, with the Red Army soldiers just a few metres from it at the time of detonation. For this crucial action -which allowed the systematic withdrawal from Poltava two days later- he was awarded the Ritterkreuz on December 1st 1943. By this time he had been credited with a personal total of 23 "kills", out of a total of 154 tanks destroyed by his batterie since the 5 of July.

On 30 January 1944 he was promoted to *Hauptsturmführer* and on June 1st he was given command of the whole abteilung. Wounded in July on the Invasion front, in August he was awarded the Deutsches Kreuz in Gold for bravery and promoted to *SS-Sturmbannführer*. He was then wounded for a second time losing an eye. Being no longer fit for front line duty he was stationed in Prague where he was reported missing on 16 May 1945.

Röhrig Oskar, born on 16 January 1911 in the village of Schweinhaus (today Swiny), seventy kilometers west of Breslau. In "Barbarossa" he fought in the central sector, and as early as November 1941 he got the EK I as a *Feldwebel* with the 11th company, Panzer-Regiment 18, 18.Panzer-Division. In the summer of 1942 he took part in the initial drive on Stalingrad. In 1943 during the battles around Orel his company (by now the 2nd company) was highly successful, with 113 tanks claimed. On 20 September *Oberfeldwebel* and zugführer Röhrig, Panzer IV commander, was awarded the Deutsches Kreuz in Gold (his gunner, *Unteroffizier* Werner Siegemund, was supposedly credited with a total of 84 gun and tank "kills" and maybe also awarded the DKiG). In late 1943 he was selected to join the schwere Panzer-Abteilung 504, which at that time was being completely refitted in the Netherlands with 45 new Tiger I, and which was sent to Italy in June. On 22 June 1944 near the village of Perolla (thirty kilometers north of Grosseto) the 1st company managed to halt a massive US armored attack of around thirty tanks aimed at breaking the Albert-Stellung. Without suffering any loss the Tigers destroy 11 Shermans, while no less than 10 Shermans are abandoned by their terrified crews. For this action platoon leader *Oberfähnrich* Röhrig was awarded the Ritterkreuz on 4 July 1944. Promoted to *Leutnant* he would see combat until the very end of the war in Italy. Still on 13 and 14 April he eliminates 2 enemy tanks; the following day his Tiger is disabled by an artillery hit and has to be blown up at the maintenance facility. On 3 May the remnants of the battalion surrender to US forces in the area of Belluno. Röhrig passed away on 4 August 1985.

Notes. According to the Tagesmeldung AOK 14 for 23.6.1944, in Perolla the Americans lost 8 tanks and 2 AT-guns destroyed, and 10 tanks captured; Röhrig being credited with five kills and with all the captured tanks.

Rohr Hans-Babo von, born on 9 October 1922 in Wolletz (seventy kilometers northeast of Berlin). He joined the Panzerwaffe in June 1941 as *Fahnenjunker* and took part in the invasion of the Soviet Union. He had been assigned to I./Panzer-Regiment 25 and became tank commander here. In early 1943 he was promoted to *Leutnant der Reserve*, he then fought in operation "Zitadelle" and in the battles in central Ukraine, receiving the EK II on 6 December 1943 followed by the EK I on 28 January 1944. During the battles for the Memel bridgehead he destroys a large number of tanks and is awarded the Ritterkreuz on 5 November 1944, as platoon leader in the 2nd company, Panzer-Regiment 25, 7.Panzer-Division.

On 14 February 1945 elements of the divisional armoured kampfgruppe, including the company now led by von Rohr, managed to penetrate into the built-up area of the enemy occupied town of Konitz (one hundred kilometers southwest of Danzig). They ferociously attacked from all sides and annihilated the Soviet tank group (belonging to the 3rd Guards Tank Corps) which was located there; with this the enemy's objective of breaking through to the north was thwarted for the time being. During this fight von Rohr destroys 8 tanks with his Panther and two more in close combat, but he is critically injured and dies the next day as a result of his wounds. He had brought his personal total of enemy tank "kills" to 58, six of them in close combat. He was posthumously promoted to *Oberleutnant* and, on 24 February, awarded the Eichenlaub.

Leutnant von Rohr and II.Abteilung commander *Major* Brandes in the evangelic church of the reconquered Konitz, 17 February 1945.

Rohrbacher Josef, born on 24 May 1920 in the town of Viernheim (ten kilometers northeast of Mannheim). At the end of March 1944 in the area southeast of Vitebsk, the Soviets achieved a break-in in the sector of the 299.Infanterie-Division capturing a commanding hilltop. Rohrbacher, with his sturmgeschütz receives the mission of covering the counterattack with flanking fire. When the German infantry fails to make any progress, he is able to approach the hill, navigating through the swampy terrain and avoiding the many scattered mines, then on his own initiative he launches a furious attack smashing bunker after bunker and forcing the enemy into cover with submachine-gun fire and hand grenades. The grenadiers are thus able to storm the hill, capturing large quantity of weapons. For this feat, as well as for the destruction of 56 enemy tanks by this time, he was awarded the Ritterkreuz on 4 May 1944 as *Oberwachtmeister* and platoon leader in the 3rd battery, Sturmgeschütz-Brigade 245. He passed away on 25 February 1982.

Rondorf Heinrich. He took part in the Polish campaign receiving the EK II on 7 December 1939. In 1943 he joined the newly formed schwere Panzer-Abteilung 503; he then fought in southern Russia and in Ukraine, and on 8 August 1943 was awarded the EK I. After the destruction of some fifty tanks he was awarded the Deutsches Kreuz in Gold on 20 May 1944 as *Oberfähnrich* in the 3rd company. Before the Allied invasion of France he may have swapped from service in Tigers and possibly served on the eastern front in command of a Jagdpanther or a StuG IV. Anyway in 1945 he moved to the schwere Panzerjäger-Abteilung 512 as platoon commander in the 1st company. With his Jagdtiger he probably had some success against Allied tanks. By the end of the war he may have been promoted to *Oberleutnant*. He passed away on 25 November 1979.

Notes. In a number of "panzer aces" lists he is credited with destroying 106 tanks. This figure probably originates from the "103 Abschüsse" (not "Panzerabschüsse") written on the back of a photo of him from early 1944. Quite obviously those "103" were tanks, vehicles and guns combined. For the remainder of the war he saw little combat, so his total shouldn't be much higher than 50. - Pictures taken after the surrender in Iserlohn in April 1945, show a number of Jagdtigers, including the vehicles he may have commanded (numbers X2 and X8), with kill rings.

Rosen Richard von, born on 28 June 1922 in Hirschsprung (thirty kilometers south of Dresden) from a German-Baltic noble family. He joined the Wehrmacht in October 1940 and in February 1941 was transferred to the 1st company of Panzer-Regiment 35, as *Gefreiter* and gunner in a Panzer III. He took part in the surprise attack (under *Oberleutnant* von Cossel) against the bridge on the Dnieper at Bykhov, and received the EK II; however in August he was injured in a road accident and would never return to the unit. In early 1942 he attended an officer course at the Panzertruppenschule Wünsdorf and on June 1st was promoted to *Leutnant*; he then joined the newly formed schwere Panzer-Abteilung 502 as half/platoon leader in the 2nd company. The company was rushed to southern Russia as an indipendent unit and incorporated into the schwere Panzer-Abteilung 503 as the 3rd company; from early January 1943 it fought at the Proletarskaya bridgehead to the east of Rostov, and then during the retreat to the Mius. In "Zitadelle" von Rosen led his platoon of four Tigers in the advance northward along the Donets, however on 11 July he was severely injured; while in hospital he received the EK I on 23 July. In Normandy he had his first encounter with Allied forces on 11 July 1944. As acting commander of the entire company (*Hauptmann* Scherf was replacing the sick battalion commander) he counterattacks a British/Canadian force which had broken through north of Colombelles (a suburb of Caen, to the west of the town): in a thirty minutes battle, without any losses, 11 Shermans and five AT guns are eliminated; another two Shermans abandoned by their crews in panic are captured intact. After the bombing raids of 18 July the company relinquished its remaining panzers to the 2nd company and the personnel relocated to Mailly-le-Camp. In September the abteilung was re-equipped with 45 new Tiger IIs and in mid-October was hurried to Hungary and immediately employed in the attack from the Szolnok bridgehead on the Tisza towards Debrecen. On November 1st, von Rosen was promoted to *Oberleutnant*. In late November he led a kampfgruppe in the battle for Gyöngyös, then in December-January in numerous counterattacks in the area of Zámoly and Stuhlweissenburg. In mid-February with the whole abteilung he was transferred north of the

213

Danube for the offensive against the Soviet bridgehead on the west bank of the Gran (Hron); here on 20 February he was wounded by artillery shell splinters in the left elbow and had to leave the front. On 28 February he was awarded the Deutsches Kreuz in Gold for his cleaver leadership as well for a personal total of over 20 enemy tank "kills". After the war he reached high command positions in the Bundeswehr retiring in 1982 with the rank of *Generalmajor.* He passed away on 26 October 2015.

On 25 September 1944 at Sennelager an unusual parade was organized for Die Deutsche Wochenschau with the participation of the 3rd company and parts of the 1st company. Here von Rosen, leader of the 3rd company, gives the order "Panzer Marsch!" and the vehicles begin rolling behind his Königstiger 300. [See also Knispel, photo page 159].

Roy Rudolf, born on 15 August 1920 in Spandau, Berlin, the son of a bricklayer. He was trained as a machine locksmith, however in November 1938 volunteered to join the Waffen-SS. In 1941 he was assigned to the SS-Panzerjäger-Abteilung LSSAH, taking part in "Barbarossa" and being awarded the EK II. In January 1943 he was promoted to *SS-Unterscharführer* and transferred to the 1st battery; in September he received the EK I. In early 1944 the entire battalion was transferred to *Hitlerjugend*; it was still forming at the time of the Allied landing so it did not reach the front until July; it was then quickly sent into action and credited with being largely responsible for the failure of "Totalise" over the period 8 to 10 August. During the morning hours of 9 August, British tanks broke through the strongpoint-like German frontline near the hamlet of Soignolles (halfway between Caen and Falaise) and into the rear of Kampfgruppe Waldmüller; they took up position on Hill 111 dominating all supply routes. Roy receives the order to attack; taking advantage of the speed and low profile of his Jagdpanzer IV he is able to destroy 9 tanks in a short time. At 21:30 in the evening, as the kampfgruppe began its withdrawal, 15 enemy tanks launched a surprise thrust. On his own initiative Roy advances into the flank of the enemy knocking out another 13 tanks. In five days of combat he had accumulated 26 "kills" bringing his total of destroyed Soviet and Allied AFVs to 36. On 16 October he was awarded the Ritterkreuz as *SS-Oberscharführer* and platoon leader in the 1st company, SS-Panzerjäger-Abteilung 12. His gunner *SS-Rottenführer* Fritz Eckstein was awarded the Ritterkreuz on 18 November. He is killed on 17 December 1944 in the Ardennes, during a march on a narrow forest lane, shot in the head by a sniper of the US 99th Infantry Division while looking out of his tank's hatch. He was posthumously promoted to *SS-Untersturmführer.*

Rubbel Alfred, born on 28 June 1921 in Senteinen, a district of Tilsit (today Sovetsk), East Prussia. At eighteen he volunteered for the Wehrmacht and after basic training, in June 1941 he was transferred to the Panzer-Regiment 29 of the 12.Panzer-Division. In September he was seriously wounded by grenade splinters in the area of Leningrad; he returned to his unit in January 1942 and took part in the fighting at the Volkhov. After a period of rebuilding in Silesia his company was transferred to Panzer-Regiment 4. During the advance towards the Caucasus he was in command of a long barreled Panzer IV. In December he joined the schwere Panzer-Abteilung 503 and with the Tiger he fought during the retreat to the west, then in operation "Zitadelle" and in the battle for the Cherkassy Pocket. In 1944 he was promoted to *Leutnant der Reserve* and employed in Hungary with the Tiger II, until the surrender to US forces. He was allegedly credited with a total of 57 "kills" in the course of 79 separate armored engagements. He was a close friend of Kurt Knispel as well as his superior. From 1956 to 1978 he served in the Bundeswehr reaching the rank of *Oberstleutnant*. He passed away on 8 August 2013.

Notes. His higher award was the EK I; 57 kills may be vehicles and guns combined. - He received the Panzerkampfabzeichen Stufe 50 on February 1st 1945.

Sauer Konrad, born on 29 January 1915 in the village of Roth an der Lahn (seventy kilometers north of Frankfurt). He joined the Wehrmacht in 1936 taking part in the Polish campaign with Artillerie-Regiment 206 and in the battle of France with Artillerie-Regiment 304. In November 1941 he volunteered for the Sturmartillerie, receiving the EK II on 10 May 1942 and the EK I on 31 July 1942. In the battles for Rzhev he reached a total of 39 enemy tanks destroyed, and was thus awarded the Ritterkreuz on 26 September 1942 as a *Wachtmeister* and zugführer in the 3rd battery, Sturmgeschütz-Abteilung 209.

In mid-September 1944 during the retreat from the Dorpat Stellung his battery manages to prevent a breakthrough of the enemy, who attacked with 12 rifle divisions and 2-3 armoured formations. In two days his vehicles wiped out 14 Soviet tanks. Sauer, with a personal total of 65 "kills", was awarded the Eichenlaub on 30 September 1944, as a *Leutnant der Reserve* in command of the 1st battery, Sturmgeschütz-Brigade 393. Promoted to *Hauptmann*, in 1945 he was posted as instructor at the Sturmgeschütz-Schule Burg. In April he was in combat with Kampfgruppe Burg south of Berlin, receiving his fifth wound of the war. From 1956 to 1968 he served in the Bundeswehr reaching the rank of *Oberstleutnant*. He passed away on 12 July 1986.

Schäfer Georg, born on the 1st of August 1914 in the village of Berfa (fifty-five kilometers northeast of Gießen). Unfortunately few is known about this soldier. Early in the war he received both classes of the EK. He took part in the invasion of the Soviet Union fighting in the northern sector of the front and then in the battle of Moscow. In late 1942 the 1.Panzer-Division was engaged in the central sector in the defense of the supply lines of the 9.Armee, and on 17 December Schäfer was awarded the Ritterkreuz as *Feldwebel* and platoon leader in the 2nd company, I.Abteilung, Panzer-Regiment 1. During these battles he was most probably in command of a Panzer IV. Promoted to *Oberfeldwebel* he was further awarded the Deutsches Kreuz in Gold. He was killed in action on 18 January 1945 near Nagybajom, Hungary. He was credited with destroying more than 40 enemy tanks.

Notes. He was mentioned in the Armeetagesbefehl n. 66 for destroying 14 tanks in few days of combat in late October-early November 1942 (allegedly reaching a total of 41 tank "kills"). - In November 1943 the I.Abteilung was converted to the Panther. - According to another source he was killed in action on 13 October 1944.

Schäfer Oskar, born on 16 January 1921 in the small town of Nixdorf (today Mikulášovice), Sudetenland, forty-five kilometers east of Dresden. In November 1938 he volunteered to join the SS-VT and was assigned to the 12th company, SS-Standarte "Deutschland". He took part in the Poland campaign and in the Battle of France. During "Barbarossa", as an infantryman in the SS-Division *Reich*, he was wounded in the head; after recovering he was transferred to the SS-Panzer-Abteilung 5 of *Wiking* which was in action in southern Russia. In the first part of the war he was awarded both classes of the EK. In 1943 he was posted back to Germany to help train and form the new schwere SS-Panzer-Abteilung 103. Promoted to *SS-Untersturmführer*, in 1945 he deployed back to the eastern front in command of the 3rd company of the renamed schwere SS-Panzer-Abteilung 503. He fights in Arnswalde where he is again seriously wounded. He manages to escape from the Soviet encirclement at Kolberg and to reach Greifswald. During the Battle of Berlin he destroys several more Soviet tanks and on 29 April he is awarded the Ritterkreuz. On 2 May, during the breakout attempt his Tiger II leads the Mohnke group, but while crossing the Heerstraße it is hit by a IS-2 (or by a 8,8-cm-PaK manned by Russians). Two men are killed and Schäfer suffers severe burns, temporarily loosing his sight and memory. He remained in hospital and was released in 1947. By the end of the war he had been credited with destroying over 50 Soviet tanks. He passed away on 22 November 2011 in Berlin.

Scharf Heinz, born on 22 April 1920 in the small town of Lichtenstein (ten kilometers northeast of Zwickau). Early in the war he received the EK II and the EK I. On 28 May 1944 he was awarded the Deutsches Kreuz in Gold as *Wachtmeister* in the 3rd battery, Sturmgeschütz-Brigade 202. In August 1944 during the retreat through Latvia and northern Lithuania, the "202" had to be committed to the support of the 215.Infanterie-Division and 290.Infanterie-Division in their positions north of Birsen (Biržai). On the 8 of that month only two sturmgeschütze remained in the area of the regiment the Brigade was originally attached to. Out of nowhere enemy tanks appeared heading straight for the regimental command post; Scharf eliminates 5 of them (while the other vehicle eliminates 4); he then pushes forward to relieve the German troops in the advanced positions destroying three more tanks (gunner Wulf). With these 8 "kills" he had brought his total to 40, and on 17 August was awarded the Ritterkreuz, being also promoted to *Fahnenjunker-Oberwachtmeister*. He passed away on 13 July 2001.

Scherer Fritz, born on 26 August 1910 in Mannheim. He joined the Reichswehr in april 1931, being assigned to the Artillerie-Regiment 35; with this unit he took part in the battle of France. He then volunteered for the sturmartillerie and fought in the invasion of the Soviet Union as *Leutnant* and platoon leader in the 3./Sturmgeschütz-Abteilung 189 which was employed in the central sector. He received the EK II on 6 December 1941 and the EK I on 30 April 1942. Promoted to *Oberleutnant* he was further awarded the Deutsches Kreuz in Gold on 13 November 1942. After recovering from wounds he was promoted to *Hauptmann* and was given command of the 2./Sturmgeschütz-Abteilung 236, which was being formed at the time. In mid July 1943 the abteilung left Jüterbog for the Mius front, and on the 20 was unloaded at the railway station in Amvrosievka, taking position in a orchard near Biloyarivka. Its mission was to assist the 16.Panzergrenadier-Division in its defense of the high ground 2 kilometers north of "Kalinowka" (11 km northwest of the large village of Kuybyshevo), against strong enemy attacks (supported by aircrafts, tanks and artillery) from the north and northeast. Already on the next day the abteilung counterattacked the broken-in enemy along a broad front, and in a very short time the said high ground was back in friendly hands. On the 22, when the enemy armoured masses launched a surprise attack from the north, Scherer with cold blooded determination decided to let the T-34s to come into a favourable range, and only then he gave the order to fire. When tank terror set in among the grenadiers, he disembarked from his Sturmgeschütz, took control of the disorganized friendly infantry and decided on his own initiative to begin a counterthrust. Despite the lack of support he drove

forward with his six vehicles, crushed the foremost enemy foxholes, rolled over and destroyed several dug-in enemy AT guns and was able to acquire a commanding view (Hill 196.0) that would later be of decisive importance in dealing with the still oncoming enemy tanks. On this day he personally destroyed 13 tanks (out of a total of 52 by his battery); on the following day the battery repelled another enemy attack supported by armour. In total, in four days the 22 Sturmgeschütze of the abteilung were able to knock out 139 tanks for the total loss of just one of their own.

Scherer was awarded the Ritterkreuz on 14 December 1943. Until February 1944 he was involved in heavy combat on the Dnieper and in Krivoy Rog. The destroyed abteilung was then withdrawn from the front and sent to Germany for reconstruction as Sturmgeschütz-Brigade 236. For a short period Scherer took command of this unit; then from July to September 1944 of the Sturmgeschütz-Brigade 303 in Finland, where presumably he was severely injured. After recovering, in the last period of the war he was assigned as chief instructor to a course for artillery commanders. After the war he joined for a few years the Bundeswehr retiring in 1960. He passed away on 8 May 1998.

Notes. On 1st May 1943 StuG-Abteilung 189 handed over its third battery for the formation of StuG-Abteilung 236. - In 1944 Scherer may have been promoted to *Major*.

Scherf Fritz, born on 19 June 1915 in the small town of Geithain (forty kilometers southeast of Leipzig). He served during the Polish and French campaigns as an *Unteroffizier* with the 7th company of the Panzer-Regiment 1, receiving both classes of the EK. In August 1940 he was transferred to the Panzer-Regiment 18 and in 1942 to the newly formed Panzer-Abteilung 103. He escaped the Stalingrad pocket after being credited with destroying 22 tanks in the battle. In Italy he knocked out at least 6 tanks. In one action his 3 vehicles had withstood for hours an attack of fifty enemy tanks against Velletri and Genzano. He fell on 29 May 1944 during the Allied breakout at Anzio. With a personal total of 42 enemy tank "kills", he was posthumously awarded the Ritterkreuz on 30 September 1944 as *Oberfeldwebel* and platoon leader in the 2nd company, Panzer-Abteilung 103, 3.Panzergrenadier-Division.

Notes. The Panzer-Abteilung 103 was created in February 1942 from the II.Abteilung of Panzer-Regiment 18, and fought during the advance in southern Russia attached to the 3.Infanterie-Division (mot.). It ceased to exist in Stalingrad. It was reactivated in France in March 1943 fully equipped with StuG IIIs and sent to Italy in September with the newly formed 3.Panzergrenadier-Division.

StuG III, Panthers and grenadiers (of the 26.Panzer-Division) near Anzio-Nettuno, March 1944.

Scherf Walter, born on 21 February 1917 in Gießen. He took part in the Battle of France and in the Balkan campaign, receiving the EK II on 21 May 1940 and the EK I on 22 December. He then fought in "Barbarossa". Promoted to *Oberleutnant*, in 1942 he was transferred to the schwere Panzer-Abteilung 502 -then in the process of formation at Fallingbostel- as leader of the 2nd company's 1st platoon. He fought in southern Russia and in March 1943 was made company commander. During "Zitadelle" he led his unit along the Donets as spearhead of the 7.Panzer-Division. On 7 October 1943 he was awarded the Deutsches Kreuz in Gold as *Oberleutnant der Reserve* and commander of the 3rd company, schwere Panzer-Abteilung 503. Promoted to *Hauptmann*, on 23 February 1944 he was awarded the Ritterkreuz for his successes during the operation to relieve the men trapped in the Korsun-Cherkassy pocket. In September he left the Tiger battalion and was transferred to Panzer-Brigade 150 as leader of Kampfgruppe Y, a unit that was briefly employed from 21 December east of Malmedy. Promoted to *Major* he became commander of the newly formed schwere Panzerjäger-Abteilung 512 equipped with the Jagdtiger. From 1939 to 1945 he commanded all type of panzers, meeting and battling practically every type of Soviet and Allied armor. By the end of the war he was credited with destroying 29 tanks. He passed away on 7 April 2003.

Notes. In mid-January 1943 the 2nd company, schwere PzAbt 502, was incorporated into schwere PzAbt 503 as 3rd company.

Schließmann Kurt, born on 6 August 1920 in the town of Friedrichshafen (on the shoreline of Lake Constance). He was awarded the Deutsches Kreuz in Gold on 5 April 1943 as *Leutnant* in the 1st battery, Sturmgeschütz-Abteilung 226. Promoted to *Hauptmann*, he was transferred to the Sturmgeschütz-Brigade 286 as commander of the 1st battery. During the defensive battles around Miskolc, on 16 November 1944 he destroys with his battery and an attached Jäger company the enemy forces who had entered the western suburb of Diósgyőr. Still in the same area, during the fighting in the Tisza bridgehead, a Jäger battalion along with a howitzer battery became trapped south of Tokaj. Schließmann with only his four vehicles plus a handful of escorting infantry goes up against an enemy force of about 600 men and 9 tanks. Taking along 2 light flak guns as well as horses for the trapped howitzers he charges into the enemy occupied village achieving total surprise: without casualties the small kampfgruppe allows the trapped elements to make it back to German lines and prevents the enemy from breaking out to the north. For this feat and for having reached a personal total of 29 enemy tank "kills", he was awarded the Ritterkreuz on 18 January 1945. He passed away on 16 January 2005 in his native town.

Schmalz Eberhard, born on 20 March 1919 in Thorn (today Toruń), West Prussia. He studied engineering in Danzig, but in 1938 volunteered for the Wehrmacht. As an *Unteroffizier* in the 2./Panzerjäger-Abteilung 43, 8.Panzer-Division, he was awarded the Deutsches Kreuz in Gold on 24 December 1942 for destroying during the Battle of Velikiye Luki twelve T-34s over a nine-day period with his Marder III (the type that mounted the modified Soviet 76.2 mm). The last enemy tank he engaged managed to ram the Marder disabling the traverse mechanism; the German crew aimed the gun at the T-34 by looking through the barrel. In addition to the DKiG he was sent to an officer candidate school in Prague. Promoted to *Leutnant*, he was briefly assigned to the 5.Jäger-Division where he witnessed a demonstration of the new Tiger I; however he considered the StuG III more reliable, easy to train soldiers to operate, and effective against all types of Soviet armour. In the winter of 1944 he finally joined the Panzer-Jäger-Kompanie 1102 of the 102.Infanterie-Division as a zugführer. Whit this unit he destroyed another 29 enemy tanks; he was thus awarded the Ritterkreuz, which he received on 11 March 1945 while recovering from wounds. Few days later on the 23 of March near Heiligenbeil, an Il-2 strafed his Kübelwagen to pieces. Badly injured in the legs, he was abandoned in the town by the hospital staff as the Soviets closed in. He was rescued by the crew of a Schnellboot, who piled the wounded soldiers onto the boat and shipped to a friendly German port. After the war he moved to Sao Paulo, Brazil, and then to Cincinnati, Ohio, in 1959, changing his name to Hardy Svenson and becoming an American citizen in 1965. He was project manager for Boeing of the Saturn V rocket system. He passed away on 16 October 2002 in Arlington, Virginia; he left a son. His ashes were placed with his wife's at the Eilendorf cemetery in Aachen.

Notes. In October 1944 Sturmgeschütz-Abteilung 1102 (of the Panzerjäger-Abteilung 102) received 10 StuG IVs, however according to Schmalz the kompanie had only StuG IIIs.

Schramm Richard, born on 8 July 1913 in the village of Langburkersdorf (thirty-five kilometers east of Dresden). He joined the Reichswehr in March 1933 in the Artillerie-Regiment 4; in August 1938 he was promoted to *Wachtmeister*. In August 1940 he was posted as instructor to the Artillerie-Lehr-Regiment in Jüterbog and in October promoted to *Oberwachtmeister*. Finally in September 1941 he was transferred to the newly formed Sturmgeschütz-Abteilung 202. He distinguished himself in the fighting west of Moscow and received the EK II on 30 November 1941 and the EK I on 17 July 1942. In late 1942, during the hard-fought defensive battles near Sychyovka (50 km south of Rzhev) his 1st battery was detached to help elements of the 5.Panzer-Division against an enemy breakthrough on the Vazuza river. Schramm, as platoon leader, in seventeen days of combat destroyed a large number of tanks (12 on 12 December alone) rising his total to 37. As a result on 23 December 1942 he was awarded the Ritterkreuz. In March 1943 he was seriously wounded, however after a period spent in the Sturmgeschütz-Ersatz-und-Ausbildungs-Abteilung 500 he returned to his unit, by then upgraded to Brigade. He went missing in action on 17 June 1944 near Priekule, southwestern Latvia; his remains were never found. By this time he had been credited with around 40 (probably 44) enemy tank "kills". Last rank: *Leutnant*.

Schumacher Kurt, born on 8 March 1923 in Hannover. He joined the SS in November 1939; in 1942 he graduated from Bad Tölz being promoted to *SS-Untersturmführer* on 21 June. For his successes as Panzer IV commander in the 3rd company, SS-Panzer-Regiment 5 "Wiking" during the advance towards the Caucasus, he was awarded the Deutsches Kreuz in Gold on 30 December 1943. In 1944 during the battle of the Korsun-Cherkassy pocket, on 13 February two Soviet battalions attacked the village of Nova Buda (midway between Korsun and Lysianka) in order to increase the gap between the trapped Germans and the relief forces. Schumacher and one other panzer advanced and drove the enemy out of the village. The Soviets counterattacked, this time supported by around 15 T-34s. With his Panzer IV he wiped out eight tanks that had penetrated the village, then, emerging from the outskirt, destroyed two more. The enemy however was determined to drive the Germans back and re-launched its attack on the following day, this time with 11 tanks. The second panzer had been damaged, leaving Schumacher alone; yet he launched a flank attack on the advancing Soviets knocking out seven of them. With no armour-piercing ammunition left he continued with high-explosive shells. This was ineffective against the armour of the T-34s, however some crews assumed they had been hit and bailed out. The arrival of another German panzer gave Schumacher cover to finish off one of the abandoned tanks; he finally destroyed another T-34 attempting to work its way around his flank from the rear. Over the two days, thirty-two T-34s had been reduced to wrecks around the village, about half of them by Schumacher alone. For his actions at this critical time he was awarded the Ritterkreuz on 4 May 1944.

Wiking grenadiers and panzers near Korsun, early February 1944.

Promoted to *SS-Obersturmführer* he was killed on 20 March 1945 near Stuhlweissenburg, Hungary. By the time of his death he had partecipated in over fifty separate armoured engagements.

Notes. The circumstances of his death -happened at night- are disputed. Possibly he was sleeping under the hull of a panzer and was crushed when the vehicle moved to change position. According to *SS-Obersturmbannführer* Fritz Darges, commander of the panzer regiment, he was hit by enemy fire while on a Kübelwagen.

At right, with *SS-Obersturmführer* Willy Hein.

Schumacher (on the right) in Poland, late October 1944. At this time he was acting as temporary battalion commander.

Schwalb Helmut, born on 17 October 1915 in the small town of Wassertrüdingen (sixty kilometers southwest of Nürnberg). He took part in the Battle of France with Artillerie-Regiment 103, then in 1941 he joined the Sturmgeschütz-Abteilung 190; he fought in "Marita" and received the EK II on 14 April. As StuG commander in the 1st battery he took part in the invasion of the Soviet Union; he fought in the southern sector and, in 1942, in the assault on Sevastopol. In 1943 his unit was deployed in the central sector; he was promoted to *Leutnant* and on 21 September received the EK I. On 20 January 1944 he was awarded the Deutsches Kreuz in Gold and on March 1st was promoted to *Hauptmann*. Against operation "Bagration" his 1st battery was attached to the 337.Infanterie-Division which was being pushed back with high losses in men and materiel. Schwalb leads his sturmgeschütze in rearguard actions allowing the remaining divisional elements, including the divisional staff, to escape over the Dnieper at Mogilev. In another action he leads a very successful counterattack to retake a village resulting in enemy losses of over 40 tanks and numerous AT guns. On 23 August 1944 he was awarded the Ritterkreuz as commander of the 1st battery, Sturmgeschütz-Brigade 190. In December he was promoted to *Major* and was given a post of chief instructor. He was credited with destroying 40 Soviet tanks. He passed away on 31 May 2006.

Notes. In 1945 he may have been in command of the 2nd battery, Sturmgeschütz-Schule "Burg" (formerly Sturmartillerie-Schule "Zinna").

Schwarzenbacher Josef, born on 17 March 1919 in the village of Eisentratten (sixty kilometers northwest of Klagenfurt, Carinthia). Early in the war he received both classes of the EK. During the fighting of the Sturmgeschütz-Brigade 912 north of the Lithuanian town of Biržai (Birsen in German) in mid-August 1944, as *Unteroffizier der Reserve* in the 1st company, he takes on a Soviet attack entirely on his own, destroying 11 tanks out of a group of 15, and preventing an enemy break-in. He is killed in action a few days later, on 16 August. By the time of his death he had been credited with destroying 43 tanks as gunner of the battery commander's StuG, and about 25 tanks as StuG commander. He was posthumously awarded the Ritterkreuz on 27 August and promoted to *Wachtmeister*.

Seibold Emil, born on 26 February 1907 in Basel, Switzerland. He joined the NSDAP on April 1st 1933, and on 10 April 1940 he volunteered for the Waffen-SS. He was first posted as infantryman to the SS-Division *Totenkopf*, then in December transferred to *Reich* (later *Das Reich*) in the 3rd battery of the Panzerjäger-Bataillon as a motorcyclist. In "Barbarossa" he was in command of one of the battery's guns and on 23 August 1941 was awarded the EK II. In March 1943 the division captured about fifty T-34s, and with half of them formed a third battalion for the SS-Panzer Regiment 2. Seibold, after being awarded the EK I on 20 April, was selected to command one of these modified and refurbished tanks and was transferred to the 8th company. From July to August he would fight with the captured T-34; in "Zitadelle" and following battles he destroys 24 enemy tanks. Later that year he was given command of a Panzer IV. On 4 June 1944 he was awarded the Deutsches Kreuz in Gold as *SS-Oberscharführer* in the 8th company, SS-Panzer-Regiment 2, 2.SS-Panzer-Division *Das Reich*. In Normandy and in the Ardennes he may have achieved some successes against Allied tanks because in January he was recommended for the Ritterkreuz. In "Frühlingserwachen" he eliminates few more Soviet tanks and on 12 March 1945 his total of "kills" had reached 65. In the last days of the war he destroys another 4 tanks and he is finally awarded the Ritterkreuz on 6 May as *SS-Hauptscharführer* and platoon leader in the 8th company. After the war he may have settled in Austria. He passed away on 11 September 1990 on the Ligurian coast, Italy.

Notes. His Ritterkreuz was one of several high awards made by "Sepp" Dietrich at the very end of the war, which were tecnically invalid as they were not authorized by the SS-Personalhauptamt or Heerespersonalamt. He was however member of the OdR and, de facto, a Ritterkreuzträger. - Other sources give Hesse, Germany, as place of death.

Seibold (at right) with his crew.

Senghas Paul, born on 31 January 1916 in the village of Böttingen (eighty kilometers south of Stuttgart). In July 1935 he volunteered to join the Waffen-SS. With the SS-VT he fought in the Poland campaign and the Battle of France receiving the EK II in June 1940. He was then posted in the newly formed SS-Division *Wiking* as a *Scharführer*, taking part in "Barbarossa" and being awarded the EK I in December 1941; in 1942 he fought in the Caucasus. On 9 June 1943, after the destruction of over 30 enemy tanks, he was awarded the Deutsches Kreuz in Gold as *SS-Hauptscharführer* in the 1st company, I.Abteilung, SS-Panzer-Regiment 5; he was also selected to become an officer and promoted to *SS-Untersturmführer* in July 1943.

During the battles northeast of Warsaw, on 18 August 1944 the Soviets are advancing towards the Warsaw-Radzymin-Wyszków road with massive forces and strong air support. *SS-Obersturmführer* Senghas stands with his Stabskompanie in the village of Zazdrość (1,5 km east of Niegów). At 11:00 he receives a message which reports the enemy as having broken through in battalion strength to a point 1 km east of the railway embankment. A wide gap is forming and there is the danger that the enemy would block the main road and thrust into the left flank of the division. With the handful of men of the supply unit, he goes into position at the embankment and defends for the remainder of the day and also the two following days, fighting off strong enemy attacks with only rifles, sub-machine guns and close combat weapons. With the help of two conditionally operational Panzer IVs, 2 Shermans and 1 T-34 are eliminated, the Soviets take heavy losses and cease their attacks. On 11 December 1944 he is awarded the Ritterkreuz as commander of the 1st company, SS-Panzer Regiment 5 "Wiking". Promoted to *SS-Hauptsturmführer*, in the last days of the war he leads his men, fighting as infantry, in the area of Truppenübungsplatz Sennelager (just north of Paderborn). He is severely wounded on April 1st 1945 and evacuated to hospital at Warendorf where he is captured by the advancing American forces. He was released from captivity in June 1946. During the course of the war, as Panzer IV commander he was credited with a total of 49 tank "kills". He passed away on 6 November 1996.

Senghas (second from right) and his crew east of Maykop, late 1942.

Sowada Bernhard, born on 13 August 1920 in the village of Chrzumczütz (today Chrząszczyce; from 1933 to 1945 Schönkirch), six kilometers south of Oppeln, Upper Silesia. On the eastern front he received the EK II on 13 October 1942. In September 1943 he was *Leutnant der Reserve* and leader of the 2nd platoon in the 1st battery, Sturmgeschütz-Abteilung 237 (it was the battery led by Bodo Spranz). He distinguished himself during the German withdrawal from the area of Smolensk and in particular during the figthing of the battalion to cover the retreat of the IX.Armeekorps. On September 4 he had already received the EK I. Then on September 18 he knocks out a KV-1 and seven T-34s; on the 20 two KV-1s, eight T-34s and two M3s "Lee". By this time he had reached a total of 21 enemy tanks destroyed and was thus awarded the Ritterkreuz on 12 October 1943. He was killed on 25 December 1944 in Vértessomló near Tatabánya, Hungary.

Spielmann Johannes (or Johann), born on 29 December 1916 in the small town of Laufenburg (fifty kilometers south of Freiburg im Breisgau). He joined the Wehrmacht in 1937 being posted to Artillerie-Regiment 5 in Ulm; with Artillerie-Regiment 206 he took part in the Battle of France. He fought in "Barbarossa" receiving the EK II on 13 July 1941, followed by the EK I on 26 September. In early 1942 he was *Leutnant* and platoon leader in the 1st battery, Sturmgeschütz-Abteilung 197. At the start of the second Soviet offensive in the Kerch peninsula (eastern Crimea), between 13 and 15 March his platoon destroys 34 enemy tanks, including six KV-1s, damages two more and also eliminates an enemy artillery battery. Spielmann, who has raised his total of tank "kills" to 35 (fourteen T-34s in the first day alone) is mentioned by name in the Wehrmachtbericht of 15 March and awarded the Ritterkreuz on 27 March 1942. Promoted to *Oberleutnant*, for another action near Sevastopol on 8 June, he is again mentioned in the Wehrmachtbericht. In April 1943 the "197" became the schwere Panzerjäger-Abteilung 653 and was re-equipped with 45 new Panzerjäger Tiger (P) (called Ferdinand; Elefant after May 1944). Spielmann, promoted to *Hauptmann* is given command of the 1st company, but at the beginning of "Zitadelle", on 6 July, he is severely wounded by an antipersonnel mine while dismounted and guiding his Ferdinand 101. In 1944 he was promoted to *Major* and in September put in command of the whole Sturmgeschütz-Brigade 202, to be employed in the northern sector. During the third battle of Courland his unit fought in the most critical sector south of Frauenburg and north of Doblen, and in three days destroyed 44 enemy tanks and 10 AT guns (with this, the total number of tanks eliminated by the unit rose to 1017). Spielmann always led his sturmgeschütze from the front and by the end of the battle had reached a personal total of 48 enemy tank "kills"; he was thus awarded the Eichenlaub on 28 March 1945. He passed away on 14 August 2005 in his native town.

Spranz Bodo, born on the 1st of January 1920 in Nordhausen. He joined the Wehrmacht in November 1938 as *Fahnenjunker* in the Artillerie-Regiment 12. Promoted to *Leutnant* early in 1940, he took part in the Battle of France as platoon commander within the IV.Abteilung, Artillerie-Regiment 209. On 23 June 1940 he received the EK II. He was then trained on the StuG III and assigned as platoon commander to the Sturmgeschütz-Abteilung 185 on the eastern front. On 2 July 1941 he was awarded the EK I, followed by the Deutsches Kreuz in Gold on 6 May 1942. He was wounded multiple times and spent long periods as instructor in a replacement and training unit in Schweinfurt. In June 1943 he is back to the front, in the area east of Smolensk, as *Oberleutnant* and commander of the 1st battery of the newly formed Sturmgeschütz-Abteilung 237. In September he is recommended to the Ritterkreuz for 50 tank "kills" since the start of the war, as well as for the outstanding performance of his unit, which in six days of combat, end of August/start of September 1943, has eliminated 61 enemy tanks. Few days later his seven serviceable vehicles defeat a fierce Soviet armoured attack destroying 27 tanks without any friendly losses. By 17 September Spranz has raised his personal total to 76 tanks (of which 4 were eliminated in close combat on 27 August), so on the day of the award of the Ritterkreuz, 3 October 1943, he receives

simultaneously the Eichenlaub! By this time he had been promoted to *Hauptmann* and wounded for the ninth time in the war. In November he got married; but at the beginning of 1944 his wife, a nurse, died of a jaundice she had contracted on the eastern front. Spranz was posted at first as instructor at the Sturmgeschütz-Schule in Burg, later at the Oberkommando des Heeres. In Berlin he managed to escape the Soviets and surrender to US forces on 6 of May. From 1962 to 1984 Prof. Dr. Spranz was the director of the museum of Natural History in Freiburg. He passed away on September 1st 2007.

With his crew, near Yelnya in mid-September 1943.

Awarded the Eichenlaub by Hitler.

Staudegger Franz, born on 12 February 1923 in the village of Unter-Loibach (forty kilometers east of Klagenfurt, Austria), the son of a pub owner. He finished the school in 1940 and immediately volunteered for the Waffen-SS, being assigned to the *Leibstandarte*. He took part in the invasion of the Soviet Union as *SS-Schütze* in the 1st company, I.Bataillon (thereafter Infanterie-Regiment 1). In late 1942 he joined the newly formed Tiger company, as *SS-Rottenführer* in command of a Panzer III in the light platoon; it was one of the few tanks of the company to see action during the counterattack at Kharkov, attached to Peiper's armored troop carrier battalion. Staudegger was promoted to *SS-Unterscharführer* and awarded the EK II for bravery on 20 March 1943, at the same time he switched to the Tiger tank.

July 5, first day of "Zitadelle". In the evening Staudegger is driving alone to rejoin the company when, in the darkness, he almost collides with another tank. He jumps from the turret only to realize that what he is facing is a T-34; controlling his fear he arms a hand grenade tossing it into the open hatch of the enemy tank, he then runs toward a second T-34 climbing on to it with another grenade. The next day he is awarded the EK I. On July 8 he is setting around in Teterevino waiting for his damaged Tiger being fixed; here he is told that a group of about fifty to sixty T-34s is approaching from the northeast. Employing all available means he makes the vehicle drivable and immediately sets out. His crew: driver *SS-Sturmmann* Herbert Stellmacher, gunner *SS-Panzerschütze* Heinz Buchner, loader *SS-Panzerschütze* Walter Henke, radio operator *SS-Panzerschütze* Gerhard Waltersdorf. They arrive just in time to rescue elements of "Deutschland" to be overrun, then in a two hours battle they eliminate 17 tanks; the enemy formation subsequently breaks off and withdraws into a gully. Without waiting for orders Staudegger now decides to attack; advancing far beyond friendly lines and without support he destroys 5 more tanks. With its armor-piercing ammunition expended, the Tiger begins firing HE rounds: four additional T-34s are seen to be hit. A patrol dispatched by the 2nd company of "Germania" later confirmed the 22 kills. On 10 July he was awarded the Ritterkreuz; he was then summoned by Hitler at the Führer Headquarters for a detailed account of the battle. While at home he received a voucher for a Volkswagen car and gave several speeches on the Tiger, he also sent several packages to his company at the front.

In 1944 on account of illness he was forced to leave a course for officer candidates, however promoted to *SS-Standartenjunker* he joined the 1st company of the newly formed schwere SS-Panzer-Abteilung 101. He was entrusted with training and organizational tasks and took little or no part in the fighting in Normandy and in the Ardennes. On 17 January 1945 a understrenght company with six Tiger IIs and other vehicles departed from support base Schloß Holte and was transported to Breslau; here the train sat idle for several days, until it was sent onward to Hungary arriving in Raab (Győr). In the course of several engagements Staudegger destroys numerous enemy tanks; finally on 18 April during the retreat from Wilhelmsburg (ten kilometers south of Sankt Pölten) a bridge collapsed beneath his Tiger. After the war he settled in Germany. He passed away on 16 March 1991.

Stehle Werner, born on 21 May 1923 in the small town of Müllheim (twenty-five kilometers southwest of Freiburg im Breisgau). He fought with the 97.Jäger-Division in the southern sector of the eastern front receiving the EK II on 22 January 1943. Soon after he may have been transferred as *Gefreiter* in the 21.Luftwaffen-Feld-Division in the area of Leningrad; in November however, he was injured and evacuated to the Reich. He then volunteered for the Sturmartillerie and was transferred to the Fallschirm-Sturmgeschütz-Brigade 12 which would be employed on the western front. On November 1st 1944 he was promoted to *Leutnant*. As platoon leader in the 3rd battery, he distinguished himself during the defensive combat which took place along the German-Dutch border on the northern bank of the Rhein in late March 1945. On the 19 he had already been awarded the EK I; in the following days he held the main battle line at the southern edge of the village of Loikum, alone against the almost continuously artillery, mortars, tanks and armoured cars fire. Despite the fractured state of the frontline (which in some places didn't even exist at all) he advanced twice with his sturmgeschütz a kilometre in front of the line without any infantry protection. In this way he destroys 5 armoured cars (of a force of twenty) on the 26 March and 2 Shermans on the following day. Through this outstanding attitude he prevented a breakthrough in the left flank of the 7.Fallschirmjäger-Division. On the 30 March a strong enemy tank force crossed the border by the customs house on the road Bocholt-Winterswijk. Positioned completely alone and without escorting infantry Stehle drives 2 km in front of the main battle line. Here he destroys 3 armoured cars and a

Sherman: the enemy did not attack at this position again, and a rollup of the front in the sector of the neighbouring division was prevented. On April 1st he is severely wounded by a hit from an enemy AT-gun. In total he had eliminated 19 tanks and 8 armoured cars, and on 28 April 1945 was awarded the Ritterkreuz. He passed away on 4 March 1993.

Men of Fallschirm-Sturmgeschütz-Brigade 12. The one on the right could be Stehle.

Stier Gottwald (or Gottwalt), born on 17 March 1919 in the village of Zoghaus (ninety kilometers southeast of Erfurt). In 1943 he was *Unteroffizier der Reserve* in the 2nd battery, Sturmgeschütz-Abteilung 667. In the central sector of the eastern front, on 9 August the Soviets succeeded in breaking into the defence of Grenadier-Regiment 468 northwest of Nadzyeya (in German reports: "Nadezhda"), to the east of Mogilev. A platoon of sturmgeschütze was sent to help the infantry recapture the lost territory, however en route two of the vehicles bottomed out in some soft ground. Unfortunately at this exact moment the Soviets launched a major attack against the left wing of the regiment and managed to encircle the two battalion command posts as well as the two immobilized sturmgeschütze. The platoon commander informed his company via radio that the two vehicles would have to be blown up as their recovery was now impossible. Stier, who had been left behind as security, listened to the conversation. He rallies some nearby infantry and attacks under heavy artillery and small arms fire breaking through to the rest of his platoon. Once there, he dismounts his gun and organizes the recovery of the two vehicles by using his own sturmgeschütz to pull them out. He then takes up the fight and eliminates 5 enemy tanks routing their escorting infantry. With this the German grenadiers are able to recapture their old positions. For this feat he was awarded the Ritterkreuz on 13 August 1943. Promoted to *Oberwachtmeister*, by the end of the war he had been credited with destroying over 30 enemy tanks. He passed away on 21 August 1994 in his native village.

Notes. According to other sources he was in the 1st battery.

244

Stock Hans-Christian, born on 21 November 1919 in the village of Liebstadt (twenty kilometers southeast of Dresden). He joined the Wehrmacht in 1938 being posted to Artillerie-Regiment 60; he took part in the Polish campaign receiving the EK II on 22 September 1939. In February 1941 he moved to the Sturmgeschütz-Abteilung 184 and with this unit he fought in the central sector of "Barbarossa". On September 1st was promoted to *Leutnant der Reserve* and on 13 February 1942 awarded the EK I. In December he was transferred to the newly formed Sturmgeschütz-Abteilung 270 as platoon leader in the 2nd battery. In 1943, after the battle of Kursk, in the Orel salient the headquarters of the LIII.Korps found itself encircled by the enemy and was able to escape only through the assistance of Stock's sturmgeschütze. In the following four days of combat he personally eliminates 19 enemy tanks before his own vehicle is hit. On the way back to the workshop company he encounters a Soviet breakthrough force; despite being totally alone and with a damaged vehicle, with his crew he immediately engages the enemy: 6 tanks are destroyed and the rest is forced to flee; swiftly assembled reserves of the 112.Infanterie-Division are called up and succeed in sealing off the penetration. For this important local victory he was decorated with the Ritterkreuz on 22 August 1943, and in October promoted to *Oberleutnant*. In June 1944 the abteilung was upgraded to Brigade, only to be renamed Panzerjäger-Abteilung 152 in August; by this time Stock had been promoted to *Hauptmann* and was in command of the 2nd battery. For his successes during the elimination of the Soviet bridgehead over the Vistula at Annopol on 30 and 31 August, and for

reaching a total of 58 enemy tank "kills" he was awarded the Eichenlaub on 23 October. In the following months he led the entire abteilung, which was attached to the 1.Skijäger-Division, in heavy combat in Slovakia. He was killed in action on 12 January 1945 near the village of Mokrance (German Mokrantz, Hungarian Makranc), twenty kilometers southwest of Košice. He was posthumously promoted to *Major*.

Straub Johann, born on 6 June 1912 in the village of Oberglashütte (forty-five kilometers south of Tübingen). He entered the Reichswehr in 1934; he took part in the Polish campaign and in the battle of France receiving the EK II followed by the EK I in May 1940. On the eastern front he fought in the Panzerjäger-Abteilung 7 of the 7.Infanterie-Division. On January 1st 1943 he was promoted to *Leutnant* and on 23 May 1944 was awarded the Deutsches Kreuz in Gold as platoon leader in the "Sturmgeschütz-Abteilung 1007" company. After the start of the Soviet operation "Bagration", he greatly distinguished himself during the fighting retreat of the division through Pinsk and in the direction of the river Bug. In the time period 9-27 July 1944, with his StuG III he personally destroyed 18 enemy tanks (out of a total of 44 by the whole abteilung). He was thus awarded the Ritterkreuz on 12 August 1944. Later that year he was wounded and in October he was transferred to the Ersatz-Abteilung. In 1956 he joined the Bundeswehr retiring in 1966 with the rank of *Major der Reserve.* He passed away on 12 July 1996.

Strippel Hans, born on the 1st of December 1912 in the village of Obergeis (forty-five kilometers south of Kassel). He joined the Reichswehr in 1932 in the 3rd company, 5.Kraftfahr-Abteilung; in 1935 he was transferred to the newly formed Panzer-Regiment 1. He took part in the Poland campaign receiving the EK II on 24 September 1939. After the Battle of France he fought in "Barbarossa" in command of a Panzer III and was awarded the EK I on 21 July 1941 as *Oberfeldwebel* in the 3rd company, Panzer-Regiment 1, 1.Panzer-Division. On 24 December 1941, as platoon leader, he was awarded the Deutsches Kreuz in Gold. After the battles in the area of Toropets and the destruction of 36 enemy tanks he received the Ritterkreuz on 22 January 1943. During the relief effort towards the Korsun-Cherkassy pocket, in command of a Panther he eliminates another 37 T-34s, and on 4 June 1944 he is awarded the Eichenlaub. By the end of the war he had been promoted to *Leutnant* and credited with a total of over 70 tank "kills", possibly 77. He passed away on 26 November 1983.

Notes. The figure of 77 is given in the book "The 1st Panzer Division: A Pictorial History, 1935-1945".

Tadje Friedrich "Fritz", born on 23 November 1914 in the village of Feggendorf (twenty-five kilometers west of Hannover). He was posted to the Artillerie-Regiment in Münster. Early in the war he was wounded several times and received both classes of the EK. On 2 July 1942 he was awarded the Deutsches Kreuz in Gold as *Oberwachtmeister* in the 2nd battery, Sturmgeschütz-Abteilung 190. In September 1942 the Germans had planned to retreat from their bridgehead east of the Don at Voronezh, but the Soviets beat them to it and broke into the positions of the 323.Infanterie-Division. The division was able to contain the attack but not eliminate it on its own, so Sturmgeschütz-Abteilung 190 and an infantry regiment were sent as reinforcements. On 22 September these units counterattacked with the goal of capturing a brickyard, however their progress was halted by two dug-in Soviet tanks. Tadje leads his assault gun out of its firing position moving 150 meters in front of the infantry, and in a firefight at close range is able to destroy the enemy. However, immediately after the second tank is knocked out, his sturmgeschütz receives a direct hit; all of the crew is killed and Tadje seriously wounded. For this action as well for reaching a total of 39 tank "kills" he was awarded the Ritterkreuz on 21 October 1942 as *Leutnant* and leader of the 2nd battery. By the end of the war he had been promoted to *Hauptmann*. He surrendered to the British being held captive until 1947. He passed away on 26 January 1981.

Teriete Heinrich, born on 20 February 1915 in the small town of Rhede (sixty-five kilometers north of Düsseldorf). With the Sturmgeschütz-Abteilung 197 he fought in the southern sector of "Barbarossa", then in 1942 in the siege of Sevastopol and in the area of Orel. He received the EK II and the EK I and was promoted to *Wachtmeister*. In January 1943 his unit was reorganized as schwere Sturmgeschütz-Brigade 197, then in April after being equipped with the new Ferdinand tank destroyer, received its final designation of schwere Panzerjäger-Abteilung 653. For "Zitadelle" the battalion moved to Russia, detraining south of Orel and reaching the start point in Glazunovka, directly on the Orel-Kursk rail line. On 14 July, at "Shelyaburg" (actually Zhelyabuga, forty kilometers east of Orel) the 36.Panzergrenadier-Division was the target of a frontal attack by almost 400 Soviet tanks. By this time the serviceable Ferdinands have been regrouped under the command of *Leutnant* Teriete. The enemy is repulsed, with Teriete personally destroying 22 tanks (vehicle 121, gunner *Unteroffizier* Kurt Titus, driver Alois Schafer). He was awarded the Ritterkreuz on 22 July, however during the following battles on the Dnieper he was wounded. After a long stay in a field hospital he was transferred to the 2nd company, of which he became acting commander. On 18 July 1944 he was again seriously wounded at Kabarovce (Kabarivtsi, northwest of Ternopil). He then returned to the 2nd company, now an indipendent unit renamed Heeres schwere Panzerjäger-Kompanie 614 and equipped with 4 Elefants. In early 1945 the vehicles retreated through Silesia; in February were under maintenance in Stahndorf, southwest of Berlin. During the battle of Berlin, *Oberleutnant* Teriete led his unit in the area of Wünsdorf, south of Zossen; here his Elefant was knocked out and he was captured. He returned home in November 1949. He passed away on 17 November 2002.

Ferdinand of schwere Panzerjäger-Abteilung 653 at Kursk.

Elefant in western Ukraine (or possibly Italy), 1944.

Timpe Heinz, born on 12 October 1923 in Karnap (a district of Essen). He was directly transferred to the front as artilleryman with the 29.Infanterie-Division (mot.) during the advance on Stalingrad. He was wounded and escaped the fate of his division. After recovering he volunteered for the Sturmartillerie and fought in the central sector as platoon leader in the Sturmgeschütz-Abteilung 667. Again wounded he was transferred to the newly formed Sturmgeschütz-Abteilung 300 (in February 1944 upgraded to Brigade; in late March 1945 reorganized as Heeres-Sturmartillerie-Brigade 300). This unit fought in the battles west of Kiev, in the area of Vinnytsia and then during the long retreat through the Carpathians to the Reich. On 28 February 1945 Timpe was awarded the Deutsches Kreuz in Gold, as *Leutnant* in the 1st company. His accomplishments culminated with his outstanding performance as company commander during the battle to recapture Bautzen, in the period 20-27 April. By this time he had personally destroyed a total of 59 enemy tanks, and on 7 May was awarded the Ritterkreuz. Prior to this he had already been recommended twice. From 1956 to 1983 he served in the Bundeswehr reaching the rank of *Oberst*. He passed away on 15 May 2015.

Notes. The presentation of the Ritterkreuz was authorized via radio message from the Heeresgruppe Mitte and made by *Feldmarschall* Schörner.

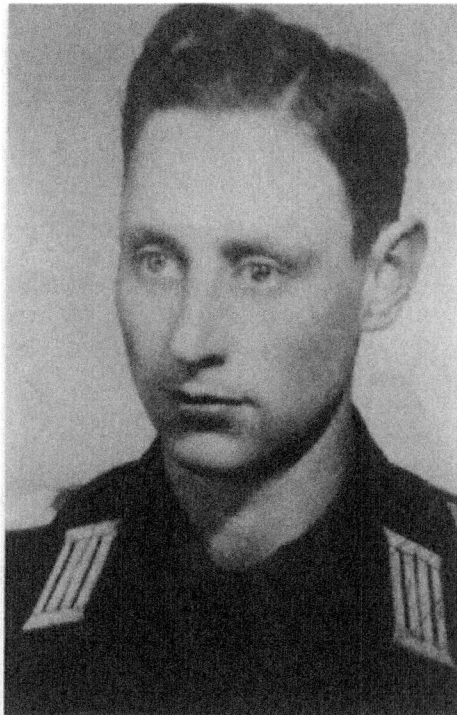

Tornau Gottfried, born on 20 December 1919 in Hamburg. He took part in the Battle of France as *Leutnant* in the Artillerie-Regiment 20, receiving the EK II on 9 July 1940. In "Barbarossa" he fought in the central sector, in the 3rd battery, Sturmgeschütz-Abteilung 184, being wounded twice in late August 1941 and receiving the EK I on 9 September. In the course of 1942 he was again repeatedly wounded and promoted to *Oberleutnant*. On 28 May 1943 he was awarded the Deutsches Kreuz in Gold and then promoted to *Hauptmann*. In 1945 in Pomerania, near the village of Nantikov (today Nętkovo), seventy kilometers east of Stettin, he leads a counterattack against an advancing Soviet armoured unit, allowing thousands of wounded soldiers and civilians to flee west; he is thus awarded the Ritterkreuz on 5 March as leader of the Heeres-Sturmartillerie-Brigade 911 assigned to the Führer-Grenadier-Division. He ended the war with the rank of *Major* and credited with personally destroying 40 Soviet tanks. After the war he served in the Bundeswehr reaching the rank of *Oberst*. He passed away on 9 February 1992.

Trägner Josef, born on 10 February 1915 in the small town of Podersam (today Podbořany, Czech Republic), seventy-five kilometers west of Prague. *Wachtmeister* in the 1st battery, Sturmgeschütz-Abteilung 667, during the defensive battles west of Smolensk in the sector of the 268.Infanterie-Division he destroys a total of 30 enemy tanks. He is thus awarded the Ritterkreuz on 23 August 1943. His last rank was *Oberwachtmeister*. He passed away on 20 January 1974.

Truxa Rolf, born on 6 June 1921 in Berlin-Schöneberg. He received the EK II on 27 August 1941 and the EK I on 18 July 1943. As *Oberleutnant* in the Sturmgeschütz-Abteilung 190 he was awarded the Deutsches Kreuz in Gold on 29 October 1943; he was then given command of the entire 2nd battery. In November during the German attempt to recapture Nevel, the sturmgeschütze had the mission of supporting the 252.Infanterie-Division. After overcoming the Soviet minefields the grenadiers became pinned down in their efforts to take the high ground at "Sui Shmotki" (possibly Smol'niki, twelve kilometers northwest of the town). At this point Truxa was able to rally them and then proceed to capture the heights in a sharp attack. By the evening the Soviets had been pushed back 6 km. Despite the overall failure of the German operation, Truxa was nonetheless decorated with the Ritterkreuz on 17 December 1943. Promoted to *Hauptmann*, by the end of the war he had reached a total of no less than 25 enemy tank "kills". He passed away on 3 February 1983.

Veith Johann (or Hans), born on 27 July 1916 in the village of Albersweiler (eighty-five kilometers southwest of Mainz). He took part in the French campaign and received the EK II on 5 June 1940. On the eastern front he was awarded the EK I on 26 April 1943. He distinguished himself in the Ardennes as *SS-Obersturmführer* and commander of the 3rd company, SS-Panzer-Regiment 2 "Das Reich". On 25 December 1944 in the area of Manhay he made the indipendent decision to attack in order to take advantage of a success in the neighbouring sector. Carrying the grenadiers with him, he captures Grandménil in a bold action that sees his Kompanie destroy 20 Shermans (of which he is responsible for 5). On 3 January 1945 near the hamlet of Beffe the enemy started an advance with about 60 tanks along a narrow front; the grenadiers were forced to displace and took heavy losses from artillery drumfire. The danger now existed that the enemy would be able to reach the west-east La Roche-Salmchâteau road and cut off major German elements. Veith with his small force of just 4 Panthers attacks into the middle of the US tank formation forcing it to retreat: 22 Shermans are knocked out (9 personally by him) and the accompanying infantry is eliminated by well-laid fire. He was killed in action on 7 January. On the request of SS-Panzergrenadier-Regiment 3 "Deutschland" he was posthumously awarded the Ritterkreuz, 14 February 1945.

Wagner Klaus, born on 30 October 1917 in the small town of Schmalkalden (fifty kilometers southwest of Erfurt). In August 1942 in the area of Rzhev he was *Oberleutnant* and leader of the 3rd battery, Sturmgeschütz-Abteilung 667. During the battles in support of the 161.Infanterie-Division his battery destroyed 83 Soviet tanks; he and his crew alone destroyed 18 on the 29/30 August. For these successes he was awarded the Ritterkreuz on 4 September. By the end of the war he had been promoted to *Hauptmann* and credited with a total of 22 tank "kills". He passed away on 24 April 2002.

Warmbrunn Karl-Heinz, born on 15 October 1924 in Nürnberg. In 1943 he joined the newly formed *LSSAH* Tiger company as *SS-Panzerschütze* and had his baptisme of fire in March 1943 during the recapture of Kharkov, as gunner with the commander Kling. He eliminates several tanks and AT guns and on 20 March he is awarded the EK II. Promoted to *SS-Sturmmann*, in "Zitadelle" he was credited with destroying 13 tanks and 38 AT guns. In the battles west of Kiev he eliminates tank after tank, on 21 November 1943 alone thirteen T-34s and seven AT guns (gunner with Wittmann that day). On 5 December he is awarded the EK I and promoted to *SS-Rottenführer*. When the bulk of the exausted *LSSAH* was entrained to Belgium for reorganization, one small group from the Tiger company under Wendorff remained in action near Proskurov. Warmbrunn is given command of his own Tiger, and during the fighting in the Hube pocket destroys 6 enemy tanks and several AT guns. Many anti-tank fronts have to be overcomed: on 7 April alone, at the Seret, his Tiger receives eleven hits. After the breakout, the rest of the company left, but Warmbrunn took his Tiger to *Frundsberg* with the task of training a new crew. On 16 April he supports an attack which crushes the Soviet bridgehead over the Strypa, north of Bučač, personally destroying a T-34 and a Sherman, and bringing his "kills" to 51. As the last member of the 13th company to return from the Soviet Union he joined the newly formed 2nd company, schwere SS-Panzer-Abteilung 501, under Wittmann. On June 1944 he was promoted to *SS-Unterscharführer*.

In Kharkov's Red Square, renamed "Platz der Leibstandarte" after the city was retaken. (Fourth from the right, gunner in the Tiger of *SS-Unterscharführer* Höld).

In France on the road to the front, in the forest of Versailles, commanders Warmbrunn, Woll, Höflinger and Seifert, shoot down an Allied fighter-bomber with their machine-guns on anti-aircraft mounts. On 17 July southwest of Caen, Warmbrunn eliminates 3 enemy tanks; the day after, in action against "Goodwood", he hits a Sherman exactly in the turret ring: the turret is blown straight up into the air. Shortly afterwards Wendorff climbs into the Tiger and Warmbrunn has to move to the gunner's position; he destroys a last Sherman, then as he's taking aim at another one, the Tiger is hit on the gun mantlet. The force of the impact drives the eyepiece of the telescopic sight into Warmbrunn's right eye. Suffering from double vision he is sent near Berlin for special treatment. Back to the battalion in late August, he is given a special mission. Two times, on the 21 (in a Schwimmwagen) and the 23 (with a truck and two men), he drives into partisan-dominated Paris retrieving important documents on the Tiger tank and other material, and also rescuing a German female agent. Still unfit for front-line service he would spend the remainder of the war in Schloß Holte. With most of the men of the battalion he was taken prisoner by the Americans in April. On the eastern front, as gunner he destroyed 44 tanks, 62 AT guns, two 122 mm guns, seven bunkers, ten flamethrowers and one armored car; as commander eight more tanks and six AT guns. During the relief of the Cherkassy pocket on 10 February 1943 he even shot down an Il-2 with machine gun fire. He may have been the youngest Tiger commander of the war. He never received the DKiG, nor was recommended for the RK.

Tiger commander in 1944.

258

Wegener Paul, born on 7 September 1920 in Berlin-Lichtenberg. *Wachtmeister* and StuG commander in the 1st company, Sturmgeschütz-Abteilung 237, he was particularly successful during the hard defensive fighting in the area of Smolensk in September 1943 (for example, on the 19 he destroyed one KV-1 and three T-34s). For the elimination of a total of over 40 enemy tanks he was awarded the Ritterkreuz on 18 October. Promoted to *Oberwachtmeister*, he was most probably posted as instructor in a Sturmgeschütz-Schule. He passed away on 5 July 1997 in his native city.

Weinert Konrad, born on 12 August 1920 in the village of Randsdorf (today Wieszowa), twenty-five kilometers northwest of Katowice. Early in the war he was awarded the EK II. He is killed in action near Znamianka (northeast of Kirovograd) on 3 December 1943 as *Leutnant* in the 3rd company, schwere Panzer-Abteilung 503 (Tiger number 311). Awarded posthumously the Deutsches Kreuz in Gold on 10 January 1944 for the destruction of 59 enemy armored vehicles.

Weißflog Hans-Joachim, born on 24 February 1923 in the small town of Lommatzsch (thirty-five kilometers northwest of Dresden). On December 1st 1940 he joined the Panzer-Regiment 1 of the 1.Panzer-Division. He took part in the invasion of the Soviet Union receiving the EK II on 14 November 1941. In June 1942 the I.Abteilung of Panzer-Regiment 1 was renamed Panzer-Abteilung 116 and transferred to the 16.Infanterie-Division (mot.), (later 16.Panzergrenadier-Division). With this unit he fought in the Caucasus and on the Mius, receiving the EK I on 31 July 1943. He then fought on the Donets, at Zaporizhia and in the battles of Krivoy Rog and Nikopol. In early 1944 the remnants of the battalion were finally sent to France for reorganization and conversion to the Panther tank. On 28 April 1944 Weißflog was awarded the Deutsches Kreuz in Gold, as *Leutnant* in the 2nd company of the newly formed I.Abteilung, Panzer-Regiment 16, 116.Panzer-Division. With the Panther he fought in Normandy and during the retreat to Germany.

During the Ardennes counteroffensive, on 26 December at 18:30 he was in position in the woods one kilometer north of Verdenne (half way between Bastogne and Namur). He is ordered to take the last 9 Panthers of his regiment to spearhead the breakout of Panzergrenadier-Regiment 60 towards friendly lines. In a swift advance they manage to crash through the fortified village of Marenne and exit to the other side without losses; here they are halted by AT gun fire and are ordered to bypass the enemy by moving through the woods south of Menil. Under enemy fire they approach the village, but the two lead Panthers are knocked out. With the kampfgruppe surrounded on all side, he orders his remaining panzers to advance towards the enemy positions on their right. Though the area is mined they manage to bull through and crush six AT guns. At this moment three US tanks appear on the left, however with his crew Weißflog is able to destroy them. With this, the kampfgruppe reaches safety while taking all the wounded with it. For this action he was promoted to *Oberleutnant* on January 1st 1945; then on 5 March for reaching a total of 47 enemy tanks destroyed he

was awarded the Ritterkreuz. At the end of the war after being wounded for the eleventh time he was captured by American troops and then transferred to Soviet custody. However he was later released because of the severity of his condition. He passed away on 11 August 1995.

Panther Ausf.G in the Ardennes.

Wendorff Helmut, born on 20 October 1920 in the village of Grauwinkel (seventy kilometers south of Berlin), the son of a farmer. In 1939 he graduated from the Napola in Naumburg, and on 4 September joined the *LSSAH*. In June 1940 he was assigned to the newly formed Sturmgeschütz battery as a *Sturmmann* and saw action in the Balkans and in "Barbarossa". On 14 September 1941 he was awarded the EK II and promoted to *SS-Oberscharführer*. On 1 November he was sent to the SS-Junkerschule in Bad Tölz, returning to the battalion in April 1942 as an *SS-Untersturmführer*. On December 1942 he was reassigned to the 13th Tiger company of the *LSSAH* in command of a platoon. He took part in the Manstein counterattack at Kharkov. He was wounded and put out of action on the first day of "Zitadelle". On 16 September he received the EK I.

In the battles west of Kiev he leads the 1st platoon. In November and December 1943, during the northward advance, he stands out for his bravery. He is now known in the Tiger unit as a daring commander -second only to the incomparable Wittmann- much loved by his men for his kindness and his sense of humor. On 27 December in the area of Korosten with his platoon of 4 Tigers he is instructed to intercept the enemy armoured spearheads and protect the division's withdrawal to the south. In ambush position he destroys two T-34s, he then drives into an enemy occupied village where he eliminates eleven more T-34s; after his return he is sent towards another advancing enemy force and destroys three more tanks; in the afternoon he stands fast at an important crossing point allowing the safe retreat of the units. The day after, with the remaining three Tigers put out of action, he drives alone and destroys once again eleven T-34s preventing the enemy from breaching the division's flank. His total of "kills" is now fifty-eight. On January 1st he destroys another five tanks. Promoted to *SS-Obersturmführer*, beginning of February 1944 he is in action in the relief of the Cherkassy pocket, and on the 12 of the same month he is awarded the Ritterkreuz. From 29 February to 9 April he would still lead a small group from the company in the area of Proskurov and Ternopol.

263

On the Invasion front, on 14 July 1944 he becomes the new commander of the 2nd company; the same day with three Tigers he attacks in the area of Maltot and destroys several Cromwells; on 18 July against "Goodwood" he destroys a Sherman (aboard Warmbrunn's tank). On 8 August he leads the attack which smashes the English bridgehead at Grimbosq: many AT guns and armoured vehicles are eliminated and prisoners taken; in the evening his crew destroys one more tank and an AT gun. On 12 August northeast of Falaise he destroys 7 Canadian tanks in the morning, few hours later he attacks again and destroys 8 more tanks plus many fuel trucks (gunner *SS-Rottenführer* Lau). He is killed in action on 14 August three kilometers west of Maizières, Calvados, when suddenly confronted by two Shermans in a bend of the road; the Tiger scores a direct hit on the first, but is knocked out by the second.

Notes. At the time of his death he had been credited with 84 enemy tank "kills", a figure which seems to be close to the truth. The recommendation for his Ritterkreuz reads that end of December 1943 his personal total had raised to fifty-eight. In the following battles of January-February he may have destroyed some ten tanks; then in Normandy at least another fifteen. W. Schneider's estimate of 95 "kills", without further clarification, is too high.

Kharkov, April 1943. On the left, with *SS-Obersturmführer* Schütz and *SS-Untersturmführer* Wittmann.

Witte Albert, born on 5 December 1916 in Münster. Early in the war he received both the EK II and EK I. In operation "Nordwind", during the fighting for Sessenheim, a unit of fallschirmjägern is pinned down by heavy fire outside the town. On his own initiative *Oberwachtmeister* Witte, platoon leader in the 1st company, Sturmgeschütz-Brigade 394, leads his assault guns forwards to engage the enemy AT guns and tanks, destroying several of them at close range. On 11 March 1945 he was awarded the Ritterkreuz and promoted to *Leutnant*. By the end of the war he had been credited with a personal total of 56 enemy tank "kills". He passed away on 11 February 2009, aged 92.

Wittmann Michael, born on 22 April 1914 in the Bavarian village of Vogelthal (thirty kilometers north of Ingolstadt and of the Danube), the son of a farmer. In late 1934, after six months into the Reichsarbeitsdienst, he volunteered for the German army. Two years later he left the service as *Unteroffizier*, but to re-enlist soon after in the SS. On April 1937 he was accepted in the 17.Kompanie of the élite *Leibstandarte SS Adolf Hitler* [from now *LSSAH*] with the rank of *SS-Mann*. Leaving Bavaria for the first time, he joined the company in training at the famous Lichterfelde Barracks in Berlin.

Promoted to *SS-Sturmmann* in November 1937, in March 1938 he became a member of the NSDAP; in April 1939 he was promoted -by two grades- to the rank of *SS-Unterscharführer*. He entered the war as leader of an armoured car in the Panzerspäh-Zug of the *LSSAH*, then in April 1940 he was transferred to the SS-Sturm-Batterie in command of a StuG III Ausf.A. In "Marita" with the assault gun battalion he took part notably in the crucial attack on the Klissura Pass.

During "Barbarossa" on 12 July 1941 north of Odessa he eliminates six T-34s in a single action (gunner *Sturmmann* Brüggenkamp, driver *Uscha* Fritz) and is presented with the EK II. On 8 September he is awarded the EK I for his actions in the crossing of the Dnieper and for the destruction of other enemy tanks and AT guns near Melitopol. Promoted to *SS-Oberscharführer*, from 4 June to 5 September 1942 he attended an officer candidate course at the SS-Junkerschule in Bad Tölz. On 21 December he was promoted to *SS-Untersturmführer* and 3 days later he joined the *LSSAH* Tiger company. He was in the light platoon, in command of a long barreled 50 mm gun Panzer III Ausf.J. The platoon was essentially a defensive screen for the Tigers against close range attack, offensive operations were secondary; even so Wittmann soon became a well-liked leader on account of his correct and reserved manners. In February and March 1943 the platoon remained in Poltava and didn't take part in the recapture of Kharkov. On 5 April new vehicles arrived and finally Wittmann became a Tiger commander at the head of the 3rd Zug within the new 13.Kompanie. His Tiger was designated number 1331, 13 for the company, 31 (in small) for the platoon and the position of platoon leader.

With his StuG Ausf.A, nicknamed "Bussard", in Russia, 1941.

"Zitadelle", 5 July. The Tigers under *SS-Hauptsturmführer* Kling have redied themselves on a broad plain. It is still dawn, in the sky the wall of smoke of the rocket salvoes is just subsiding and already the Stuka squadrons are making their appearance. At the same moment the panzers move off. Wittmann's Tiger (gunner *Sturmmann* Woll) is the first one to cross the antitank ditch that the panzergrenadiers have sized in the night and that the pioneers have just rendered passable maneuvering a T-34 into it. The Tigers deploy in inverted wedge formation, at hight speed, against an unprecedented anti-tank system protecting the large village of Bykovka. There are also many T-34s dug-in with only their turrets showing. Enormous quantity of ammunition are expended and the panzers have to pull back several times to rearm. By the evening Wittmann has knocked out eight tanks and seven AT guns. On the second day the Tiger company is to take the mined and heavily fortified position on Hill 243.2. On 7 July Teterevino is conquered amidst fierce Soviet counterattacks; Wittmann leads his platoon and destroys another 7 tanks (2 T-34s, 2 SU-122s, 3 T-60/70s), then he drives on a mine; the Tiger, immobilized with a wrecked right track, is hit in the front several times, another Tiger takes the crippled machine under tow and pulls it out of the line. The following days the Tigers are employed in support of a general attack of both *LSSAH* panzergrenadier regiments, firing H.E. rounds at the Soviet bunkers. It begins to rain heavily, many enemy guns and tanks are also destroyed; the attack is rolling and a breakthrough appears imminent.

On 11 July, under heavy thunderstorms the few serviceable Tigers join the advance; they destroy a very large numbers of T-34s and guns; Kling is severely wounded and Wittmann assumes command of the company. On 12 July, after *Totenkopf* has eliminated the flanking threat at the Psel, the *Leibstandarte* is to take the small town of Prokhorovka in a frontal assault with *Das Reich* in covering position to the right. The long-awaited tank battle takes place early in the morning when the Waffen-SS units, still in their assembly area, are surprised by waves of T-34s carring infantry and firing with all weapons. Hurriedly the Germans deploy in an all-round defence and in desperate combat -the intervention of the Luftwaffe proves crucial- manage to stop the Red Army soldiers who, in self-sacrificing attacks, are trying to ram the panzers and the Sd.Kfz. troop carriers. The four serviceable Tigers are in screening position and Wittmann (gunner *Uscha* Gräser that day) keeping manoeuvring destroys a number of tanks, engaging even the enemy artillery with long-range shots. On 13 July the *LSSAH* armoured group sets out to attack the hills north west of Oktyabrsky collective farm under heavy enemy artillery fire, Wittmann himself while taking a short walk -he is with Warmbrunn- is caught by a salvo from Katyusha rocket launchers and almost killed on the spot. The reinforced reconnaissance battalion enters the hamlet of Mikhailovka, on the Psel, but is expelled by an immense barrage from the hills. On 14 July heavy rain has completely softened the roads and rendered them impassable; the Tiger company has five serviceable tanks, they are to lead the attack on Iamki (at the southern outskirts of the town), but the SS-Panzerkorps decides not to carry on the advance when it becomes apparent that the enemy intends to cut off the salient held by the *Leibstandarte*. On 15 July there is strong enemy activity in the air, Soviet forces probe the German lines all day; the Tiger company guards the railway line, there is no combat. On 16 July the pressure on the German main line of resistence becomes untenable. The *Leibstandarte* helds the line Teterevino-Prokhorovka; after darkness falls the SS units begin to move into the area west of Belgorod. In all the *LSSAH* has eliminated 501 Soviet tanks by 14 July; the Tiger company has destroyed 151 enemy tanks, 87 heavy anti-tank guns and four batteries of artillery, as well as countless bunkers and field positions; it has lost five killed; not a single Tiger has to be written off as a total loss. Wittmann alone has destroyed thirty enemy tanks, twenty-eight AT guns and two batteries.

After a period spent in upper Italy in occupation duty and for reorganizing and training, in early November 1943 the *LSSAH* leaves again for the east. With its 27 Tigers (5 in each of the five platoons, 2 command tanks) the company possess now enormous striking power and represents an imposing force; the Tigers are also given new turret designations, the number 13 being replaced by the letter S for schwere. Wittmann is in command of the 2nd Zug with Tiger S21.

30 January 1944, Peiper (seen from behind) congratulates Wittmann and his crew.

On 15 November, west of Kiev, the Tigers move into position right in the tick of the Soviet advance, and the day after they are committed en masse in the attack northward towards Brusilov. Wittmann takes part in every action and has already destroyed a considerable number of enemy vehicles and guns in these first days. His tactics make him an example to the men; he favors stealth over open-field battles, most of his kills are the results of outflanking manoeuvres followed by a sudden approach. On the 21 he has a fever but nevertheless carries on. With Warmbrunn at the gunner's position he takes by surprise an entire Soviet armoured unit and destroys thirteen T-34s and seven anti-tank guns that day. After Brusilov is taken, the *LSSAH* proceeds with its action of encirclement and turns to the west. On muddy roads and difficult forest terrain the Tiger company leads the attack on Radomyshl. On 6 December as dawn is breaking, the Tigers deploy in wedge formation; they halt, fire, then move off again immediately as not to offer a stationary target. Several guns are destroyed by Wittmann together with entire columns of supply vehicles. The armoured group, under *SS-Sturmbannführer* Peiper, drives through several more positions; the command posts of four Red Army rifle divisions are overrun. Wittmann has knocked out three T-34s and destroyed an entire anti-tank front. On early December the attack has reached the area of Korosten, the Soviets had already been forced to evacuate the city and are now prevented from establishing a bridgehead over the Teterev. On 9 December Wittmann engages a group of twenty enemy tanks destroying six of them at extremely close quarters. In the middle of the month the German attempts to break through to Kiev are stopped, and on 24 December the enemy starts his own general offensive to the southwest. Until 5 January the *LSSAH* fights off enemy attacks north of Berdichev then redeploys to the south.

On 8 January Wittmann leads his panzer at maximum speed against an enemy incursion in Sherepki, he eliminates 3 tanks and an assault gun. On 9 January he is the first to make contact with the enemy destroying 6 tanks in rapid succession. On 10 January he is finally recommended by divisional commander *SS-Oberführer* Wisch for the prestigious Ritterkreuz after the destruction of 66 enemy AFVs since July 1943. The following days he engages the Soviet spearheads that have broken through the German positions and have blocked a main supply road. Over the 12th and 13th January alone he destroys sixteen T-34s and three assault guns. His score is now eighty-eight enemy tanks. The next day in a brief ceremony he is awarded the Ritterkreuz. Few hours later he destroys several more tanks in a general attack of the armoured kampfgruppe south of Zhytomyr that puts the Soviets in full flight. Just in the period between 5 December and 17 January the few serviceable Tigers of the company have eliminated 146 enemy AFVs and 125 AT guns. In furious counterattacks in the area of Vinnytsia lasting from 25 to 29 January Wittmann destroys additional vehicles and guns. In 22 days, since January 7, he has wiped out 61 tanks rising his final total as Tiger commander in the east to 117 "kills". On 30 January he is sent a telegram from Hitler's headquarters confirming the Eichenlaub to the Ritterkreuz. He would receive the award together with the promotion to the rank of *SS-Obersturmführer* personally from the Führer on 2 February 1944.

Michael and Hilde, 1 March 1944.

Wittmann is now a national hero, the living embodiment of the "last hope". His achievements obtained against overwehlming odds, are due to a unique combination of unsurpassed conscientiousness and personal courage. In the evening he sats in front of the map evaluating all the possibilities for the coming action, then he listens to the opinion of other experienced commanders; then, after much consideration he makes his decision. Before an attack he almost always drives forward to the crest of a hill in his tank to reconnoiter the enemy situation, then gives his orders. In the attack he is in the lead vehicle. Nothing was left to chance. As one of his men recalled: "It simply had to succeed and it did succeed".

April 1944, Wittmann speaks to workers involved in production of the Tiger. Henschel factory, Kassel.

He is now in command of the 2nd company of the newly formed schwere SS-Panzer-Abteilung 101. The battalion is assigned to the I.SS-Panzerkorps as a corps asset, never permanently attached to any division or regiment. From the end of April the company establishes itself in the Chateau Elbeuf, located between Rouen and Beauvais. The chateau is empty, save for the caretakers, with the surrounding woods offering excellent cover for the Tigers.

7 June 1944, 2nd company en route to Morgny. He is standing in the turret of Tiger 205.

By the night of 12-13 June, Wittmann has arrived at the front near Bayeux. In the morning he takes up position with only half a dozen serviceable Tigers on the Villers-Bocage ridge, close to the Vire-Caen road. The Allies are about to launch a massive thrust with the aim of outflanking both *Panzer-Lehr* and *Hitlerjugend* panzer divisions. On the morning of 13 June, the available *LSSAH* panzer unit commanders are with Sepp Dietrich to discuss the plan of action. Wittmann suggests that his Tigers carry out a proper reconnaissance of the area. He sets out towards Villers-Bocage at around 06:00 moving alongside a wooded area south of the Route Nationale 175. Some 150 meters from Hill 213 he's informed by a Wehrmacht Unteroffizier of the presence of a large number of unfamiliar vehicles in the vicinity. He then spotts what looks like a never-ending convoy of British and American type vehicles casually rolling along the highway, heading out towards Villers-Bocage: it is the lead element of the 22nd Armoured Brigade of the highly-trained British 7th Armoured Division. With his own command Tiger out of commission he sprints at the closest available one (probably Tiger 222). By chance his gunner that day may have been Woll, his driver *Uscha* Müller. Wittmann orders all the remaining Tigers to stay in position. The time is now 08:35 and he goes on the attack. First he destroys a stationary Cromwell and a Sherman Firefly at the rear of the advanced column in order to prevent any retreat by the remaining vehicles, afterwards he continues parallel to the road towards Villers-Bocage. He demolishes the majority of the 1st Rifle Brigade: along the road eight M5 half-tracks, four carriers and three M3 Stuart light tanks; on the edge of the town three Cromwells of the regimental headquarters, the scout car of the Intelligence Officer, the M5 half-track of the Brigade surgeon and another carrier, followed by two artillery observer tanks (a Cromwell and a Sherman). The vehicles burst into flames as their fuel tanks are ruptured by machine gun and high explosive fire. In the town centre he duels briefly without success with a Firefly, then he turns around and rushes back. Another Cromwell, whose two armor-piercing rounds fired at short distance failed to penetrate the panzer, is destroyed. Finally the Tiger is immobilized by an AT gun hit on the left front drive sprocket. The crew bails out and sneaks throught to the command post of the *Panzer-Lehr*, some seven kilometers to the north. Few days later, on 16 June in the Forest of Grimbosq, Wittmann may have destroyed at least another English tank. On 22 June he is awarded the Schwertern to the Ritterkreuz and promoted to *SS-Hauptsturmführer* (the award is presented on 29 June at Berchtesgaden). He was given a post of instructor, but he did not abandon his men and was back to Normandy in July as commander of the entire Abteilung.

On 8 August the Allies would launch "Totalize", an outbreak from Caen with the aim of sealing the pocket in the area around Falaise. Wittmann's eight serviceable Tigers are attached to the 12.SS-Panzer-Division Hitlerjugend. They are earmarked to push forward towards the village of Cintheaux, which stood on the RN 158 between Caen and Falaise, and to win back the heights to the north from the British and Canadian units. In the early afternoon he meets *Hitlerjugend* commander *SS-Oberführer* Meyer, then for the last time he climbs aboard. Meyer: "...we observed a lone bomber flying over us a couple of times dropping flares. It seemed to us that it was some sort of flying command post and I ordered an immediate attack to get the units out of the bombing zone.". The attack sees Wittmann (turret number 007) move north on the right side of the RN 158 out of Cintheaux. Suddenly the Tigers are hit by flanking fire; from the west by a Sherman Firefly belonging to the 27th Canadian Armoured Regiment (the Sherbrooke Fusiliers) which has positioned itself in the hamlet of Gaumesnil; from the opposite side by another Firefly from a squadron of the British 1st Northants Yeomanry. Wittmann's Tiger is immobilized but apparently still intact, no one bails out. Then there is a blaze, followed by an internal explosion which blows the turret clean out of the hull. After the battle the bodies were hastily buried by local civilians. In 1983 he and his crew were reinterred together at the Soldatenfriedhof at La Cambe.

Notes. In "Zitadelle" he destroyed 30 tanks; in the offensive phase of the counterattack west of Kiev at least 22 (on 9 December he reached 56 and was proposed for the Ritterkreuz); and 61 in the defensive phase up to 29 January 1944. On 29 January he was officialy credited with 117, but for this figure 4 kills are lacking. These 4 kills cannot be the 7+ StuG ones. They were probably additional kills he made in November 1943 in the early days of the counterattack. - The destruction of an English tank on 16 June was reported by *SS-Hauptscharführer* Menninger of the Kurt Eggers SS propaganda unit, who in those days had joined the crew of Wittmann's panzer (in Agde, "Michael Wittmann").

13 June, after Villers-Bocage.

Wolf Walter, born on 7 February 1919 in the village of Steinpleis (eight kilometers west of Zwickau). He joined the Wehrmacht in November 1937 and took part in the Poland campaign as divisional messenger. Promoted to *Feldwebel* he fought in the battle of France as gunner in a Panzer IV in the 8th company, Panzer-Regiment 35, 4.Panzer-Division (according to another version he was already in command of a Panzer III). In Sedan he destroyed an AT gun, and soon after two French tanks at close range: a H39 and a B1; in Béthune 3 British tanks and 5 AT guns. On 24 August 1940 he received the EK II. During "Barbarossa" he knocked out several AT guns and a T-34 in Orel, and a KV-1 and three T-34s in Mtsensk. In February 1942 in the area of Bryansk he took command of his own Panzer IV. In June, in view of the offensive towards Voronezh, the II.Abteilung was transferred to the 11.Panzer-Division, becoming the III.Abteilung of Panzer-Regiment 15. On 27 August, positioned on a narrow forest lane, he destroyed six T-34s and the following day was awarded the EK I. At the beginning of December near Surovikino on the Chir river, during a three days battle he wiped out a KV-1, six T-34s, two light tanks and seven 76-mm guns. On the 25 January 1943 he led the attack against the village of Manychskaya (on the Don, east of Rostov) personally destroying a KV-1, three T-34s and seven AT guns. On the 8 February he succeeds in eliminating three T-34s that had broken through; when his panzer is disabled by a direct hit he dismounts carrying the severely wounded gunner, then still under enemy fire he goes back to rescue the driver. Promoted to *Oberfeldwebel* he fought in operation "Zitadelle" as platoon leader in the 9th company, being credited with 11 enemy tanks. With over 40 tank "kills", on 13 August 1943 he was awarded the Deutsches Kreuz in Gold.

In late September 1943 the III.Abteilung was returned to its old 4.Panzer-Division, becoming the I.Abteilung, Panzer-Regiment 35, equipped with Panther tanks; Wolf was platoon leader in the 4th company. On 14-18 September 1944 in the battle around Doblen (Dobele) in central Latvia, he is able to capture the key position of Hill 92, however on the last day he is killed by a Soviet sniper. He was credited with a total of 52 enemy tanks and on 16 October was posthumously awarded the Ritterkreuz.

Woll Balthasar, born on the 1st of September 1922 in the village of Wettemsweiler (fifteen kilometers north of Saarbrücken), the son of a worker. He qualified as an electrician before volunteering for the Waffen-SS on 15 August 1941. During "Barbarossa" he fought in the Demyansk pocket as a *MG-Schütze* in the 3rd company, SS-Totenkopf-Infanterie-Regiment 1. He was severely wounded there and evacuated to a hospital in Germany. Promoted to *SS-Oberschütze* he received the EK II on 23 July 1942 and trained as a tank gunner. In late 1942 he was assigned to the Tiger company of the *LSSAH*. He took part in the counterstroke at Kharkov in March, then he become the gunner in Wittmann's Tiger. After "Zitadelle" he was awarded the EK I on 14 October 1943 and promoted to *SS-Rottenführer* on 9 November. By the end of January 1944 he had eliminated 80 tanks, 107 AT guns, 2 artillery batteries, five flamethrowers, a heavy mortar position, two prime movers and one armored car. On 16 January he received the Ritterkreuz, the first gunner in the entire panzer arm to be awarded the high decoration. Woll used a simplified firing tecnique: the range setting on his telescopic sight remained set at 800 meters even when the target was farther away or closer; this shortened preparations to fire, but required the gunner to be able to make the necessary adjustments, aiming high or low, almost by instinct. In France Woll, now *SS-Unterscharführer*, was assigned his own Tiger in Wittmann's 2nd company. During the transfer to the front his Tiger got damaged and he may easily have been the gunner of Wittmann in Villers-Bocage. Few days later, on 16 June still as gunner he may have destroyed at least another English tank. The same day during an enemy artillery barrage he gets to his feet as if to leave cover, Wittmann just manages to catch him. Suffering from an old head wound and great mental strain he is taken to hospital and from there to Germany. On October 1st he was promoted to *SS-Oberscharführer*, however he would not return to Normandy. For the rest of the war he remained in Schloß Holte (few kilometers south of Bielefeld), the support base of the battalion, training recruits. After the war he worked as electrician. He passed away on 18 March 1996.

Tiger commander in Normandy.

Zillmann Erich, born on 10 January 1912 in the village of Kuschten (today Kosieczyn), one hundred and seventy kilometers east of Berlin. He fought in southern Russia and received the EK II on 30 November 1941 followed by the EK I on 20 August 1942. On 23 February 1944 he was awarded the Deutsches Kreuz in Gold as *Stabswachtmeister* in the 3rd battery, Sturmgeschütz-Abteilung 245 (later redesignated Sturmgeschütz-Brigade 245). In August 1944, northeast of Vilnius the 252.Infanterie-Division finds itself unexpectedly with its southern flank exposed, with the Soviets advancing towards the rear. Zillmann, now platoon leader, is sent with his assault guns and an attached pioneer platoon to stop them and permit the division to retreat. Upon contact he destroys 3 AT guns, then when the enemy attempts to bypass his small kampfgruppe with about 2 companies, he launches his own attack into their flank putting them to flight. The next day around noon seven Soviet tanks with limbered AT guns in tow succeed in reaching and cutting off the division's escape route. Zillmann quickly counterattacks and with his platoon destroys 4 tanks as well as 2 AT guns that were trying to deploy. He is thus awarded the Ritterkreuz on 8 August. He was credited with a total of 48 tank "kills". He passed away on 9 August 1986.

StuG III of Sturmgeschütz-Abteilung 245 next to a captured Soviet SU-152 self-propelled heavy howitzer, 1943.

Zitzen Kurt, born on 25 March 1916 in the small town of Lobberich (thirty-five kilometers northwest of Düsseldorf). He took part in the invasion of the Soviet Union and was awarded the EK II on 21 October 1941 and the EK I on 19 January 1942. In 1943, during operation "Zitadelle" he was *Oberleutnant der Reserve* and leader of the 2nd battery, Sturmgeschütz-Abteilung 177. On 10 July his unit was in action near Ponyri. In the late afternoon, with five assault guns he moves forward against an enemy assembly area in front of German lines. While he is advancing he notices 30 Soviet tanks assembling in the area as well; he withdraws and sets up ambush positions in the anticipation of their attack. Sure enough shortly after dusk the Soviets rolled forward. He waits until these tanks are only 200 meters away before giving the order to open fire. In a furious firefight at ranges as little as 30 meters, 15 tanks are destroyed -6 of them personally by Zitzen- and 4 more immobilized. For this important local success he was awarded the Ritterkreuz on 4 August 1943. Promoted to *Hauptmann* he was captured in September 1944 by Soviet troops and held until 1953. He was credited with a total of 22 tank "kills". He passed away on 24 August 1993.

APPENDICES

Misinterpreted or dubious or inexplicable number of kills.

Arndt Ernst August. *Leutnant* and platoon leader in the 1/Panther-Sperber-Kompanie, II./Panzer-Regiment "Müncheberg" (former I./Panzer-Regiment 29). According to a post-war account this infrared panther, turret number 121, destroyed 48 Soviet tanks from 16 April to 2 May 1945 (gunner Leo Tyma; from 20 to 24 April the vehicle was under the command of another soldier). Arndt may have been awarded the EK I, he received no higher decorations.

Giesen Arno. A mysterious "ace" usually credited with 111 enemy tanks destroyed. His name appeared in "The Defense of the Vienna Bridgehead", an article published by Armor Magazine, January-February 1986. According to that story *Ostuf*. Giesen was a Panther tank commander and Ritterkreuz recipient. He had 97 "kills" by 12 April 1945, scoring 14 more on the next day, for a total of 111. Unfortunately there is no document, no record giving him a position as a commander or gunner in "Das Reich" Tiger or Panther units. No soldier with that name has ever received the RK or the DKiG. Historian D. Nash provides a convincing argument: Arno Giesen was infact Arno Friesen, an *SS-Fahnenjunker*, actually an officer cadet, who really did serve in SS-Pz.Rgt 2 "Das Reich" during the battle for Vienna. After the war he settled in the US and changed his name to avoid close scrutiny.

Junge Walter. Sometimes credited with over 57 "kills". In late 1942 he joined the newly formed schwere Panzer-Abteilung 503 as *Gefreiter* and gunner in Panzer III Ausf.N of *Leutnant* Jammerath, the commander of the 1st company's light platoon. From the end of April 1943 the companies would be equipped exclusively with Tigers. From August 1944 onwards he was gunner or commander in the 3rd company (a known wartime photo shows him in Sailly, northwest of Paris, in front of Tiger II turret number 301). He didn't receive any high awards.

Kauerauf Friedrich-Wilhelm "Fritz". Born in Berlin-Neukölln on July 1st 1922. Promoted to *SS-Untersturmführer* on September 1st 1944, in 1945 he joined the 1st company, schwere SS-Panzer-Abteilung 503. He is sometimes credited with 28 tank "kills", however his higher award was probably the EK II. On 2 February in Pomerania he was seriously wounded when his panzer was hit near Klein Silber. Severe burns, his left leg amputated. He passed away on 18 November 1987.

Klaucke Werner. On the Invasion front he was platoon leader in the 3rd company, Panzer-Jäger-Abteilung 200, and under his command 29 British tanks were destroyed in the area of Caen. *Leutnant der Reserve*, he was awarded the Ritterkreuz on 4 July 1944; he was killed on 14 September near Epinal. He is usually credited with a personal total 29 tank kills, but this figure is obviously a misunderstanding. Previously he had been awarded both classes of the EK. His real number of kills is unknown.

Knecht Walter. *SS-Oberscharführer* in schwere Panzer-Abteilung 102, he is sometimes credited with 51+ "kills". This figure derives from a misinterpretation of a wartime photo which shows his Tiger, turret number 132, with 51 kill rings. However this was the total number of enemy tanks eliminated in Normandy by the whole company. In Normandy he may have destroyed some 5-10 tanks (gunner *SS-Rottenführer* Rudolf Wuester) and in total some 10-20 tanks. *SS-Unterscharführer* Ernst Glagow (usually also credited with the same 51+ "kills"!) may have been also in command of Tiger 132.

Kniep Walter. His name appears in a number of "panzer aces" lists, credited with 129 "kills"; however this number has a different explanation. On 15 November 1941, as *Hauptsturmführer* in the 3rd company of SS-Regiment "Der Führer", he was awarded the DKiG, the first member of the division to be so honoured; then he went on to command the III.Bataillon, SS-Regiment "Deutschland". In 1942 he took over command of the SS-Sturmgeschütz-Abteilung 2. On 8 July, on his own initiative he decided to gather together the already engaged three batteries of his unit; from an assembly area to the rear he then moved out against an attacking enemy force of about 170 tanks. In the ensuing four hours battle his Sturmgeschütze destroyed 51 enemy tanks (5 by him and his crew) for the loss of just one of their own. In all during "Zitadelle" and up to 17 July the Abteilung was able to eliminate 129 enemy tanks for the loss of only two vehicles. On 14 August 1943 *SS-Sturmbannführer* Kniep was awarded the Ritterkreuz. In 1944 he was given command of the SS-Sturmgeschütz-Abteilung 17 of the newly formed 17.SS-Panzer-Grenadier-Division "Götz von Berlichingen". He died on 22 April 1944 at Thouars, France, from the accidental discharge of his pistol during target practice.

Krönke Horst. He was assigned to Panzer-Regiment 6, 3.Panzer-Division and experienced the opening of the war in Russia. He was in action on the eastern front through the end of 1942, at which time he was sent back to Germany to attend officer cadet and then officer's schools. Upon his return to the front to Panzer-Regiment 6 he was incorporated into schwere Panzer-Abteilung 503. He was introduced to the new Tiger tank, then transferred to schwere Panzer-Abteilung 505 in command of a Tiger II (turret number 124) serving until the end of the war with the rank of *Leutnant*. However he didn't receive any high award; W. Schneider in "Tigers in Combat I" doesn't speak of him. His name appears in several lists credited with 50 "kills"; this figure seems to come from a book about his war experience in which he simply mentioned a total of 50 tank kills, but without telling nothing about any engagements.

Lang Fritz. Usually credited with 113 enemy tanks destroyed as StuG III commander on the eastern front. He allegedly ended the war as *Wachtmeister* and platoon leader in the 3rd battery of Sturmgeschütz-Brigade 232. He didn't get the Ritterkreuz, neither the DKiG, so the 113 "kills" seem to be a fabrication. Here too it can be assumed that some overall score of his unit was associated with his name only. However he received a rare award, the Anerkennungsurkunde des Oberbefehlshabers des Heeres, a certificate of particular appreciation for prominent achievements on the battlefield. Nothing else is known about this soldier.

Lobmeyer Jacob. Credited with 50+ kills as StuG III and Hetzer commander. Early in the war he received the EK II and EK I. In early 1945, as *SS-Hauptsturmführer* he was given command of a StuG batterie, but this unit was combined with other elements on the Oder front, redesignated SS-Panzerjäger-Abteilung 561 (in part because it actually used Hetzers) and assigned to V.SS-Freiwilligen-Gebirgskorps [according to other versions the unit's designation was SS-Jäger-Panzerabteilung 561 or SS-Jagd-Panzer-Abteilung 561]. He is supposed to have been awarded the RK on 28 April 1945; he may have received a lawful presentation via the Heerespersonalamt or a direct presentation from Hitler, however no evidence can be found in the German Federal Archives. In his later years he also claimed to have received the DKiG as well as the Eichenlaub (!) on 2 May.

Lochmann Franz-Wilhelm. Sometimes credited with destroying over 75 enemy tanks. This figure stems from a misunderstanding: in 1945 he received the Panzerkampfabzeichen (panzer badge) Stufe "75" for taking part in 75 separate armoured engagements. *Unteroffizier* in the 1st company, schwere Panzer-Abteilung 503, he was the driver and/or radio operator of the company commander's Tiger. His higher award may have been the EK I.

Luithle Emil. In 1944 he was *Oberfeldwebel* in the 5th company, Panzer-Regiment "Großdeutschland", Panzergrenadier-Division "Großdeutschland". His name is usually associated with the destruction of over 70 enemy tanks. Nothing is known of his actions as Panzer IV commander; his higher award was the EK I. He also received the rare Anerkennungsurkunde des Oberbefehlshabers des Heeres.

Ludwig Hubert. He is sometimes credited with over 70 tank "kills". In one day alone, in September 1943, as *SS-Unterscharführer* in the 2nd company, SS-Panzer-Regiment 2, in command of Panther 335, he allegedly destroyed 23 enemy tanks near the village of Kolomak (seventy kilometers west of Kharkov). For this feat he was promoted to *Oberscharführer* receiving (or being recommended for) the DKiG by *SS-Sturmbannführer* Weiss on 17 December 1943. He was then killed in action in Normandy near Perrières on 28 July 1944. Nothing else is known about him, and in fact he was never awarded the DKiG. According to another version he served with *Wiking*, in the 5th company, SS-Panzergrenadier-Regiment 10 "Westland" and died from wounds on 3 October 1943 in southern Ukraine.

Möbius Rudolf "Rolf". Usually credited with destroying 125 (!) enemy AFVs.

He had been awarded the DKiG on 28 March 1943 as *SS-Hauptsturmführer* in the Flak-Abteilung "LSSAH". In November 1943 he joined the Tiger battalion, in command of the headquarters company. In early 1944, during the reorganization in Belgium, he assumed command of the 1st company. In November, in view of "Wacht am Rhein", he was transferred to the 2nd company of the now renamed schwere SS-Panzer-Abteilung 501. He personally destroyed around 8 tanks in Normandy and at least one tank in the Ardennes. "125" was possibly the total number of enemy tank "kills" credited to the whole 1st company in the fighting in Normandy.

Oberhuber ? . In several lists he is credited with the destruction of 127 (!) enemy tanks. He served in the 2nd company, schwere SS-Panzer-Abteilung 102. He is mentioned by Schneider (Tigers in Combat II): "18 July 1944 … Tiger 224 [sic] of *SS-Unterscharführer* Oberhuber knocks out three tanks and one antitank gun."; "25 July 1944 … Tiger 222 of *SS-Unterscharführer* Oberhuber is hit; the radio operator is killed."; "26 July 1944 … Tiger 222 … is knocked out by antitank-gun fire from the flank.". He destroyed at least another tank on 19 August in Trun-Vimoutiers. According to the Wehrmachtbericht of 8 October 1944 the entire Abteilung destroyed "227" tanks from 10 July to 20 August. Maybe by mistake "227" became "127", and then this wrong figure was somewhat attributed to this single commander of the 2nd company.

Ohler Kurt. Sometimes credited with destroying 47 enemy tanks. However he never received the Ritterkreuz, nor the DKiG. Little is known about him. *Unteroffizier* in the Sturmgeschütz-Abteilung 270, in September 1943 he was assigned to the 1st company of the Skijäger-Brigade. When the latter was upgraded to 1.Skijäger-Division in June 1944, his unit was renamed Panzerjäger-Abteilung 152. He may have fought in the central sector of the eastern front, then in Slovakia, and finally in Southern Poland and Upper Silesia.

Sametreiter Kurt. Usually and erroneously credited with 24 "kills". In "Zitadelle" he was *Oberscharführer* and platoon leader in the 3rd company, SS-Panzerjäger-Abteilung LSSAH. On 12 July 1943, south of Prokorhovka, he advanced with his 4 self-propelled 7.5 cm guns against the enemy which was attacking out of "Storostrowoje" (actually Storozhevoye) with around 40 tanks. The German vehicles drove past the outermost friendly lines continuously shooting at the enemy for over an hour and destroying in the end 24 tanks. For this action he was awarded the Ritterkreuz on 31 July 1943. His real personal total achieved during the course of the war is unknown.

Sandrock Hans. He is usually credited with 123 (!) "kills". But here again, this is nothing but the overall number of enemy tanks destroyed by the whole Abteilung under his command during the fighting north of Radom in August 1944. He fought in the Poland campaign as *Oberleutnant* and platoon leader in the 2nd company, Panzer-Regiment 5, receiving the EK II. During the Battle of

France he was in command of a tank. In late 1940 Panzer-Regiment 5 was removed from the 3.Panzer-Division and attached to the 5.leichte Division as part of the DAK; in the summer of 1942 it was reformed within the 21.Panzer-Division. During his service in North Africa Sandrock was awarded the EK I, then the DKiG on June 1st 1942, as *Hauptmann* in the I.Abteilung. In El Alamein he was severely wounded and then evacuated to Germany. In July 1943 he joined the Fallschirm-Panzer-Division 1 Hermann Göring in a Sturmgeschütz detachment which was employed in many major battles in Italy. In June 1944 the division moved to Poland. On 18 October 1944 Sandrock was awarded the Ritterkreuz as *Major* and commander of the III.Abteilung, Fallschirm-Panzer-Regiment Hermann Göring. In April 1945 after being wounded he was posted to the regiment's reserve detachment; from there he made his way west, surrendering to US forces. During the war he took part in over 50 separate armored engagements, however the number of tanks destroyed by him is unknown.

Scholz Paul (or Hans-Joachim). He commanded a Tiger I of schwere Panzer-Abteilung 505, and is credited in several lists with destroying no less than 46 Soviet tanks. However he didn't receive any high award. In a book titled "Tiger I on the Eastern Front" by author J. Restayn, it is stated that from 3 to 10 February 1944, during the fighting in Toporino sector, the Tiger of *Leutnant* Scholz, 2nd company, took part in the destruction of 46 T-34s. W. Schneider (Tigers in Combat I) writes for 3 February: "... Tigers 200 and 213 (Leutnant Scholz) bring enemy attacks to a halt near Ssubadschewa.".

Schroif Martin. The mysterious *SS-Untersturmführer* Schroif is credited in a number of "panzer aces" listings with 161(!) -sometimes 127- "kills". In Normandy he was leader of the first platoon in the 2nd company, schwere SS-Panzer-Abteilung 102 "Das Reich", and he may have destroyed 14 tanks. On 19 August his Tiger 241 was set on fire by two AT gun hits. In early March 1945, in command of a Tiger II he fought on the Oder with the 2nd company, in the "502". On 21 April his Tiger II was knocked out west of Seelow after having eliminated several Soviet tanks. There is not even certainty about his name; sometimes he is called Walter, maybe making confusion with Walter Scherf, chief of the 3./schwere Panzer-Abteilung 503. W. Schneider in his books on the Tigers doesn't mention Schroif as one of the top scorers. No soldier with that name has ever received the Ritterkreuz. One can guess that in some post-war publications, by mistake, some overall score of his unit was associated with his name only.

Warnick Heinrich. In a number of lists he is credited with destroying 77 tanks (and 44 guns). He was *SS-Oberscharführer* and Panther commander in the 3rd company, SS-Panzer-Regiment 2 "Das Reich". Later he joined the Tiger Abteilung (Tiger I, turret numbers 812 and 833). His higher award was the EK I; nothing more is known of him.

Pending Biographies.

Altmann Karl, born in 1909 in Babkowitz (1939-1945 Frauendorf, today Babkowice), bezirk Posen. *Gefreiter* and gunner in the 3./Panzerjäger-Abteilung 160 of the 60.Infanterie-Division (mot.), he was awarded the Deutsches Kreuz in Gold on 18 October 1942. *Unteroffizier* and gunner of a Jagdpanther (*Feldwebel* Faltinski) in Kampfgruppe Feldherrnhalle 14/XX, on 4 March 1945 fighting in the sector of the 35.Infanterie-Division (in the Danzig pocket) he destroyed 8 tanks, reaching a personal total of 42 (or 37) kills.

Bauer Ludwig (1923-2020). Awarded the Ritterkreuz on 29 April 1945 as a *Leutnant* in command of the 1st company, Panzer-Regiment 33, 9.Panzer-Division. In "Barbarossa" he operated a Panzer II, in 1942/43 he was given command of a Panzer III, and in early 1944 of a Panzer IV. He took part in the Ardennes offensive with a StuG III, and by the end of the war he had transitioned to the Panther. He received the second level of the Panzerkampfabzeichen (for 25 separate armoured engagements) and was severely wounded seven times, managing to bail out nine times of a burning panzer. He may have destroyed no less than thirty enemy tanks.

Beise Walter, born in 1918. As an *Unteroffizier* with 1./Sturmgeschütz-Abteilung 197 he got the EK II on 13.7.1941 and the EK I on 31.10.1941. Promoted to *Leutnant* he was transferred to the Sturmgeschütz-Abteilung 904 in command of the 1st (or the 2nd) battery. In one action on September 1st 1943 he destroyed 6 tanks for his 42nd kill. He was awarded the Deutsches Kreuz in Gold on 25 October 1943. Fate unknown.

Beloch Ernst. Awarded the DKiG on 19 October 1944 as *Feldwebel* in the 2nd company, schwere Panzer-Abteilung 509 (turret number 212). Allegedly credited with 103 "kills" (probably tanks, vehicles and guns combined. W. Schneider in "Tigers in Combat I" doesn't mention him as one of the abteilung's top scorers). He was killed in late 1944.

Beutler Walter (1914-1995). *Oberwachtmeister* in the 3./Sturmgeschütz-Abteilung 245, on the 9 and 10 August 1943 he destroyed 14 Soviet tanks enabling the 260.Infanterie-Division to stabilize its frontline situation. He was thus awarded the RK on 13 August. Previously he had received both classes of the EK. In 1944 he fought as platoon leader in the Sturmgeschütz-Brigade 667.

Bleyer Werner, born in 1920. He scored his first successes with a Marder in the 3./Panzerjäger-Abteilung 616. In January 1945 this company was equipped with Jagdpanthers and subordinated to the 4th company of the schwere Heeres-Panzerjäger-Abteilung 563. In February in East Prussia, in three days of combat to the north of Mehlsack (today Pieniężno) in support of the 131.Infanterie-Division, *Feldwebel* and zugführer Bleyer reportedly knocked out 33 enemy T-34s. For this feat and for reaching a total of 49 tank "kills" he received the

Ritterkreuz on 24 February. He was killed four days later near Wormditt (today Orneta).

Bloos Ludwig (1915-1991). *Oberfeldwebel* and platoon leader in the 8th company, Panzer-Regiment 11, 6.Panzer-Division, he was awarded the DKiG on 9 June 1943 followed by the Ritterkreuz on 6 April 1944. On 5 March 1944 during the battle of the Kamenets-Podolsky pocket, in one action with his Panzer IV he had personally destroyed seven T-34s. He scored at least two more tanks on 30 October. Final total likely to exceed 30. After the war he joined the Bundeswehr reaching the rank of *Hauptfeldwebel.*

Burmester Hans-Jürgen (1916-1998). Awarded the EK I in May 1942 as panzer commander in the 23.Panzer-Division; the DKiG in August 1943 as company commander in the s.Pz.Abt 503; the RK in September 1944 as *Hauptmann* and commander of the s.Pz.Abt 509. In August 1944 he received the Panzerkampfabzeichen Stufe "50". His total of tank kills is unknown.

Buss Wilhelm (1918-1991). Awarded the Ritterkreuz in December 1944 as *Oberfeldwebel* in Panzer-Regiment 31. He had been panzer commander in the same unit since the start of the invasion of the Soviet Union and had already received the EK I in july 1942. He was recipient of the Panzerkampfabzeichen Stufe "50".

Dehmel Ernst, born in 1915. Awarded the Ritterkreuz on 15 August 1943 as *SS-Hauptsturmführer* and acting commander of SS-Sturmgeschütz-Abteilung 3 "Totenkopf". In a single action on the Psel on the 11 July, his unit destroyed 25 tanks; later a renewed enemy attack was crushed with the loss of a further 22 T-34s. His final personal score is unknown. He was beaten to death on 7 August 1945 by French soldiers.

Düe Rolf (1915-2005). After a course at the Kriegsoffizier-Lehrgang, Panzertruppenschule Wünsdorf, in June 1940 he joined the Panzerjäger-Abteilung 19 of the 19.Panzer-Division. He would fight with this unit on the eastern front until the very end of the war. He received the EK II on 21 July 1941 and the EK I on 5 November 1943 as an *Oberleutnant* and chief of the 1.Kompanie (probably Marder IIIs). Promoted to *Hauptmann*, in mid February 1945 with his company (by this time probably equipped with Jagdpanzer IVs) he held the village of Wernersdorf, Lower Silesia, for three days inflicting heavy losses (including around twenty-four T-34s) and preventing an enemy breakthrough towards Schweidznitz that would have led to a catastrophe for the XVII.Armeekorps. On 23 March he was awarded the Ritterkreuz. Already in command of the whole Abteilung, on 20 April he obtained the fourth level of the Panzerkampfabzeichen for the participation in over 75 separate armoured engagements. Personal total of tank "kills" unknown.

Engel Heinrich (1914-2004). *Unteroffizier der Reserve* in the 2nd battery,

Sturmgeschütz-Abteilung 259, on the 8 September 1943, southeast of Stalino, he personally destroyed 16 enemy tanks. For this feat, on 2 November he was awarded the Ritterkreuz. He had taken part in the French campaign and in "Barbarossa" as assault-gun driver in the Sturmgeschütz-Batterie 660, one of the first three assault-gun batteries created by the German Army. In 1942 health problems removed him from the front line. After the RK he returned to Germany due to continued problems with sciatica and spent the remainder of the war serving with various training units. Last rank *Wachtmeister*.

Eysser Oskar (1911-1959). He took part in the Polish campaign and in the Battle of France, being awarded the EK II on 27 November 1939 and the EK I on 6 September 1940. As *Leutnant* in the 3rd company, Panzer-Regiment 31, 5.Panzer-Division he received the Deutsches Kreuz in Gold on 13 May 1942. Promoted to *Hauptmann* and in command of the company he distinguished himself in the defensive battles north of Memel in October 1944, where his 15 Panthers destroyed a total of 173 enemy tanks. For his leadership he received the Ritterkreuz on 3 November. His personal total of tank "kills" should be well above 20.

Fechtel Walter (?-?). *Wachtmeister* in the 3rd battery, Sturmgeschütz-Abteilung 189, he was awarded the Deutsches Kreuz in Gold on 9 April 1943. On 27 April 1945, while serving as *Oberfeldwebel* in the 2./Panzerjäger-Abteilung 70, 4.Kavallerie-Division, he got the fourth level of the Panzerkampfabzeichen for the participation in 75 separate armoured engagements (!). Personal total of tank kills unknown.

Feldheim Hermann, born in 1919. *Leutnant* in schwere Panzerjäger-Abteilung 654, in the battle of Kursk with his Ferdinand he was credited with destroying 16 enemy tanks. In 1944 with his battalion he transitioned to the Jagdpanther. In the west he achieved further success (at least 2 tank kills) and on 20 January 1945 was awarded the DKiG. Credited with another tank kill in April 1945.

Fendesack Hans, born in 1914. *Oberfeldwebel* in the 1st company, schwere Panzer-Abteilung 503, on 7 October 1943 he was awarded the DKiG. During the employement within Kampfgruppe Bäke, in early February 1944 in two separate actions he claimed 18+ and 24 tanks respectively. After reaching a personal total of 86 "Abschüsse" (likely tanks and AT guns combined) he was proposed for the RK but received instead the Ehrenblattspange. He was a close friend of Knispel. He fell on 16 August 1944 in France.

Fiebig Erich Walter (1913-2000). Credited with destroying over 50 tanks. In Russia he received the EK II and the EK I. In 1944 he fought in the area of Tarnopol, and on 30 September was awarded the DKiG, as *Wachtmeister* in the 1st battery, Sturmgeschütz-Brigade 301. His last name is sometimes mispelled as Feibig. With 50+ tank "kills" in a StuG, he would have largely obtained the Ritterkreuz; probably it was all vehicles and guns combined.

Fischer Hans (1922-2005). *SS-Oberscharführer* in the 2.Kompanie, SS-Panzer-Regiment 5, SS-Panzer-Division "Wiking", he was awarded the Deutsches Kreuz in Gold on 28 February 1945. By the end of the war he had also received the fourth level of the Panzerkampfabzeichen for the participation in 75 separate armoured engagements (!). Personal total of tank kills unknown.

Frosch Horst. *Oberleutnant der Reserve* in the Sturmgeschütz-Abteilung 244, he was awarded the Deutsches Kreuz in Gold on 10 January 1944. Promoted to *Hauptmann*, after allegedly reaching a total of over 70 armoured kills he may have been proposed for the Ritterkreuz.

Gebhardt Rolf (1915-2010). *Feldwebel* in the 2nd company, schwere Panzer-Abteilung 507, he was awarded the DKiG on 28 April 1944 and the Ritterkreuz on 30 September. In a letter dated 8 May 1944, *General der Panzertruppe* Raus praised him for the elimination of 20 tanks in the difficult fighting around Tarnopol and Brody. The recommendation for his Ritterkreuz seems to mention 27 enemy tanks and 35 AT guns destroyed since April.

Gerlach Karl (1914-1991). *Oberleutnant* and leader of the 4./Panzer-Regiment 35, in mid-March 1945, in the area of Danzig with his Panther and with the collaboration of just another Panther, in a three-days battle he managed to prevent the decisive breakthrough planned by the enemy, destroying 21 Soviet AFVs in the process. For this feat he was awarded the Ritterkreuz (the date is disputed). He had already received the DKiG in January 1942, as *Feldwebel* in the 8th company. During the course of the war he supposedly parteciped in "almost 150 armoured attacks".

Gruber Walter (1920-1982) from Linz. *SS-Unterscharführer* in the 3rd company, SS-Panzerjäger-Abteilung 3, he was awarded the Deutsches Kreuz in Gold on 17 September 1944 and promoted to *Oberscharführer*, for destroying with his Sturmgeschütz, since 5 July 1943, a total of 26 enemy tanks and 30 AT-guns.

Hecker Otto (?-?). Awarded the EK I in 1942 as *Unteroffizier* with 2./Sturmgeschütz-Abteilung 197 (possibly as a gunner). During operation "Zitadelle", *Feldwebel* in command of Ferdinand 232 in the 2nd company, schwere Panzerjäger-Abteilung 653, he was allegedly credited with destroying 27 tanks. His vehicle was captured in the Soviet counteroffensive in September. Promoted to *Oberfeldwebel* he continued to serve until 1944 at least. It is not known if he was ever recommended for the DKiG.

Henke Max (1909-?). At the start of Barbarossa he was *Oberfeldwebel* with 3./Panzer-Regiment 7. He then transferred to the Panzer-Abteilung 118, 18.Panzergrenadier-Division; on 18 May 1944 he received the EK I. *Stabsfeldwebel* and zugführer in the 1st company, in one week period in

October in the area of Ebenrode (east Prussia, near the border with Lithuania; today Nesterov) he was allegedly credited with the elimination of 28 enemy tanks. For this feat, on 26 December 1944 he was awarded the Ritterkreuz. In 1945 still in the same area, in one action on 13 January with his Sturmgeschütz he destroyed six ot of nine attacking T-34s. His final total of tank kills could be more than 40. He survived the war.

Jauss Karl (1922-2003). Awarded the Deutsches Kreuz in Gold on 18 December 1944, as *SS-Oberscharführer* in the SS-Panzer-Regiment 5, 5.SS-Panzer-Division "Wiking". In 1942-43 he was in command of a Panzer III in the 2nd company, and during the fighting retreat from the Caucasus he earned the EK I on 30 January 1943. In 1944 he transitioned to the 8th (Panther) company. Promoted to *Untersturmführer* on 30 January 1945, in April 1945, in command of a Jagdpanther with the kampfgruppe led by Nicolussi-Leck against US forces in northern Germany, he destroyed 2 Shermans. During the war he took part in some fifty armoured engagements and was allegedly credited with the elimination of 26+ tanks (20 of Soviet type, 6 of American type) and 40+ AT-guns and artillery guns.

Job Eduard. He got the EK II on 20.10.1941 while serving with 1./Pz.Jg.Abt. and the EK I on 23.12.1944 with 3./Panzerjäger-Lehr-Abteilung 130. Promoted to *Unteroffizier* he distinguished himself in 1945 during the fighting on the Lower Rhine region. When Schiefbahn (a suburb of Willich) was taken back, he destroyed 5 enemy tanks in heavy night combat allegedly bringing his total of kills as a gunner in Jagdpanzer IV and Jagdpanther to 38. He was thus awarded the Deutsches Kreuz in Gold on March 1st. His tank commander in the abteilung was *Oberfeldwebel der Reserve* Erich Stolz (born in 1914), awarded the Deutsches Kreuz in Gold on 11 February 1945 and with a presumed final score of no less than 39 enemy tanks.

Kändler Willi (1920-1986). He came to 12.SS-Panzer-Division "Hitlerjugend" from LSSAH. Promoted to *SS-Untersturmführer* on 10 March 1944, in Normandy he was in the 5./SS-Panzer-Regiment 12 (first a zugführer, later he took over the Kompanie). Awarded the EK II on 3 July and the EK I on 24 July. On 8 July in the battle of Buron with five panzers he rejected many attacks of Allied infantry and tanks; two days later north of Maltot he destroyed 8 Churchills. In a personal photo he has 24 kill rings on his Panzer IV.

Kageneck Clemens-Heinrich von (1913-2005). After positions as Nachrichtenoffizier in the Panzer-Regiment 6 of the 3.Panzer-Division, he was promoted to *Oberleutnant* and in March 1942 he became chief of the 4th company; on 28 November 1942 he received the DKiG. In 1943, already credited with 18 tank kills during the fighting for the Caucasus, he was promoted to *Hauptmann* and given command of schwere Panzer-Abteilung 503. With this unit he greatly distinguished himself in operation "Zitadelle", being awarded the Ritterkreuz on 4 August 1943. Promoted to *Major* he was further awarded the Eichenlaub on 26 June 1944. With the Tiger he may have personally destroyed no less than 12 tanks. In western Ukraine, in January 1944 he had been severely wounded; after recovering he was assigned to a Panzertruppenschule.

Kauermann Helmut, born in 1917. *Feldwebel* in the II.Abteilung, Panzer-Regiment 2, 16.Panzer-Division, he received the Deutsches Kreuz in Gold on 12 October 1943. Promoted to *Oberfeldwebel*, during the battle of the Korsun-Cherkassy pocket, as a zugführer in the 7th company, he destroyed 12 enemy tanks and one self-propelled gun. For this feat and for reaching a total of 52 tank kills he was awarded the Ritterkreuz on 20 March 1944. He fell in battle on 24 April 1945, in Kotzen, Brandenburg.

Klimas Peter (?-?). *Unteroffizier* and sturmgeschütz commander in the 1./Panzerjäger-Abteilung 12 of the 12.Infanterie-Division, he was awarded the DKiG on 14 March 1944 for reaching a total of 22 enemy tank kills on the eastern front. In 1944 during the Allied attack on Aachen, *Feldwebel* Klimas with his StuG IV destroyed 2 enemy tanks near Alsdorf on 7 December.

König Georg (1914-1995). Already awarded the EK I as a panzer driver, in June 1943 he became *Feldwebel* and platoon leader in the 1st company, Panzer-Abteilung 18, 18 Panzer-Division. On 17 July 1943 he shot 9 out of twenty-five T-34s within five minutes. For this feat and for reaching a total of over 12 tank kills, on 13 September he was awarded the Ritterkreuz. In early 1945 he supposedly was with the 1st company, Panzer-Abteilung Kummersdorf, and on 17 April he may have scored another 14 kills with a Tiger II. In this action he was severely injured losing an eye.

Kohlke Helmut. Awarded the DKiG on 16 October 1942 as *Unteroffizier* in the 3rd company, Panzerjäger-Abteilung 561. Photos taken in spring 1943 show him and his crew on their famous "Kohlenklau" Marder II with 19 kill rings. By the end of the war he may have destroyed well over 20 enemy tanks.

Kosar Karl, born in 1920. In mid-January 1944, during the fighting north of Kirovograd he destroyed 16 enemy tanks within three days (out of a total of 31 tanks by the whole Zug of three sturmgeschütze under his command). He was thus awarded the Ritterkreuz on 7 February as *Leutnant der Reserve* in the 2./Panzer-Abteilung 7, 10.Panzergrenadier-Division. He was killed in action in January 1945 near Radom, Poland.

Kreßmann Erwin (1918-2017). *Oberfeldwebel*, he fought in Demyansk being awarded both classes of the EK. In May 1942 he was sent to the Panzerjäger-Abteilung 24, taking part in the conquest of Sevastopol and being promoted to *Leutnant*; in January 1943 he was promoted to *Oberleutnant* and was given command of the 2nd company. After recovering from wounds, in July he was transferred to the schwere Panzer-Jäger-Abteilung 519. In the area of Vitebsk the 1st company under his command was credited with 63 enemy tanks in just ten days of combat. He was thus awarded the DKiG on 16 January 1944 and promoted to *Hauptmann*. In September the 1st company was equipped with the new Jagdpanzer V and employed in the west. He distinguished himself in the Aachen combat area, knocking out numerous Shermans and inflicting heavy losses on the American troops. On 9 December 1944 he was awarded the RK. In February 1945 he was again on the eastern front. At the beginning of May he destroyed two T-34s in close combat.

Kreutzberg (or Kreuzberg) Anton (1914-1988). Awarded the Ritterkreuz on 21 September 1944 as *Unteroffizier* in the 2nd company, schwere Panzerjäger-Abteilung 525, while in Italy. Promoted to *Feldwebel der Reserve*. In command of a Nashorn he may have destroyed over 36 enemy tanks.

Langanke Fritz (1919-2012). *SS-Standartenoberjunker* and platoon leader in the 2./SS-Panzer-Regiment 2 "Das Reich", in Normandy on the night of the 29-30 July he led a kampfgruppe in a successful breakout via St.Denis, personally destroying with his Panther 13 tanks and 4 AT guns (as well as numerous halftracks and trucks). For this feat he was awarded the Ritterkreuz on 27 August 1944 and promoted to *SS-Untersturmführer* on September 1st. He had been transferred to the divisional panzer abteilung in 1942. On 25 December 1944 he was given command of the 2.Kompanie. In April 1945 he was promoted to *Obersturmführer*. Final total of tank kills unknown.

Lange Gerhard (1916-1996). Awarded the Ritterkreuz on 28 March 1945 as *Hauptmann* and leader of the II./Panzer-Regiment 35, and further awarded the DKiG on 28 April. During the war he took part in over 50 separate armoured engagements (Panzerkampfabzeichen Stufe "50" received in March 1945) and was wounded five times.

Langkeit Willy (1907-1969). Awarded the Eichenlaub on 7 December 1943 as *Oberstleutnant* and leader of Panzer-Regiment 36, 14.Panzer-Division. Previously he had received the DKiG in July 1942 as II.Abteilung commander and the RK in December 1942 as I.Abteilung commander. By the end of the war he had directly partecipated in over 75 separate armoured engagements.

Lehrter Günther (1922-?). While serving with Panzer-Regiment 27, 19.Panzer-Division, he received consecutively the EK II on 12 August and the EK I on 6 September 1943. Promoted to *Leutnant der Reserve* he distinguished himself during the defensive fighting in central Poland, where as a zugführer in the 5.Kompanie, on 22 August 1944 with his Panzer IV he knocked out six T-34s. For this feat and for achieving a total of 41 kills he was awarded the Ritterkreuz on 2 September. Fate unknown.

Lex Hans (1916-1994). *Oberleutnant* in the 7th company, Panzer-Regiment 203, he was awarded the DKiG on 8 December 1942. He then transferred to

Panzer-Regiment "Großdeutschland" and during operation "Zitadelle" he commanded the 7th company. On 15 July with his Panzer IVs he launched a surprise attack against an enemy assembly area destroying 16 tanks without any loss. For this feat and for reaching a personal total of over 20 kills he was awarded the Ritterkreuz on 10 September 1943. Promoted to *Hauptmann der Reserve*, on 27 April 1944 he received the second level of the Panzerkampfabzeichen, for the participation in over 25 separate armoured engagements.

Liethmann Günter (1918-1999). EK II on 13 October 1941 and EK I on 14 July 1942. As an *Oberleutnant* in the 3./Sturmgeschütz-Abteilung 237, he was awarded the Deutsches Kreuz in Gold on 31 August 1943. Promoted to *Hauptmann* and in command of the battery, he further distinguished himself few weeks later during the defensive combat west of Yelnya (in the area of Smolensk). On 20 September against a massive Soviet attack, he destroyed 11 tanks bringing his personal total to 53. For this action, in which he was severely wounded, he was awarded the Ritterkreuz on 26 October 1943. In February 1944 he returned to his old unit (by this time upgraded to Brigade) and later became Kommandeur of Sturmgeschütz-Brigade 184.

Lüders Friedrich (1918-1993). *Oberleutnant* in the 2nd company (Marder II), Panzerjäger-Abteilung 654, he was awarded the DKiG on 12 February 1943. During operation Zitadelle, on 6 July he knocked out 8 tanks with Ferdinand "601". After being promoted to *Hauptmann* and given command of the company, he further distinguished himself in Normandy in 1944. On 18 July he personally destroyed one M4 flamethrower; on the 30 with three Jagdpanthers he ambushed an enemy tank brigade south of Caumont destroying 11 Churchills; the day after 2 more tanks; on 3 August 6 tanks. For these successes he received the Ritterkreuz on 30 September 1944. On 21 November he personally destroyed yet another tank. His total of kills is likely to have exceeded twenty.

Mahlstedt Heinrich, born on 30 August 1911. *Oberfeldwebel* and platoon leader in the 3rd company, Panzer-Abteilung 8, 20.Panzergrenadier-Division, he was awarded the EK I on 5 January 1944 for the elimination of six enemy tanks near Kirovograd. Few months later, in the time period 20 July-5 August 1944, in the area of Lemberg and Sambor with his sturmgeschütz he was credited with destroying 20 tanks. He died of wounds on 27 August. Posthumously awarded the Ritterkreuz on 30 September 1944.

Masemann Willi (1919-1975). *Unteroffizier* in the 4./Panzer-Jäger-Abteilung 15 (L) of the 15.Luftwaffen-Felddivision, he was awarded the Ritterkreuz on 25 June 1944 for the elimination of 18 Soviet tanks from summer 1943. Promoted to *Feldwebel* he went on to serve in another unit in the west. In October 1944 in one action north of Geilenkirchen with his sturmgeschütz he destroyed 4 American tanks before being seriously wounded.

Mennel Hans, born on 25 November 1921. After promotion to *SS-Untersturmführer*, in September 1942 he joined the 6th company, SS-Panzer-Regiment "Das Reich". In operation "Zitadelle" with his Panzer IV he was allegedly credited with destroying 24 tanks, before being killed in action on 14 July. Already awarded the EK I, he was also posthumously included in the Ehrenblatt des Deutschen Heeres (Honour Roll). His total score over enemy tanks could be more than 25.

Meyer Herbert. *Leutnant der Reserve* in schwere Panzer-Abteilung 502, on 11 February 1943 in one action near Mischkino with his Tiger he destroyed 7 Soviet tanks (out of a total of 32 by the zug under his command), thus receiving the EK I. Few days later he personally destroyed another ten KV-1s (out of a total of 14 by his kampfgruppe; his gunner *Unteroffizier* Pfeffer got the EK I). After further successes, on 30 December 1943 he was awarded the Deutsches Kreuz in Gold. He died in Gatchina on 21 January 1944 (he shot himself refusing to be captured). Posthumously included in the Ehrenblatt des Deutschen Heeres. He could have over 30 tank kills to his credit.

Naber Josef (1916-1992). During the battle of Kursk he commanded a captured T-34 in the 9th company, SS-Panzer-Regiment 2 "Das Reich", destroying many tanks. He was awarded the Deutsches Kreuz in Gold on 8 September 1943 as an *SS-Oberscharführer* in the SS-Panzerjäger-Abteilung 2. Promoted to *Hauptscharführer* he received the Panzerkampfabzeichen III for the participation in fifty separate armoured engagements. His final total of tank kills should be well over twenty.

Nowaczyk Paul (?-?). *Feldwebel* in the 1./Panzerjäger-Abteilung 255, 255.Infanterie-Division, he distinguished himself in the battles in the area of Kharkov being awarded the Deutsches Kreuz in Gold on 7 October 1943 for the destruction of 27 Soviet tanks. He may have scored most of his kills with the Marder tank destroyer. In October 1943 he left his company for the Ersatz-Abteilung 4, possibly having been severely wounded in combat.

Oberbracht Friedrich-Karl, born on 19 December 1920. While serving with Panzer-Regiment 2 he received the EK II. Promoted to *Leutnant*, he transferred to schwere Panzer-Abteilung 501, being consecutively awarded the EK I on 13 January 1944 and the Deutsches Kreuz in Gold on 9 October, as a zugführer in the 1st company. On 13 January 1945 during an attack of the abteilung against Lisów (southern Poland), with his Tiger II (turret number 111) he knocked out 12 tanks. While sitting immobilized (both tracks shot off) on the edge of the village he destroyed another 7 before being mortally wounded. His personal total of tank kills should be well over thirty.

Ott Heinz (1921-1997). Awarded the Ritterkreuz on 9 May 1945 as *Oberwachtmeister* and platoon leader in the 12th company, Panzer-Regiment

24, 24.Panzer-Division. Allegedly credited with a total of 47 enemy tank kills (in late 1944 with his Pz IV he destroyed eight T-34s in one action). He took part in over fifty separate armoured engagements.

Ott Hermann. Awarded the DKiG on 28 April 1945 as *Unteroffizier der Reserve* in the 3rd company, Panzer-Regiment 35. By this time he may have reached a total of 53 tank and 58 AT guns "kills". He took part in over fifty separate armoured engagements.

Palm Paul (1913-1990). *Oberfeldwebel* in the 6.Kompanie, Panzer-Regiment 35, 4.Panzer-Division, he was awarded the Deutsches Kreuz in Gold on 20 January 1945. During the famous action of *Oberleutnant* Gerlach in mid-March 1945 in the area of Danzig, he was in command of the second Panther, being personally responsible for the destruction of at least two tanks and several AT guns. By the end of the war he had been allegedly credited with a total of 80 kills (probably tanks and guns combined; he was also credited with a tank in close combat).

Peter Horst. Awarded the DKiG on 9 March 1945 as *Leutnant der Reserve* in the 2nd company, Panzerjäger-Abteilung 1544 (which fought against the Red Army within the 544.Volksgrenadier-Division). He may have destroyed 30+ enemy tanks.

Rade Hans-Dietrich. Awarded the DKiG on 29 October 1943 as *Hauptmann* in the Sturmgeschütz-Abteilung 244. He may have destroyed a total of 23 enemy tanks. In October 1942 as *Oberleutnant* and leader of the 2nd battery he had received the rare Anerkennungsurkunde des Oberbefehlshabers des Heeres.

Rambow Richard, born in 1917. As *Unteroffizier* in the 1st company, Panzerjäger-Abteilung 561, during the battle of Rzhev he eliminated 9 enemy tanks. In doing so he also raised his total of destroyed enemy tanks to 29, and on 19 September 1942 was awarded the Ritterkreuz. His victories were achieved both as a Pak and as a Marder gunner and commander; final total unknown. He was killed in action on 26 October 1943.

Ramin Hans-Georg von (1916-1949). He took part in the invasion of the Soviet Union as *Leutnant der Reserve* in the Panzerjäger-Abteilung 53, 5.Panzer-Division. After a period with the towed Pak he took command of a Marder. On 5 May 1943 he was awarded the Deutsches Kreuz in Gold as *Oberleutnant* in the 2nd company. In 1944 he transitioned to the Jagdpanzer IV; on 11 October 1944 north of Nattkischken (Natkiškiai, Lithuania) 6 jagdpanzers under the lead of von Ramin destroyed 16 enemy tanks. Promoted to *Hauptmann* and in command of the whole abteilung he had reached a personal total of 23 tank "kills", and on 23 October 1944 was awarded the Ritterkreuz. Last rank in 1945: *Major der Reserve.*

Ratajczak Edmund (1916-1998). He served in the panzerwaffe from the first day of WW2 until April 1945. As *Feldwebel* in the 6./Panzer-Regiment 11, he was awarded the DKiG in April 1943 for outstanding achievement during the campaign in Kharkov and Belgorod. By August of the same year he had already partecipated in over 25 separate armoured engagements. In April 1944 he volunteered to schwere Panzer-Abteilung 507. On 10 February 1945 he was awarded the RK as *Oberfeldwebel* and platoon leader in the 1st company.

Raum Otto. *Leutnant der Reserve* in the 8th company, II.Abteilung, Panzer-Regiment 3. He received both the EK II and the EK I. According to the unit history of the 2.Panzer-Division, he fell on 28 September 1943 with a total of 45 "kills" achieved as Panzer IV commander. He was posthumously awarded with the Ehrenblattspange des Heeres on 17 October.

Ribbentrop Rudolf von (1921-2019). He was the son of the Minister of Foreign Affairs Joachim von Ribbentrop. *Obersturmführer* and platoon leader in the 6./SS.Panzer-Regiment 1 of the "LSSAH", he distinguished himself during operation "Zitadelle": after having already knocked out several tanks on the 7 and 8 July, in Prokhorovka he allegedly destroyed another 14 T-34s. For these successes he received the Ritterkreuz on 15 July 1943. Transferred to "Hitlerjugend", he was further awarded the DKiG on 25 August 1944, as commander of the 3rd company, SS-Panzer-Regiment 12. Final total unknown.

Riehl Wilhelm, born in 1916. With the Sturmgeschütz-Abteilung 909 he received the EK II on 28 February 1943 and the EK I on 9 July. During the battle of Kursk, south of Orel in the time period 5 July-5 August 1943 the abteilung was credited with destroying 115 enemy tanks for the loss of only 8 veichles. In the battle *Oberwachtmeister* Riehl, Zugführer in the 2.Batterie, knocked out 21 tanks and four AT-guns; he was also responsible for the shooting down of an enemy liaison aircraft. For these successes and for reaching a personal total of 41 tank "kills" in the east, he was recommended for the Ritterkreuz, the proposal was rejected and he was instead awarded the DKiG on 15 September 1943. He was killed on 12 February 1944 in Kaimen (today Zarechje), to the east of Königsberg, East Prussia.

Roßmann Emil (1920-2003). Awarded the RK on 23 October 1944 as *Leutnant der Reserve* and commander of the 2nd company, Panzer-Regiment 26, 26.Panzer-Division. In one action, on the 6 October near Windau, Latvia, all on his own with his Panther he had destroyed 9 T-34s and over 20 AT guns. In march 1945 he was awarded the fifth level of the Panzerkampfabzeichen for the participation in over 100 separate armoured engagements. Final total of tank "kills" unknown.

Rudloff Paul, born in 1914. He joined the Wehrmacht in 1935. *Feldwebel* in the 6./Panzer-Regiment 36, he served during the Polish, French and Russian campaigns receiving the EK II in 1939 and the EK I in1941. Promoted to

Oberfeldwebel he was awarded the Deutsches Kreuz in Gold on July 1st 1942. In 1944 during heavy combat in the area of Doblen (Dobele, Latvia), as zugführer in the 4th company he reportedly reached a total of 54 tank kills. Fate unknown.

Rudolf Richard (1923-2004). *SS-Unterscharführer* and platoon leader in the 9./SS-Panzer-Regiment 12 of the "Hitlerjugend", he particularly distinguished himself with his Panzer IV in the fighting at the Carpiquet airfield just outside of Caen. Awarded the EK I on 3 July 1944 (together with the promotion to *Oberscharführer*) and the Ritterkreuz on 18 November for the destruction of a total of 20 Allied tanks (6 Shermans in one action on 4 July alone).

Schaelte Otto. He was awarded the DKiG on 30 December 1944 as *SS-Oberscharführer* in the 3./SS-Sturmgeschütz-Abteilung 1. According to the recommendation he had destroyed a tank on July 28 bringing up his score to 25 armor kills.

Scheiber Erich. He served with schwere Panzerjäger-Abteilung 654 on the eastern front in the Werkstatt-Kompanie of the Ferdinande (receiving the EK I in August 1943), then in the west with the jagdpanther. In August 1944 he destroyed some 9 tanks as a gunner and in November a further 11 tanks as a commander. On 30 December he was awarded the Deutsches Kreuz in Gold, as a *Leutnant der Reserve* and zugführer in the 3rd company. One month later on 24 January 1945 he destroyed five tanks, before being killed in the course of the same action.

Schirp Werner (1922-1993). Awarded the Panzerkampfabzeichen Stufe "50" in February 1945, followed by the Ritterkreuz on 28 March as *Hauptmann* and commander of the 4th company, Panzer-Regiment 6, 3.Panzer-Division (which was equipped with the Panther). Total of enemy tank kills unknown.

Schmitt Johann. As *Oberwachtmeister* and StuG commander in the 1st battery, Sturmgeschütz-Abteilung 210 he was awarded the DKiG on 26 November 1943. Later in the war he may have moved to Sturmgeschütz-Abteilung 261. He wasn't awarded the RK. His name is usually associated with the destruction of 75 enemy "tanks"; probably tanks, armoured vehicles and guns combined.

Schnauder Adolf. Born in Sankt Pölten, Austria. *Unteroffizier* and gunner in the 6./Panzer-Regiment 39, 17.Panzer-Division. Awarded the Deutsches Kreuz in Gold on 13 January 1944 for the destruction since 1942 on the eastern front, of 52 tanks, 3 self-propelled guns and 170 guns of various type. Fate unknown.

Schöck Fritz (1915-2003). In the panzerwaffe since the start of the war, he received the EK I in June 1940 and the DKiG in January 1943 as *Oberleutnant* in the 9./Panzer-Regiment 4, 13.Panzer-Division. He was awarded the Ritterkreuz on 5 September 1944 as *Hauptmann* in command of the 2nd company, schwere Panzer-Abteilung 507. By August 1943 he had already partecipated in over 50 separate armoured engagements. During the war he was wounded five times.

Schulz-Streeck Karlheinz (1909-1978). He took part in the invasion of the Soviet Union as a *Leutnant der Reserve* in the Sturmgeschütz-Abteilung 192, receiving the EK II on September 3rd and the EK I on November 1st 1941. Promoted to *Oberleutnant*, in 1942 he transferred to Sturmgeschütz-Abteilung 184, then in early 1943 to Sturmgeschütz-Abteilung 912, before being seriously wounded. After recovering he entered the Waffen-SS in the "Nordland" division, being awarded the Deutsches Kreuz in Gold on 19 August 1944 as *SS-Hauptsturmführer* and acting commander of SS-Sturmgeschütz-Abteilung 11; in November he was promoted to *SS-Sturmbannführer*. In the time period 1 February-4 March 1945 his unit destroyed 85 Soviet tanks (and immobilized a further 21) and 67 AT guns for minimal losses. In May he was awarded the Ritterkreuz. By the end of the war Schulz-Streeck had partecipated in over fifty separate armoured attacks and 22 infantry attacks. Personal total of tank kills unknown.

Schulze Paul (1913-1980). Awarded the Ritterkreuz on 30 December 1943 as *Hauptmann* in command of the II.Abteilung, Panzer-Regiment 21, 20.Panzer-Division. Promoted to *Major* he was awarded the Panzerkampfabzeichen Stufe "100" (!) and the Eichenlaub on 28 July 1944 in recognition for the exceptionally high number of enemy tanks knocked out by his Abteilung 21 against operation "Bagration". Previously in April 1942, he had received the DKiG as *Oberleutnant* in the Panzerjäger-Abteilung 36. His personal total of enemy tank kills is unknown. He destroyed one tank in close combat.

Serck Julius (1917-1999). Awarded the Ritterkreuz on 23 March 1945, as *Oberwachtmeister* and platoon leader in the 3rd battery, Sturmgeschütz-Brigade 300. He may have destroyed a total of 32 enemy tanks.

Siebenthaler Richard (1913-1980). *Oberfeldwebel* in the 6th company, Panzer-Regiment 2, 16.Panzer-Division, he was awarded the DKiG on 24 November 1942. In the defensive combat to the east of the Oder, as platoon leader in the same company (by this time equipped with sturmgeschütze), he destroyed several T-34s and was thus awarded the Ritterkreuz on 14 April 1945. In total in the east he was allegedly credited with 50+ enemy tank "kills".

Siegel Hans (1918-2002). *SS-Obersturmführer* with 3./SS-Sturmgeschütz-Abteilung 1, it is said that he had 11 tank kills in early 1943 in Kharkov up until wounded (EK II on 18 February 1943). Transferred to the 12.SS-Panzer-Division "Hitlerjugend", with his Panzer IV he had another 18 tank kills in Normandy (seven on 11 June alone; eleven on 27-28 June, his tank knocked out, severely burned), being awarded the EK I on 14 June 1944 and the Ritterkreuz on 23 August, as *SS-Hauptsturmführer* and chief of the 8th company. After recovering he commanded a panzer kampfgruppe of the division in 1945 in Hungary.

Soretz Hans. *SS-Untersturmführer* in the 3rd company, schwere SS-Panzer-Abteilung 102. According to his DKiG recommendation he destroyed 22 tanks, 18 AT guns and 30 vehicles (this total includes east and west fronts and was reached after the fighting on Hill 112 on July 11, 1944).

Sorge Karl-Heinz (1914-1963). Awarded the DKiG in March 1942 as *Oberfeldwebel* in the 7./Panzer-Regiment 6, 3.Panzer-Division, and the RK on 7 February 1944 as *Oberleutnant* in command of the 5th company. On 11 January 1945 he received the fourth level of the Panzerkampfabzeichen for the participation in over 75 separate armoured engagements.

Stegmaier Alfons (1914-1996). Awarded the DKiG on 4 June 1944 as *SS-Hauptscharführer* in the 3rd company, SS-Sturmgeschütz-Abteilung 2 of "Das Reich". As StuG III commander he may have been credited with 25+ tank kills.

Struck Heinz, born on 11 September 1913. *Oberfeldwebel* in the 1./Kompanie, Panzer-Abteilung 129 of the 29.Infanterie-Division (mot.), during the offensive towards Stalingrad he was credited with destroying 13 enemy tanks (reaching a total of 16; previously he had served in Panzer-Regiment 3), being awarded the Deutsches Kreuz in Gold on 13 September 1942. Over the next three months he was allegedly credited with another 11 tanks plus one in close combat. Promoted to *Leutnant* on January 1st 1943, he transferred to Panzer-Abteilung 2106 (Panther tanks), but was killed after three days of combat in the west in late 1944.

Thiele Arno, born in 1912. Already awarded with the EK II in the Polish campaign and the EK I in the battle of France, he greatly distinguished himself near Leningrad. During the battle for Tikhvin (some 200 km to the east of the city), as a *Leutnant* in the I.Abteilung, Panzer-Regiment 29, 12.Panzer-Division, he reached a total of 39 tank "kills", 22 AT-guns and 16 artillery guns, thus receiving the DKiG on 29 November 1941. In 1942, still in the sector of lake Ladoga, as a platoon leader in the 4th company (in command of a long barreled Panzer IV), over the course of a few days he destroyed 10 tanks and several bunkers before dying from a shot in the head on 3 August. Posthumously promoted to *Oberleutnant* and awarded the Ritterkreuz on 24 September 1942. Allegedly credited with a personal total of over fifty tanks.

Walz Hans (1912-1977). *Hauptfeldwebel* in the 4./Panzer-Regiment 2, he fought in the Polish campaign and in the Battle of France being awarded the EK II followed by the EK I on 28 August 1940. On the eastern front he was platoon leader in the 2./Panzer-Regiment 18, then in mid 1942 he transferred to the Panzer-Abteilung 103, 3.Infanterie-Division (mot.). In the northern sector of the battle of Stalingrad this company wiped out over 100 enemy tanks, with Walz being awarded the DKiG on 6 November 1942. Wounded three times, he was flown out of the pocket. In recognition of his bravery, on May 1st 1943 he was promoted to *Leutnant*. As a company commander he fought in Italy, then in the Ardennes where he distinguished himself being promoted to *Oberleutnant* on January 1st 1945. On 3 March 1945 in Mödrath (20 km west of Cologne) with three StuG of his 1st company he ambushed an American armoured column, knocking out 24 armoured vehicles with only one friendly loss. In another action he was credited with destroying 2 Shermans, reaching a personal total of 60 enemy tank "kills". He was thus awarded the Ritterkreuz on 14 April 1945 being also promoted to *Hauptmann*.

Weerts Hans. Awarded the DKiG on 8 February 1945 as *SS-Obersturmführer* in the 4th company, SS-Panzer-Regiment 5 of "Wiking". He commanded an assault gun and/or a Panzer IV. Allegedly, by the time he was recommended for the DKiG in November 1944, he had been credited with 39 tank kills. Fate unknown.

Wiesemann Otto (1915-1999). Awarded the Ritterkreuz on 11 December 1944 as *Feldwebel* and platoon leader in the 1st company, Panzer-Regiment 1, 1.Panzer-Division. By this time, as Panther commander he may have destroyed 50+ enemy tanks. One of the few RK bearers who stayed in the DDR after the war.

Windmüller Herbert, born on 10 June 1918. *Wachtmeister* and zugführer in the 3.Batterie, Sturmgeschütz-Abteilung 190, he was awarded the Deutsches Kreuz in Gold on 16 November 1943 for destroying a total of 25 enemy tanks over the course of 31 armoured attacks. He was killed in action on 4 April 1944 near Kovel.

Wirsching Maximilian (1919-2004). Awarded the Ritterkreuz on 7 February 1945 as *Oberleutnant* and commander of the 2nd company, schwere Panzer-Abteilung 507. In combat since the start of the invasion of the Soviet Union, by the end of the war he had partecipated in over fifty separate armoured engagements and had been wounded five times. Personal total of tank kills unknown.

Wörner Theo. *Oberwachtmeister* in the 2./Sturmgeschütz-Abteilung 189, in 1942 during the heavy defensive fighting in the area of Rzhev, in two months he destroyed 28 enemy tanks. He had already been credited with six tanks the winter before. For his total, up to October, of 34 "kills", he was awarded the Deutsches Kreuz in Gold on 21 December 1942. Fate unknown.

Wohlrab Rudolf. Awarded the DKiG on 17 September 1944 as *SS-Unterscharführer* in the 3rd company, SS-Panzerjäger-Abteilung 3 of "Totenkopf". He may have destroyed no less than 26 tanks and 28 AT-guns.

Printed in Great Britain
by Amazon